Second Edition

THE ROAD TO
THE WHITE HOUSE

The Politics of Presidential Elections

Second Edition

THE ROAD TO
THE WHITE HOUSE

The Politics of Presidential Elections

Stephen J. Wayne
The George Washington University

ST. MARTIN'S PRESS   NEW YORK

Library of Congress Catalog Card Number: 83–61600
Manufactured in the United States of America.
87654
fedcba
For information, write St. Martin's Press, Inc.,
175 Fifth Avenue, New York, N. Y. 10010

cover design: Darby Downey
book design: Bennie Arrington

cloth ISBN: 0–312–68525–4
paper ISBN: 0–312–68526–2

Acknowledgments

cover photos: Wide World Photos/Paul Conklin

To my mother and father,
Mr. and Mrs. Arthur G. Wayne,
and my grandmother, Mrs. Hattie Marks

PREFACE

It is easier to follow a political campaign than to understand it. We read about it in the press, view it on television, and occasionally even see or hear a candidate in person. What we observe, however, is usually what others want us to see—be they candidates, their advisers, reporters, or a host of other self-interested participants. We are presented with a final product and expected to use it to make a judgment on election day.

There is more, however, to presidential elections than meets the eye. Campaign planners work hard to design a strategy to maximize their vote. They understand the intricacies of the process. They know how the system works, who its beneficiaries are, and where to concentrate their campaign resources. They understand the requirements of the new finance legislation—how to comply with it, get around it, and take advantage of it. They appreciate the psychological and social motivations of voters and have a feel for which appeals are likely to be most effective most of the time. They are aware of the party reforms and the way to build a winning coalition during the primaries. They can sense the rhythm of conventions and know when events should be scheduled and how various interests need to be orchestrated. They know how to organize and plan a general election campaign and how best to present their candidate to the voters. They can usually predict what will happen in the election and interpret the results so as to enhance their political position and governing potential. They do not need to read this book.

On the other hand, people who want to get behind the scenes of presidential campaigns, who want to understand what is going on and why, who want to know the reasons for adopting particular strategies and utilizing certain tactics, should benefit from the information contained in this book. The gratifying success of the first edition indicates that the work is indeed useful.

The Road to the White House: The Politics of Presidential Elections is a straightforward "nuts and bolts" discussion of how the system is designed and how it works. It is primarily concerned with facts, not opinions;

with practice, not theory. It summarizes the state of the art and science of presidential electoral politics.

The second edition has been thoroughly updated. Like the first, it is organized in four main parts. The first discusses the arena in which the election occurs. Its three chapters examine the electoral system, campaign finance, and the political environment. Chapter 1 provides a historical overview and now covers nominations as well as elections. Chapters 2 and 3 examine recent developments. Highlighted are the political considerations which candidates need to be aware of as they plan and structure their presidential campaigns.

Parts II and III are organized sequentially. They describe the distinct yet related stages of the presidential campaign: delegate selection, nominating conventions, and the general election. Chapter 4 examines reforms in the selection of convention delegates and their impact on voters, candidates, and the parties. Chapter 5 carries this discussion to the nominating convention, describing its purposes, procedures, policies, and politics. In chapter 6, the organization, strategy, and tactics in the general election are discussed. Chapter 7 describes the creation and projection of candidate images. It examines how the media cover the campaign and the impact of that coverage on voting behavior. Detailed illustrations from recent elections are used throughout these chapters.

The fourth part looks at the presidential vote and its impact. What does the election mean? Does it provide a mandate? How does it influence the President's ability to govern?

Finally, a new afterword considers problems and reforms. It examines some of the major difficulties that have affected the political system and the proposals which have been advanced for dealing with them: how the electoral process can be made more equitable; how it can be made more responsive to popular choice; and how that choice can be conveyed more effectively to elected and appointed officials.

These questions are not easy to answer. Students of the American political system have been debating them for some time, and that debate is likely to continue. Without information on how the system works, we cannot intelligently participate in it or improve it. In the case of presidential politics, ignorance is definitely not bliss.

The road to the White House is long and arduous. In fact, it has become more difficult to travel than in the past. Yet, surprisingly, there are more travelers. Evaluating their journey is essential to rendering an intelligent judgment on election day. However, there is more at stake than simply choosing the occupants of the presidential and vice presidential offices. The system itself is on trial in every presidential election. That is why it is so important to understand and appreciate the intricacies of the process. Only an informed citizenry can determine whether the nation is being well served by the way we go about choosing our President.

Few books are written alone. This one was no exception. For the first edition I was fortunate to have had the wise counsel of Richard L. Cole (University of Texas-Arlington) and Hugh L. LeBlanc (George Washington University). Their perceptive critiques vastly improved the quality of the manuscript as did the comments of the other reviewers: Jay S. Goodman (Wheaton College), James Lengle (Georgetown University), Robert T. Nakamura (Dartmouth College), Lester Seligman (University of Illinois), Earl Shaw (University of Minnesota), and William H. Steward (University of Alabama). I also benefited from the advice and experience of two friends, Jeff Fishel of American University and Paul Wilson of Bailey, Deardourff and Associates, who were willing to share their extensive knowledge of presidential politics with me.

In revising the book for the second edition, I was again fortunate to have received close, careful, and extraordinarily helpful readings from Hugh L. LeBlanc and Earl Shaw. They corrected, corroborated, and condensed parts of the manuscript, tightening it, strengthening it, and keeping it current. James W. Davis (Washington University) also reviewed the second edition and provided me with new perspectives on several of the chapters. I would like to thank my friends Bill Adams of George Washington University, Michael Malbin of the American Enterprise Institute, and Michael Robinson of George Washington and Catholic universities for allowing me to read manuscripts they are preparing on aspects of the electoral process. Joanne Ainsworth did a superb job of copy-editing the manuscript as did the project editor, Carol Ewig.

Jane DiSalvo typed the first edition, Judith Schneider typed the second, and Peg Ruffner helped at numerous points by typing revisions of revisions of revisions. All did exceptional work, often under severe time constraints.

I wish to extend my heartfelt thanks to them, to the reviewers, to my editors at St. Martin's (first Bertram Lummus and now Michael Weber), and to my wife, Cheryl Beil, whose encouragement has been unwavering throughout. Lastly, I would like to acknowledge with gratitude the help I received over the years from my students in Political Science 116, The American Presidency. Their comments, questions, and criticisms have been a constant source of guidance to me.

Stephen J. Wayne

CONTENTS

III. THE CAMPAIGN   165

6. ORGANIZATION, STRATEGY, AND TACTICS   167

7. IMAGE BUILDING AND THE MEDIA   209

PART 1

THE ELECTORAL ARENA

Chapter 1

PRESIDENTIAL SELECTION: A HISTORICAL OVERVIEW

Introduction

The road to the White House cannot be traversed in a day. It takes months, often years, to travel and the time is getting longer. The framers of the Constitution worked for several months on the presidential selection system and their plan has since undergone a number of constitutional, statutory, and precedent-setting changes. Modified by the development of parties, the expansion of suffrage, and the revolution in the media, the system has become more open and participatory but also more contentious, more circuitous, and more expensive. Candidates need to have considerable skill and luck to travel the road successfully.

This chapter is about that system. Why was it created? What needs was it supposed to serve? What initial compromises did the original plan incorporate? How did it operate? What changes have subsequently affected that operation? Whom have they benefited? What does this suggest about parties, about the electorate, about the political system in general?

In addressing these questions, I have organized the chapter into four sections. The first discusses the creation of the presidential election process. In doing so, it explores the motives and intentions of the delegates at Philadelphia and describes the procedures for selecting the President within the context of the constitutional and political issues of the day.

The second section examines the development of a nominating system. It explores the three principal methods that have been used—partisan congressional caucuses, brokered national conventions, and state primaries and caucuses—and describes the political forces that helped to shape them and in the case of first two modes destroyed them.

The third part of the chapter discusses presidential elections. It focuses on those decided by the House of Representatives (1800 and 1824), those influenced by Congress (1876), and those actually or very nearly unreflective of popular choice (1888, 1960, 1968, and 1976). In doing so, the section highlights the evolution of the Electoral College.

The final part of the chapter examines the current operation. It describes its geographic and demographic bases, whom it benefits, and whom it hurts. The section also discusses the system's major party orientation and its effects on third-party candidacies.

THE CREATION OF THE ELECTORAL COLLEGE

Among the many issues facing the delegates at the Constitutional Convention of 1787 in Philadelphia, the selection of the President was one of the toughest. Seven times during the course of the convention the method for choosing the executive was altered.

The framers' difficulty in designing electoral provisions for the President stemmed from the need to guarantee the institution's independence and, at the same time, create a technically sound, politically efficacious mechanism that would be consistent with a republican form of government. They were sympathetic with a government based on consent but not with direct democracy. They wanted a system that would choose the most qualified person but not necessarily the most popular. There seemed to be no precise model to follow.

Three methods had been proposed. The Virginia plan, a series of resolutions designed by James Madison and introduced by Governor Edmund Randolph, provided for legislative selection. Eight states chose their governors in this fashion at the time. Having Congress choose the President would be practical and politically expedient. Moreover, members of Congress could have been expected to exercise a considered judgment. This was important to the delegates at Philadelphia, since many of them did not consider the average citizen capable of making a reasoned, unemotional choice.

The difficulty with legislative selection was the threat it posed to the institution of the Presidency. How could the executive's independence be preserved if his election hinged on his popularity with Congress and his reelection on the legislature's appraisal of his performance in office? Only if the President were to serve a long term and not be eligible for reelection, it was thought, could his independence be protected so long as Congress was the electoral body. But this also posed problems.

Permanent ineligibility provided little incentive for the President to perform well and denied the country the possibility of reelecting a person whose experience and success in office might make him better qualified than anyone else. Reflecting on these concerns, Gouverneur Morris urged the removal of the ineligibility clause on the grounds that "it . . . intended to destroy the great motive to good behavior, the hope of being rewarded by a re-appointment."[1] A majority of the states agreed. Once the ineligibility clause was deleted, however, the terms of office had to be shortened to prevent what the framers feared might become almost indefinite tenure. However, with a shorter term of office and permanent reeligibility, legislative selection was not nearly as desirable, since it could make the President beholden to the legislature.

Popular election was another alternative, although one that did not generate a great deal of enthusiasm. It was twice rejected in the convention by overwhelming votes. Most of the delegates felt that a direct vote by the people was neither desirable nor feasible.[2] Lacking confidence in the public's ability to choose the best-qualified candidate, many delegates also believed that the size of the country and the poor state of its communication and transportation precluded a national campaign and election. The geographic expanse was simply too large to permit proper supervision and control of the election. Sectional distrust and rivalry also contributed to the problem.

A third alternative was some type of indirect election in which popular sentiment could be expressed but would not dictate the selection. James Wilson first proposed this idea after he failed to generate support for a direct popular vote. Luther Martin, Gouverneur Morris, and Alexander Hamilton also suggested indirect popular election through intermediaries. However, it was not until the debate over legislative selection divided and eventually deadlocked the delegates that election by electors was seriously considered. The Committee on Unfinished Business proposed the Electoral College compromise on September 4, and it was accepted after a short debate. Viewed as a safe, workable solution to the selection problem, it was deemed consistent with the constitutional and political features of the new government.

According to the proposal, presidential electors were to be chosen by the states in a manner designated by their legislatures. In order to insure their independence, the electors could not simultaneously hold a federal government position. The number of electors was to equal the number of senators and representatives from each state. Each elector had two votes but could not cast both of them for inhabitants of his own state.[3] At a designated time the electors would vote and send the results to Congress, where they would be announced to a joint session by the President of the Senate, the Vice President. Under the original plan, the person who received a majority of votes cast by the Electoral College would be elected President, and the one with the second highest total would be Vice President. There was no separate ballot for each office. In the event that no one received a majority, the House of Representatives would choose from among the five candidates with the most electoral votes, with each state delegation casting one vote. If two or more individuals were tied for second, then the Senate would select the Vice President from among them. Both of these provisions were subsequently modified by the Twelfth Amendment to the Constitution.

The electoral system was a dual compromise. Allowing state legislatures to establish the procedures for choosing electors was a concession to the proponents of a federal system; having the House of Representatives decide if there was no Electoral College majority was designed to please those who favored a stronger national government. Designating the number of electors to be equal to a state's congressional delegation gave the larger states an advantage in the initial voting for President; balloting by states in the House if the Electoral College was not decisive benefited the smaller states.

The large-small state compromise was critical to the acceptance of the Electoral College plan. It was argued during the convention debates that in practice the large states would nominate the candidates for President and the small states would exercise the final choice.[4] So great was the sectional rivalry and distrust at the time that the prospect of a majority of the college's agreeing on anyone other than George Washington seemed remote.

THE DEVELOPMENT OF NOMINATING SYSTEMS

While the Constitution prescribed a system for electing a President, it made no reference to the nomination of candidates. Political parties had not emerged prior to the Constitutional Convention. Factions existed, and the framers of the Constitution were concerned about them, but the development of a party system was not anticipated. Rather, it was assumed that electors whose interests were not tied to the national government would make an independent judgment in choosing the best possible person as President.

In the first two elections the system worked as intended. George Washington was the unanimous choice of the electors. There was, however, no consensus on who the Vice President should be. The eventual winner, John Adams, benefited from some discussion and informal lobbying by prominent individuals prior to the vote.[5]

A more organized effort to agree on candidates was undertaken four years later. Partisan alliances were beginning to develop in Congress. Members of the two principal groups, the Federalists and the Anti-Federalists, met separately to recommend individuals. The Federalists chose Vice President Adams; the Anti-Federalists picked Governor George Clinton of New York.

With political parties evolving during the 1790s, the selection of the electors quickly became a partisan contest. In 1792 and 1796 a majority of the state legislators chose them directly. Thus, the political group that controlled the legislature also controlled the selection. Appointed for their political views, electors were expected to exercise a partisan judgment. When in 1796 a Pennsylvania elector did not, he was accused of faithless behavior. Wrote one critic in a Philadelphia newspaper: "What, do I chuse Samuel Miles to determine for me whether John Adams or Thomas Jefferson shall be President? No! I chuse him to act, not to think."[6]

Washington's decision not to serve a third term forced Federalist and Anti-Federalist members of Congress to recommend the candidates in 1796. Meeting separately, party leaders agreed among themselves on the tickets. The Federalists urged their electors to vote for John Adams and Thomas Pinckney, while the Anti-Federalists (or Republicans as they began to be called) suggested Thomas Jefferson and Aaron Burr.

Since it was not possible to indicate the presidential and vice presidential choices on the ballot, Federalist electors, primarily from New England, decided to withhold votes from Pinckney (of South Carolina) to make certain that he did not receive the same number as Adams (of Massachusetts). This enabled Jefferson to finish ahead of Pinckney with 68 votes compared with the latter's 59, but behind Adams, who had 71. Four years of partisan differences followed between a President who, though he disclaimed a political affiliation, clearly favored the Federalists in appointments, ideology, and policy, and a Vice President who was the acknowledged leader of the opposition party.

Beginning in 1800, partisan caucuses composed of members of Congress met for the purpose of recommending the party's nominees. The Republicans continued to choose candidates in this manner until 1824; the Federalists did so only until 1808. In the final two presidential elections in which the Federalists ran candidates, 1812 and 1816, top party leaders, meeting in secret, decided on the nominees.[7]

"King caucus" violated the spirit of the Constitution. It effectively provided for Congress to pick the nominees. After the decline of the Federalists, the nominees were, in fact, assured of victory—a product of the dominance of the Jeffersonian Republican party as well as the success of the caucus in obtaining support for its candidates.

There was opposition within the caucuses. In 1808, Madison prevailed over James Monroe and George Clinton. In 1816, Monroe overcame a strong challenge from William Crawford. In both cases, however, the electors united behind the successful nominee. In 1820, they did not. Disparate elements within the party selected their own candidates.

Although the caucus was the principal mode of candidate selection during the first part of the nineteenth century, it was never formally institutionalized as a nominating body. How meetings were called, by whom, and when varied from election to election. So did attendance. A sizable number of representatives chose not to participate at all. Some stayed away on principle; others did so because of the choices they would have to make. In 1816 less than half of the Republican members of Congress were at their party's caucus. In 1820 only 20 percent attended, and the caucus had to adjourn without formally supporting President Monroe and Vice President Tompkins for reelection. In 1824 almost three-fourths of the members boycotted the session.

The 1824 caucus did nominate candidates. But with representatives from only four states constituting two-thirds of those attending, the nominee, William Crawford, failed to receive unified party support. Other candidates were nominated by state legislatures and conventions, and the electoral vote was divided. With no candidate obtaining a majority, the

House of Representatives had to make the final decision. John Quincy Adams was selected on the first ballot. He received the votes of thirteen of the twenty-four state delegations.

The caucus was never resumed. In the end it had fallen victim to the erosion of the two major parties, the decentralization of political power within the country, and Andrew Jackson's stern opposition. The Federalists had collapsed as a viable political force. As the Republican party grew from being the majority party to the only one, factions developed within it, the two principal ones being the National Republicans and the Democratic-Republicans. In the absence of a strong opposition there was little to hold these factions together. By 1830 they had split into two separate groups, one supporting and one opposing President Jackson.

Political leadership was changing as well. A relatively small group of individuals had dominated national politics for the first three decades after the 1787 Constitution. Their common experience in the war, the Constitutional Convention, and the early government produced personal contacts, political influence, and public respect that contributed to their ability to agree on candidates and to generate public support for them.[8]

Their successors had neither the tradition nor the national orientation in which to cast their presidential votes. Most owed their prominence and political clout to state and regional areas. Their loyalties reflected these bases of support.

The growth of party organizations at the state and local level affected the nomination system. In 1820 and 1824 it produced a decentralized mode of selection. State legislatures, caucuses, and conventions nominated their own candidates. Support was also mobilized on regional levels.

Whereas the congressional caucus had become unrepresentative, state-based nominations suffered from precisely the opposite problem. They were too representative of sectional interests and produced too many candidates. Unifying diverse elements behind a national ticket proved extremely difficult, although Jackson was successful in 1824 and again in 1828. Nonetheless, a system that was broader based than the old caucus and that could provide a decisive and mobilizing mechanism was needed. National nominating conventions filled the void.

The first such convention was held in 1831 by the Anti-Masons. A small but relatively active third party, it had virtually no congressional representation. Unable to utilize a caucus, the party turned instead to a general meeting which was held in a saloon in Baltimore, with 116 delegates from thirteen states attending. They decided on the nominees as well as an address to the people which contained the party's position on the dominant issues of the day.

Three months later a second convention was held in the same saloon by opponents of President Jackson. The National Republicans (or Whigs as they later became known) also nominated candidates and agreed on an address critical of the administration.

The Democratic-Republicans (or Democrats as they were later called) met in Baltimore one year later. The impetus for their convention was Jackson's desire to demonstrate popular support for his Presidency as well as to insure the selection of Martin Van Buren as his running mate. In 1836, Jackson resorted to another convention—this time to handpick Van Buren as his successor.

The Whigs did not hold a convention in 1836. Believing that they would have more success in the House of Representatives than in the nation as a whole, they ran three regional candidates, nominated by the states, who competed against Van Buren in areas of their strength. The plan, however, failed to deny Van Buren an electoral majority. He ended up with 170 votes compared with a total of 124 for his three opponents.

Thereafter, the Democrats and their opponents, first the Whigs and then their Republican successors, held nominating conventions to select their candidates. The early conventions were informal and rowdy by contemporary standards, but they also set the precedents for later meetings.

The delegates decided on the procedures for conducting the convention, policy statements (addresses to the people), and the nominees. Rules for apportioning the delegates were established before the meetings were held. Generally speaking, states were accorded as many delegates as their congressional representation merited regardless of the number of actual participants. The way in which the delegates were chosen, however, was left up to the states. Local and state conventions, caucuses, or even committees chose the delegates.

Public participation was minimal. Even the party's rank and file had a small role. It was the party leaders who designated the delegates and made the deals. In time it became clear that successful candidates owed their selection to the heads of the powerful state organizations and not to their own political prominence and organizational support. The price they had to pay, however, when calculated in terms of patronage and other types of political benefits, was often high.

Nineteenth-century conventions served a number of purposes. They provided a forum for party leaders, particularly at the state level. They constituted a mechanism by which agreements could be negotiated and support mobilized. By brokering interests, conventions helped unite the disparate elements within the party, thereby converting an organization of state parties into a national coalition for the purpose of conducting a presidential campaign.

Much of the bartering was conducted behind closed doors. Actions on the convention floor often had little to do with the wheeling and dealing that occurred in the smoke-filled smaller rooms. Since there was little public preconvention activity, many ballots were often necessary before the required number, usually two-thirds of the delegates, was reached.

The nominating system buttressed the position of individual state party leaders but it did so at the expense of rank-and-file participation. The influence of the state leaders depended on their ability to deliver votes. This, in turn, required that the delegates not exercise an independent judgment. To insure their loyalty, the bosses controlled their selection.

Demands for reform began to be heard at the beginning of the twentieth century. The Progressive movement, led by Robert La Follette of Wisconsin and Hiram Johnson of California, desired to break the power of state bosses and their machines through the direct election of convention delegates, or alternatively, through the expression of a popular choice by the electorate.

Florida became the first state to provide its political parties with such an option. In 1904 the Democrats took advantage of it and held a statewide vote for convention delegates. One year later, Wisconsin enacted a law for electing pledged delegates to nominating conventions. Others followed suit. By 1912, thirteen states held some type of primary election. Oregon was the first to permit a preference vote for the candidates themselves.

The year 1912 was also the first in which a candidate sought to use primaries as a way to obtain the nomination. With almost 42 percent of the Republican delegates selected in primaries, former President Theodore Roosevelt challenged incumbent William Howard Taft. Roosevelt won nine primaries to Taft's one, yet lost the nomination. (See Table 1–1.) Taft's support among regular party leaders who delivered their delegations and controlled the convention was sufficient to retain the nomination. He received one-third of his support from southern delegations, although the Republican party had won only 7 percent of the southern vote in the previous election.

Partially in reaction to the unrepresentative, "boss-dominated" convention of 1912, more states adopted primaries. By 1916, more than half

Table 1–1   NUMBER OF PRESIDENTIAL PRIMARIES AND PERCENTAGE OF CONVENTION DELEGATES FROM PRIMARY STATES, BY PARTY, SINCE 1912

	Democratic		Republican	
Year	Number of Primaries	Percentage of Delegates	Number of Primaries	Percentage of Delegates
1912	12	32.9%	13	41.7%
1916	20	53.5	20	58.9
1920	16	44.6	20	57.8
1924	14	35.5	17	45.3
1928	17	42.2	16	44.9
1932	16	40.0	14	37.7
1936	14	36.5	12	37.5
1940	13	35.8	13	38.8
1944	14	36.7	13	38.7
1948	14	36.3	12	36.0
1952	15	38.7	13	39.0
1956	19	42.7	19	44.8
1960	16	38.3	15	38.6
1964	17	45.7	17	45.6
1968	17	37.5	16	34.3
1972	23	60.5	22	52.7
1976	29*	72.6	28*	67.9
1980	31*	74.7	35*	74.3

Sources: 1912–1964, F. Christopher Arterton, "Campaign Organizations Face the Mass Media in the 1976 Presidential Nomination Process" (paper delivered at the annual meeting of the American Political Science Association, Washington, D.C., September 1–4, 1977); 1968–1976, Austin Ranney, *Participation in American Presidential Nominations, 1976* (Washington, D.C.: American Enterprise Institute, 1977), table 1, p. 6. Reprinted with permission of the author. The figures for 1980 were compiled by Austin Ranney from materials distributed by the Democratic National Committee and the Republican National Committee.

*Does not include Vermont, which held nonbinding presidential preference votes but chooses delegates in state caucuses and conventions.

of them held a Republican or Democratic contest. More than 50 percent of the delegates to both conventions were chosen by some type of primary, although many of them were not bound to vote for specific candidates. As a consequence, primary delegates did not control the outcome of the conventions.

The movement toward popular participation was short-lived, however. Following World War I the number of primaries declined. State party leaders, who saw primaries as a threat to their own influence, argued against them on three grounds: They were expensive; they had a low voter turnout; and major candidates tended to avoid them. As a result of this opposition, some states, which had used primaries, reverted to their old méthod of selection. Others made the primaries advisory rather than man-datory. Fewer delegates were selected in them. By 1936 only fourteen states held Democratic primaries and twelve held Republican ones. Less than 40 percent of the delegates to each convention in that year were chosen in this manner. For the next twenty years the number of primaries and the percentage of delegates hovered around this level.

Roosevelt's failure in 1912 and the decline in primaries thereafter made them an auxiliary route to the nomination at best. While some presidential aspirants became embroiled in them, none who depended on them won. In 1920 a spirited contest between three Republicans (General Leonard Wood, Governor Frank Lowden, and Senator Hiram Johnson) failed to produce a convention majority and resulted in party leaders choosing Warren Harding as the standard-bearer. Similarly, in 1952, Senator Estes Kefauver entered thirteen of seventeen presidential primaries, won twelve of them, became the most popular Democratic contender, but failed to win his party's nomination. The reason Kefau-ver could not parlay his primary victories into a convention victory was that a majority of the delegates were not selected in this manner. Of those who were, many were chosen separately from the presidential preference vote. Kefauver did not contest these separate delegate elec-tions. As a consequence, he obtained only 50 percent of the delegates in states where he actually won the presidential preference vote. More-over, the fact that most of his wins occurred against little or no opposi-tion undercut Kefauver's claim of being the strongest, most electable Democrat. He had avoided primaries in four states where he feared that he might either lose or do poorly.

Not only were primaries not considered to be an essential road to the nomination, but running in too many of them was interpreted as a sign of weakness, not strength. It indicated a lack of national recognition and/or a failure to obtain the support of party leaders. As a consequence, leading candidates tended to choose their primaries carefully, and the pri-maries, in turn, tended to reinforce the position of the leading candidates.

Those who did enter primaries did so mainly to test their popularity rather than to win convention votes. Dwight D. Eisenhower in 1952, John F. Kennedy in 1960, and Richard M. Nixon in 1968 had to demonstrate that being a general, a Catholic, or a once-defeated presidential candidate would not be fatal to their chances. In other words, they needed to prove they could win the general election.

With the possible exception of John Kennedy's victories in West Virginia and Wisconsin, primaries were neither crucial nor decisive for winning the nomination until the 1970s. When there was a provisional consensus within the party, primaries helped confirm it; when there was not, primaries were not able to produce it.[9] In short, they had little to do with whether the party was united or divided at the time of the convention.

Primary results tended to be self-fulfilling in the sense that they confirmed the front-runner's status. Between 1936 and 1968, the preconvention leader, the candidate who was ahead in the Gallup Poll before the first primary, won the nomination seventeen out of nineteen times. The only exceptions were Thomas E. Dewey in 1940, who was defeated by Wendell Willkie, and Kefauver in 1952, who lost to Adlai Stevenson. Willkie, however, had become the public opinion leader by the time the Republican convention met. Even when leading candidates lost a primary, they had time to recoup. Dewey and Stevenson, defeated in early primaries in 1948 and 1956, respectively, went on to reestablish their credibility as front-runners by winning later primaries.

This situation was to change dramatically after 1968. Largely as a consequence of the Democratic convention of that year, demands for a larger voice for the party's rank and file increased. In response to these demands, the Democratic party began to look into the matter of delegate selection. It enacted a series of reforms designed to insure broader representation at the convention. To avoid challenges to their delegations, a number of states which had used caucus and convention systems changed their mode of selection to primaries. By 1980, thirty-five states, the District of Columbia, and Puerto Rico were holding delegate elections of one type or another. Approximately three-fourths of the delegates to each convention were chosen in these primary elections.

New finance laws, which provided for government subsidies of preconvention campaigning, and increased media coverage, particularly by television, also added to the incentive to enter primaries. By 1972 they became important. In that year, Senator Edmund Muskie, the leading Democratic contender at the beginning of the process, was forced to withdraw after doing poorly in the early contests, while in 1976, President Gerald Ford came close to being the first incumbent President since Chester A. Arthur in 1884 to be denied his party's nomination.

In 1972 and thereafter, primaries were used to build popularity rather than simply reflect it. The ability of lesser-known candidates, such as George McGovern and Jimmy Carter, to use the prenomination process to gain public recognition, win delegate support, and become the leading candidates testifies to this new importance of primaries in contemporary politics. Today, they are the road to the nomination. Aspirants can no longer hope to succeed without entering them; incumbents can no longer ignore them.

The impact of primaries has been significant. They have affected the strategies and tactics of the candidates. They have influenced the composition and behavior of the delegates. They have changed the decision-making character of the national conventions. They have shifted power within the party. They have enlarged the selection zone of potential nominees. They have made governing more difficult. Each of these changes will be discussed in the chapters that follow.

THE EVOLUTION OF THE GENERAL ELECTION

The general election has changed as well. The Electoral College no longer operates as it was designed. It now has a partisan coloration. There is greater public participation, although it is still not direct. The system bears a resemblance to its past. While it has become more democratic, it is still not without its biases.

The Electoral College system was one of the few innovative features of the Constitution. It had no immediate precedent, although it bore some relationship to the way the state of Maryland selected its senators. In essence, it was invented by the framers, not synthesized from British and American experience. And it is one aspect of the system that has rarely worked as intended.

Only in the first two elections, when Washington was the unanimous choice, did the electors exercise a nonpartisan and presumably independent judgment. Within ten years from the time the federal government began to operate, the party system developed and electors quickly became its political captives. Nominated by their party, they were expected to vote for their party's candidates. The outcome of the election of 1800 vividly illustrates this new pattern of partisan voting.

The Federalist party supported President John Adams of Massachusetts and Charles C. Pinckney of South Carolina. The Republicans, who had emerged to oppose the Federalists' policies, backed Thomas Jefferson of Virginia and Aaron Burr of New York. The Republican candidates won, but, unexpectedly, Jefferson and Burr received the same number of votes. All electors who had cast ballots for Jefferson also cast them for Burr. Since it was not possible to differentiate the candidates for the Presidency and Vice Presidency on the ballot, the results had to be considered a tie, though Jefferson was clearly his party's choice for President. Under the terms of the Constitution, the House of Representatives, voting by state, had to choose the winner.

On February 11, 1801, after the results of the Electoral College vote were announced by the Vice President—who happened to be Jefferson—the House convened to resolve the dilemma. It was a Federalist-controlled House. Since the winners of the 1800 election did not take office until March 4, 1801, a "lame duck" Congress had to choose the next President.[10] A majority of Federalists supported Burr, whom they regarded as the more pragmatic politician. Jefferson, on the other hand, was perceived as a dangerous, uncompromising radical by many Federalists. Alexander Hamilton, however, was outspoken in his opposition to Burr, regarding him as "the most unfit man in the United States for the office of President."[11]

On the first ballot taken on February 11, Burr received a majority of the total votes, but Jefferson received the support of more state delegations.[12] Eight states voted for Jefferson, six backed Burr, and two were evenly divided. This left Jefferson one short of the needed majority. The House took nineteen ballots on its first day of deliberations and a total of thirty-six before it finally elected Jefferson. Had Burr promised to be a Federalist President, it is conceivable that he would have won.

The first amendment to reform voting procedures in the Electoral College was enacted by the new Congress in 1803, a Congress controlled by Jefferson's party. It was accepted by three-fourths of the states in 1804. This amendment to the Constitution—the twelfth—provided for separate voting for President and Vice President. It also refined the selection procedures in the event that the President and/or Vice President did not receive a majority of the electoral vote. The House of Representatives, still voting by states, was to choose from among the three presidential candidates with the most electoral votes, and the Senate, voting by individuals, was to choose from the top two vice presidential candidates. If the House could not make a decision by March 4, the amendment provided for the new Vice President to assume the Presidency until such time as the House could render a decision.

The next nondecisive presidential vote did not occur until 1824. That year, four people received electoral votes for President: Andrew Jackson (99 votes), John Quincy Adams (84), William Crawford (41), and Henry Clay (37). According to the Twelfth Amendment, the House of Representatives had to decide from among the top three, since none had a majority. Eliminated from the contest was Henry Clay, who happened to be Speaker of the House. Clay threw his support to Adams, who won.

It was alleged that he did so in exchange for appointment as secretary of state, a charge that Clay vigorously denied. After Adams became President, however, he did appoint Clay secretary of state.

Jackson was the winner of the popular vote. In the eighteen states that chose electors by popular vote (there were twenty-four states in the Union), he received 192,933 votes compared with 115,696 for Adams, 47,136 for Clay, and 46,979 for Crawford. Adams, however, had the backing of more state delegations. He enjoyed the support of the six New England states (he was from Massachusetts), and with Clay's help the representatives of six other states backed his candidacy. The votes of thirteen states, however, were needed for a majority. New York seemed to be the pivotal state and Stephen Van Rensselaer, a Revolutionary War general, the swing representative. On the morning of the vote, Speaker Clay and Representative Daniel Webster tried to persuade Van Rensselaer to vote for Adams. It was said that they were unsuccessful.[13] When the voting began, Van Rensselaer bowed his head as if in prayer. On the floor he saw a piece of paper with "Adams" written on it. Interpreting this as a sign from the Almighty, he dropped the paper in the box. New York went for Adams by one vote, providing him with a bare majority of states.[14]

Jackson, outraged at the turn of events, urged the abolition of the Electoral College. His claim of a popular mandate, however, is open to question. The most populous state at the time, New York, did not permit its electorate to participate in the selection of electors. Rather, the state legislature made the decision. Moreover, in three of the states in which Jackson won the electoral vote but lost in the House of Representatives, he had fewer popular votes than Adams. He caputred the majority of electoral votes in two of these states because the electors were chosen on a district rather than statewide basis.[15]

Opposition to the system mounted, however, and a gradual democratization of the process occurred. More states began to elect their electors directly by popular vote. In 1800, ten of the fifteen had legislative selection. By 1832, only South Carolina retained this practice.[16]

There was also a trend toward statewide election of an *entire* slate of electors. Those states that had chosen their electors within districts converted to a winner-take-all system in order to maximize their voting power in the Electoral College. This, in turn, created the possibility that there could be a disparity between the popular and electoral vote. A candidate could be elected by winning the popular vote in the big states by small margins and losing the smaller states by large margins.

The next disputed election occurred in 1876. Democrat Samuel J. Tilden received the most votes. He had 250,000 more popular votes and 19 more electoral votes than his Republican rival, Rutherford B. Hayes. Nonetheless, Tilden was one vote short of a majority in the Electoral College. Twenty electoral votes were in dispute. Dual election returns were received from Florida (4), Louisiana (8), and South Carolina (7). Charges of fraud and voting irregularities were made by both parties. The Republicans, who controlled the three state legislatures, contended that Democrats had forcibly prevented newly freed blacks from voting. The Democrats, on the other hand, alleged that many nonresidents and nonregistered people had participated. The other disputed electoral vote occurred in the state of Oregon. One Republican elector was challenged on the grounds that he held another federal position at the time and thus was ineligible to be an elector.

Three days before the Electoral College vote was to be officially counted, Congress established a commission to examine and try to resolve the dispute. The electoral commission was to consist of fifteen members: ten from Congress (five Republicans and five Democrats) and five from the Supreme Court. Four of the Supreme Court justices were designated by the act (two Republicans and two Democrats), and they were to choose a fifth justice. David Davis, a political independent, was expected to be selected, but on the day the commission was created, Davis was appointed by the Illinois legislature to the United States Senate. The Supreme Court justices then chose Joseph Bradley, an independent Republican. Bradley sided with his party on every issue. By a strictly partisan vote, the commission validated all of the Republican electors, thereby giving Hayes a one-vote margin of victory.[17]

The only other election in which the winner of the popular vote was beaten in the Electoral College occurred in 1888. Democrat Grover Cleveland had a plurality of 95,096 popular votes but only 168 electoral votes compared with 233 for the Republican, Benjamin Harrison. Cleveland's loss of Indiana by about 3,000 votes and New York by about 15,000 led to his defeat.

While all other leaders in the popular vote have won a majority of electoral votes, shifts of just a few thousand popular votes in a few states could have altered the results. In 1860, a shift of 25,000 in New York from Abraham Lincoln to Stephen A. Douglas would have denied Lincoln a majority in the Electoral College. A change of less than 30,000 in three states in 1892 would have given Harrison another victory over Cleveland.

In 1916, Charles Evans Hughes needed only 3,807 more votes in California to have beaten Woodrow Wilson. Similarly, Thomas E. Dewey could have denied Harry S. Truman a majority in the Electoral College with 12,487 more California votes in 1948. In 1960, a change of less than 9,000 in Illinois and Missouri would have meant that John F. Kennedy lacked an Electoral College majority. In 1968, a shift of only 55,000 votes from Richard M. Nixon to Hubert H. Humphrey in three states (New Jersey, Missouri, and New Hampshire) would have thrown the election into the House—a House controlled by the Democrats. In 1976, a shift of only 3,687 in Hawaii and 5,559 in Ohio would have cost Jimmy Carter the election.[18]

Not only could the results of these elections have been affected by very small voter shifts in a few states, but in 1948, 1960, and 1968 there was the further possibility that the Electoral College itself would not be able to choose a winner. In each of these elections, third-party candidates or independent electoral slates threatened to secure enough votes to prevent either of the major candidates from obtaining a majority. In 1948, Henry Wallace (Progressive party) and Strom Thurmond (States' Rights party) received almost 5 percent of the total popular vote and Thurmond won 39 electoral votes. In 1960, fourteen unpledged electors were chosen in Alabama and Mississippi.[19] In 1968, Governor George Wallace of Alabama, running on the American Independent party ticket, received almost 10 million popular votes (13.5 percent of the total) and 46 electoral votes. It was clear that close competition between the major parties, combined with a strong third-party movement, provided the Electoral College with its most difficult test.

THE POLITICS OF ELECTORAL COLLEGE VOTING

The Electoral College is not neutral. No system of election can be. The way votes are aggregated does make a difference. It benefits some of the electorate and adversely affects others.

A direct popular election always works to the advantage of the majority; the Electoral College usually does. Most often, it exaggerates the margin of the popular vote leader. Richard Nixon's 301 electoral votes in 1968 provided him with 56 percent of the college; his popular vote percentage was only 43.4 percent. Jimmy Carter's election in 1976 resulted in a smaller disparity. He won 50.1 percent of the popular vote and 55 percent of the electoral vote. In 1980, Ronald Reagan received 51 percent of the popular vote but a whopping 91 percent of the electoral vote.

It must be recalled, however, that while the Electoral College usually expands the margin of the popular vote winner, it has also from time to time led to the defeat of the candidate with the most popular votes. On three occasions, 1824, 1876, and 1888, the plurality winner was a loser in the Electoral College. Although such an electoral loss would be less likely today because the parties are competitive in more states, it is still possible.

In general, the Electoral College works to the benefit of the very smallest states (those with less than four electoral votes), and to an even greater extent, the very largest (those with more than fourteen votes.) (See Fig 1–1.) The smallest states are aided because they are overrepresented in the Electoral College. By having three electoral votes, regardless of size, a small population state such as Alaska will have an advantage. If the state's population were divided by the number of its electoral votes, Alaska would have one elector for every 133,000 inhabitants, while California would have one for every 500,000.

The system helps the largest states not only because of the number of electoral votes they cast but because the votes are almost always cast in a bloc. The general ticket system, which elects all the electors of the candidate who receives the most popular votes within the states, maximizes the clout of the bigger states. This is why a greater share of campaign time and money is spent in these states.

When the voting power of individual states is calculated by region, a bias also occurs. According to Professor Lawrence Longley, states in the Far West and East are aided, but those in the South, Midwest, and Rocky Mountain areas are hurt.[20]

By giving an edge to the larger and more competitive states, the Electoral College also benefits groups that are geographically concentrated within those states and have cohesive voting patterns. Those who live in the central cities and suburbs have a particular advantage. Jews and urban blacks fall into this category. However, the black population in general does not because many blacks live in rural and smaller states, particularly in the South.[21] The advantage given to the urban-suburban areas because of their population density has tended to give the Electoral College a liberal bias and may explain why many minority groups oppose changing the system.

The Electoral College also works to the benefit of the two major

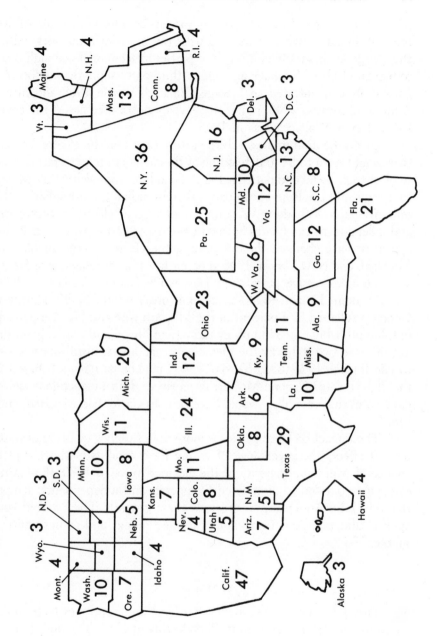

Figure 1–1   STATE SIZE ACCORDING TO POPULATION: THE 1984 ELECTORAL VOTE

parties and to the detriment of the minor parties. The winner-take-all system within states, when combined with the need for a majority within the college, makes it difficult for third parties to accumulate enough votes to win an election. To have any effect, third-party support must be geographically concentrated, as George Wallace's was in 1968 and Strom Thurmond's was in 1948, rather than evenly distributed across the country, as Henry Wallace's was in 1948.

Given the limitations on third parties, their realistic electoral objectives would seem to be to defeat one of the major contenders rather than to elect their own candidate. In 1912, Theodore Roosevelt's Bull Moose campaign split the Republican party, thereby aiding the candidate of the minority party, Woodrow Wilson. In more recent elections, third-party and independent candidates have cost the major parties votes but do not appear to have changed the outcome of the election. Truman's loss of Michigan and New York in 1948 apparently was a consequence of Henry Wallace's Progressive party candidacy, while George Wallace in 1968 probably denied Nixon 46 more electoral votes from the South. However, George Wallace's 11.4 percent of the Missouri vote and his 11.8 percent in Ohio probably hurt Humphrey more than Nixon and may explain the loss of these two states by the Democratic candidate. Ford's narrow victory in Iowa in 1976 (632,863 to 619,931) may be partially attributed to the 20,051 votes Eugene McCarthy received as an independent candidate, votes that very likely would have gone to Carter had McCarthy not run.

The impact on third parties is more than simply a question of numbers. It affects the psychology of voting for a candidate who has little chance of winning a majority of the electoral vote. In 1980, the Carter campaign appealed to disaffected Democrats and independents, sympathetic to John Anderson, on precisely these grounds. The "wasted vote appeal" undercut Anderson's ability to raise money and garner political support.[22]

SUMMARY

The quest for the Presidency has been and continues to be influenced by the system designed in Philadelphia in 1787. The objectives of that system were to protect the independence of the institution, to insure the selection of a well-qualified candidate, and to do so in a way that was politically expedient. It was intended to be consistent with the tenets of a republican form of government but not with those of a democracy.

While many of the objectives are still the same, the system has changed significantly over the years. Of all the factors that have influenced these changes, none has been more important than the advent of political parties. This development created an additional first step in the process—the nomination, which has influenced the selection and behavior of the electors and has affected the operation and the beneficiaries of the Electoral College itself.

The nomination process was necessary to the parties, whose principal interest is to get their leaders elected. At first, members of Congress, meeting in partisan caucuses, decided on the nominees. On the basis of common friendships and shared perspectives they reached a consensus and then used their status and influence to mobilize support for it. In effect, the system provided for legislative selection of the President in violation of the letter and spirit of the Constitution.

The caucus method broke down with the weakening of the parties, the demise of the Federalists, and the factionalization of the Republicans. It was never restored. In its place developed a more decentralized mode of selection reflective of the increasing sectional composition of the parties.

The new nomination process, controlled by state leaders, operated within the framework of a brokered national convention. There was little rank-and-file participation. The wheeling and dealing was done for the party's electorate, not by them. Demands for greater public involvement eventually opened the system, thereby reducing the influence of state leaders and decreasing the dependence of candidates on them. Power eventually shifted from the political leaders to the candidates themselves.

Similar trends, rooted in the development of parties and the expansion of suffrage, affected the way in which the electors were selected and voted. Instead of being chosen on the basis of their qualifications, electors were selected on the basis of their politics; instead of being elected as individuals, entire slates of electors were chosen; instead of exercising independent judgment, the electors became partisan agents who were morally and politically obligated to support their party's choice. The predictable soon happened: bloc voting by electors in states.

The desire of the populace for greater participation also had an effect. It accelerated the movement to choose the electors directly by the people, which resulted in an increased likelihood of the electoral vote's reflecting, even exaggerating, the popular vote. Only three times in American history was the plurality winner not elected. However, the shift of a very small number of votes in a few states could have altered the results of other elections, most recently in 1960, 1968, and 1976, thus raising doubts about the adequacy of the system.

The equity of the Electoral College itself has come into question. The way it works benefits the larger, more competitive states with the most electoral votes. Within those states, the groups which are better organized and more geographically concentrated seem to enjoy the greatest advantage. Their vote is maximized by the winner's taking all the state's electoral votes and the state's having a larger share of the total Electoral College. Candidates keep this in mind when planning and conducting their campaigns.

Would the framers have been satisfied with the changes? Does the system still operate to achieve the original goals as well as the new ones which party and public have demanded? The answers are debatable. For the most part, the system has been decisive and efficient, but there are questions about its equity. It does not jeopardize the President's independence. In fact, it may isolate his selection too much from the election of other officials for national office. It permits a partisan choice but recently has not contributed to the strength of the party. It facilitates participation but has not substantially raised the level of public involvement in the general election. The winning candidate often obtains only a bare majority or even plurality of the voters, who, in turn, constitute anywhere from 50 to 60 percent of the voting age population—hardly the mandate we might expect in a vibrant democratic society.

NOTES

1. Gouverneur Morris, *Records of the Federal Convention,* ed. Max Farrand (New Haven: Yale University Press, 1921), Vol. II, p. 33.

2. The first proposal for direct election was introduced in a very timid fashion by James Wilson, delegate from Pennsylvania. James Madison's *Journal* describes Wilson's presentation as follows: "Mr. Wilson said he was almost unwilling to declare the mode which he wished to take place, being apprehensive that it might appear chimerical. He would say however at least that in theory he was for an election by the people; Experience, particularly in N. York & Massts, shewed that an election of the first magistrate by the people at large, was both convenient & successful mode." Ibid., Vol. I, p. 68.

3. So great was the sectional rivalry, so parochial the country, so limited the number of people with national reputations, that it was feared that electors would tend to vote primarily for those from their own states. To prevent the same states, particularly the largest ones, from exercising undue influence in the selection of both the President and Vice President, this provision was included. It remains in effect today.

4. George Mason declared, "Nineteen times out of twenty, the President would be chosen by the Senate." Ibid., Vol. II, p. 500. The original proposal of the Committee on Unfinished Business was that the Senate should select the President. The delegates substituted the House of Representatives, fearing that the Senate was too powerful with its appointment and treaty-making powers. The principle of equal state representation

was retained. Choosing the President is the only occasion on which the House votes by states.

5. Thomas R. Marshall, *Presidential Nominations in a Reform Age* (New York: Praeger, 1981), p. 19.

6. Neal R. Peirce and Lawrence D. Longley, *The People's President* (New Haven: Yale University Press, 1981), p. 36.

7. Marshall, *Presidential Nominations*, p. 20.

8. Ibid., p. 21.

9. Louis Maisel and Gerald J. Lieberman, "The Impact of Electoral Rules on Primary Elections: The Democratic Presidential Primaries in 1976," in Louis Maisel and Joseph Cooper (eds.), *The Impact of the Electoral Process* (Beverly Hills, Calif: Sage Publications, 1977), p. 68.

10. Until the passage of the Twentieth Amendment, which made January 3 the date when members of Congress took their oath of office and convened, every second session of Congress was a lame duck session.

11. Lucius Wilmerding, *The Electoral College* (New Brunswick, N.J.: Rutgers University Press, 1953), p. 32.

12. There were 106 members of the House (58 Federalists and 48 Republicans). On the first ballot, the vote of those present was 53 to 51 for Burr.

13. Peirce and Longley, *The People's President*, p. 51.

14. Marquis James, *The Life of Andrew Jackson* (Indianapolis: Bobbs-Merrill, 1938), p. 439.

15. William R. Keech, "Background Paper" in *Winner Take All: Report of the Twentieth Century Fund Task Force on Reform of the Presidential Election Process* (New York: Holmes and Meier, 1978), p. 50.

16. South Carolina clung to this system until 1860. After the Civil War, it too instituted popular selection.

17. The act that created the commission specified that its decision would be final unless overturned by both houses of Congress. The House of Representatives, controlled by the Democrats, opposed every one of the commission's findings. The Republican Senate, however, concurred. A Democratic filibuster in the Senate was averted by Hayes's promise of concessions to the South, including the withdrawal of federal troops. Tilden could have challenged the findings in court but chose not to do so.

18. Richard M. Scammon and Alice V. McGillivray, *America Votes 12* (Washington, D.C.: Congressional Quarterly, 1977), p. 15.

19. In Alabama, slates of electors ran against each other without the names of the presidential candidates appearing on the ballot. The Democratic slate included six unpledged electors and five loyalists. All were elected. The unpledged electors voted for Senator Harry Byrd of Virginia, while the loyalists stayed with the Kennedy-Johnson ticket. In Mississippi, all eight Democratic electors voted for Byrd.

20. Lawrence D. Longley, "Minorities and the 1980 Electoral College" (paper delivered at the annual meeting of the American Political Science Association, Washington, D.C., August 28–31, 1980), p. 13.

21. Ibid., pp. 14–21.

22. Independent and third-party candidates have also been hurt by early filing deadlines in certain states. In 1980, Anderson was forced to devote several months and a million dollars to overcoming such legal obstacles. In 1983 the Supreme Court vindicated his efforts. It held that early deadlines, which limited participation by independent and

third-party candidates, violated their first amendment guarantees of freedom of association. A majority of the court declared that minority party candidates should be able to get on state ballots after the two major parties have chosen their nominees (*Anderson v. Celebrezze* 460 U.S.).

Selected Readings

American Bar Association. *Electing the President: A Report of the Commission on Electoral College Reform.* Chicago: American Bar Association, 1967.

Best, Judith. *The Case Against Direct Election of the President: A Defense of the Electoral College.* Ithaca, N.Y.: Cornell University Press, 1975.

Bickel, Alexander M. *Reform and Continuity: The Electoral College, the Convention, and the Party System.* New York: Harper & Row, 1971.

Chase, James S. *Emergence of the Presidential Nominating Convention, 1789–1832.* Urbana: University of Illinois Press, 1973.

Congressional Quarterly. *Presidential Elections Since 1789.* Washington, D.C.: Congressional Quarterly, 1979.

Longley, Lawrence D., and Alan G. Braun. *The Politics of Electoral College Reform.* New Haven: Yale University Press, 1972.

Marshall, Thomas R. *Presidential Nominations in a Reform Age.* New York: Praeger, 1981.

Peirce, Neal R., and Lawrence D. Longley. *The People's President.* New Haven: Yale University Press, 1981.

Roseboom, Eugene H. *A History of Presidential Elections.* New York: Macmillan, 1957.

Sayre, Wallace S., and Judith H. Parris. *Voting for President.* Washington, D.C.: Brookings Institution, 1970.

Sterling, Carleton W. "The Electoral College Biases Revealed, the Conventional Wisdom and Game Theory Models Notwithstanding." *Western Political Quarterly,* 31 (1978), 159–177.

U.S. Congress. House. Committee on the Judiciary. *Electoral College Reform.* Hearings. 91st Cong., 1st sess. Washington, D.C.: Government Printing Office, 1969.

———. Senate. Committee on the Judiciary. *Electing the President.* Hearings. 91st Cong., 1st sess. Washington, D.C.: Government Printing Office, 1969.

———. Senate. Committee on the Judiciary. *The Electoral College and Direct Election.* Hearings. 95th Cong., 1st sess. Washington, D.C.: Government Printing Office, 1977.

———. Senate. Committee on the Judiciary. *Hearings on Direct Popular Election of the President and Vice President of the United States.* 96th Cong., 1st sess. Washington, D.C.: Government Printing Office, 1979.

Chapter 2

CAMPAIGN
FINANCE

Introduction

Running for President is very expensive. In 1980 a whopping $128 million was spent by major party candidates in their quest for the nomination. Another $74 million was expended by the three principal candidates in the general election. National, state, and local party committees, political action committees (PACs), and individuals also spent considerable sums on behalf of the Republican and Democratic nominees. According to Herbert E. Alexander, expenditures totaled $275 million for the 1980 presidential election, $115 million more than in the previous election.[1]

The magnitude of these expenditures poses serious problems for presidential candidates, who must raise considerable sums, monitor their expenses closely, make important allocation decisions, and conform to the intricacies of finance laws. Moreover, such expenditures raise important issues for a democratic selection process. This chapter will explore some of those problems and issues.

The chapter is organized into five sections. The first details the costs of presidential campaigns, paying particular attention to the increase in media expenditures since 1960. The next section looks briefly at the relationship between spending and electoral success. Can money buy elections? Have the big spenders been the big winners? The third section focuses on the contributors, the size of their gifts, and the implications of large donations for a democratic selection process. What is more important—the individual's right to give or the government's desire to set limits? Attempts to control spending and subsidize elections are discussed in the fourth section. The final section examines the impact of the new election laws on presidential campaigning and the party system.

THE COSTS OF CAMPAIGNING

Candidates have always spent money in their quest for the Presidency, but it was not until they began to campaign actively that these costs rose sharply. In 1860, Lincoln spent an estimated $100,000. One hundred years later, Kennedy and Nixon were each spending one hundred times that amount. In the twelve years following the 1960 general election, expenditures quadrupled. Table 2–1 lists the costs of the major party candidates in presidential elections from 1860 to 1980.

Prenomination costs have risen even more rapidly than those in the general election. Until the 1960s, large expenditures were the exception not the rule. General Leonard Wood spent an estimated $2 million in an unsuccessful quest for the Republican nomination in 1920. The contest between General Dwight D. Eisenhower and Senator Robert A. Taft in 1952 cost about $5 million, a total that was not exceeded until 1964, when Nelson Rockefeller and Barry Goldwater spent approximately twice that amount.

In recent years prenomination expenditures have skyrocketed. The increasing number of primaries, participatory caucuses, and candidates has been largely responsible for the rise. In the 1950s these preconvention contests were optional; in the 1970s and 1980s they have not been. Even incumbent Presidents have to enter.

To campaign effectively in several states simultaneously requires considerable money to pay for professional services, large organizations, and media advertising. As a consequence, preconvention costs by the candidates in 1968, 1976, and 1980 actually exceeded those in the general election. Table 2–2 lists the totals spent in the last five prenomination campaigns. These costs are not likely to decrease if both parties continue to have spirited contests for their nomination.

Inflation has also contributed to rising expenditures. Goods and services cost more than twice as much as they did a decade ago. From 1972 to 1980 the consumer price index doubled, the value of the dollar was halved, and approximately 20 million more votes were cast in the primaries and general election.

Table 2-1   COSTS OF PRESIDENTIAL GENERAL ELECTIONS, 1860–1980, MAJOR PARTY CANDIDATES

Year	Republican		Democratic	
1860	$ 100,000	Lincoln*	$ 50,000	Douglas
1864	125,000	Lincoln*	50,000	McClellan
1868	150,000	Grant*	75,000	Seymour
1872	250,000	Grant*	50,000	Greeley
1876	950,000	Hayes*	900,000	Tilden
1880	1,100,000	Garfield*	335,000	Hancock
1884	1,300,000	Blaine	1,400,000	Cleveland*
1888	1,350,000	Harrison*	855,000	Cleveland
1892	1,700,000	Harrison	2,350,000	Cleveland*
1896	3,350,000	McKinley*	675,000	Bryan
1900	3,000,000	McKinley*	425,000	Bryan
1904	2,096,000	T. Roosevelt*	700,000	Parker
1908	1,655,518	Taft*	629,341	Bryan
1912	1,071,549	Taft	1,134,848	Wilson*
1916	2,441,565	Hughes	2,284,590	Wilson*
1920	5,417,501	Harding*	1,470,371	Cox
1924	4,020,478	Coolidge*	1,108,836	Davis
1928	6,256,111	Hoover*	5,342,350	Smith
1932	2,900,052	Hoover	2,245,975	F. Roosevelt*
1936	8,892,972	Landon	5,194,741	F. Roosevelt*
1940	3,451,310	Willkie	2,783,654	F. Roosevelt*
1944	2,828,652	Dewey	2,169,077	F. Roosevelt*
1948	2,127,296	Dewey	2,736,334	Truman*
1952	6,608,623	Eisenhower*	5,032,926	Stevenson
1956	7,778,702	Eisenhower*	5,106,651	Stevenson
1960	10,128,000	Nixon	9,797,000	Kennedy*
1964	16,026,000	Goldwater	8,757,000	Johnson*
1968†	25,402,000	Nixon*	11,594,000	Humphrey
1972	61,400,000	Nixon*	30,000,000	McGovern
1976	21,786,641	Ford	21,800,000	Carter*
1980	29,188,888	Reagan*	29,352,768	Carter

Source: Herbert E. Alexander, *Financing Politics* (Washington, D.C.: Congressional Quarterly, 1980), p. 5. Copyrighted material reprinted with permission of Congressional Quarterly Inc. The 1980 figures come from the Federal Election Commission.

*Indicates winner.

†George Wallace spent an estimated $7 million as the candidate of the American Independent party in 1968, while John Anderson spent $14.4 million as an independent candidate in 1980.

The media, particularly television, account for much of the spending. When campaigns were conducted in the press, expenses were relatively low. Electioneering, carried on by a highly partisan press prior to the Civil War, had few costs other than the occasional biography and campaign pamphlet, printed by the party and sold to the public at less than cost.

With the advent of more active public campaigning toward the middle of the nineteenth century, candidate organizations turned to buttons, billboards, banners, and pictures to symbolize and illustrate their campaigns. By the beginning of the twentieth century, the cost of this type of advertising in each election exceeded $150,000—a lot then, but a minuscule amount by contemporary standards.[2]

In 1924, radio was employed for the first time in presidential campaigns. The Republicans spent approximately $120,000 that year, while the Democrats spent only $40,000.[3] Four years later, however, both parties combined spent over $1,000,000. Radio expenses continued to equal or exceed a million dollars for the next twenty years.[4]

Television emerged as a vehicle for presidential campaigning in 1952. Both national party conventions were broadcast live by television as well as radio. While there were only 19 million television sets in the United States, almost one-third of the population were regular television viewers. The number of households with television sets rose dramatically over the next four years. By 1956 an estimated 71 percent had television and by 1968 the figure was close to 95 percent. A 1969 report by the Nielsen Company found the average set in operation forty-three hours per week, or over six hours a day.[5]

The first spot commercials for presidential candidates appeared in 1952. They became regular fare thereafter, contributing substantially to campaign costs. Film biographies, interview shows, political rallies, and election-eve telethons were all seen with increasing frequency.

In 1948 no money was spent on television by either party. Twenty years later, expenses exceeded $18 million for radio and television combined, approximately one-third of the total cost of the campaign. (See Table 2–3.)

Table 2–2 COSTS OF PRESIDENTIAL NOMINATION CAMPAIGNS, 1964–1980 (IN MILLIONS OF DOLLARS)

Year	Republican	Democratic
1964	$10	(uncontested)
1968	20	$25
1972	(virtually uncontested)*	33.1
1976	26.1	40.7
1980	86.1	41.7

Sources: 1964–1972, Herbert E. Alexander, *Financing Politics* (Washington, D.C.: Congressional Quarterly, 1976), pp. 45–47. Copyrighted material reprinted with permission of Congressional Quarterly Inc. 1976–1980, Federal Election Commission, Final Reports.
*Representative John M. Ashbrook spent $740,000 and Representative Paul N. McCloskey spent $550,000 in challenging President Richard M. Nixon for the nomination. Alexander, *Financing Politics*, p. 46.

Table 2–3   RADIO AND TELEVISION EXPENDITURES FOR PRESIDENTIAL GENERAL ELECTION CAMPAIGNS, BY PARTY, 1952–1980

Year	Republican	Democratic
1952	$ 2,046,000	$ 1,500,000
1956	2,886,000	1,763,000
1960	1,865,000	1,142,000
1964	6,370,000	4,674,000
1968	12,598,000	6,143,000
1972	4,300,000	6,200,000
1976	7,875,000	9,081,321
1980	14,600,000	19,500,000

Source: Herbert E. Alexander, *Financing Politics* (Washington, D.C.: Congressional Quarterly, 1980), p. 10. Copyrighted material reprinted with permission of Congressional Quarterly Inc. Figures for 1980 provided to the author by Professor Alexander.

Outlays for television dropped in 1972, largely as a consequence of Richard Nixon's use of free television time as President. In 1976 and again in 1980, they increased. Higher production costs and charges for air time combined with greater reliance on the media by the candidates contributed to the rise. As a consequence larger portions of campaign budgets have had to be allocated to media expenses with the bulk of this money going to television, In 1980 Carter spent $20 million on media, Reagan $17 million, and Anderson $2.4 million.

The use of modern technology has also increased expenditures. In 1968, Humphrey and McGovern spent between them $650,000 on polling, while in 1972, the Nixon campaign alone spent over $1.6 million.[6] These expenses have remained relatively constant at the presidential level. In 1980 the major party candidates spent approximately $2 million each.

Finally, the costs of fund raising have increased. In the past, candidates depended on a relatively small number of large contributors. They could personally solicit funds. Today, they depend on a relatively large number of small contributors. Mass appeals must be made. Direct mail is the principal mechanism for doing so.

Eisenhower was the first presidential candidate to make use of the direct-mail technique. His letter to *Reader's Digest* subscribers promising to go to Korea to end the war generated a substantial legacy for his campaign. In 1964 and again in 1972, Barry Goldwater and George McGovern, unable to obtain support from their party's regular contributors, targeted appeals to partisans and other sympathizers. Their success, combined with changes in the law that prohibited large gifts yet ultimately required more spending, has made direct-mail solicitation the order of the day for parties and candidates alike.

The costs of these mailings can be considerable. When the price of obtaining the lists is added to the expense of designing, producing, addressing, and sending the letter, the total spent can exceed the amount raised. Philip Crane, the first declared candidate for the 1980 Republican nomination, spent $2 million to raise $1.7 million from 70,000 contributors.[7] (See pages 104–105 for a discussion of direct mail techniques.)

Three major issues arise from the problems of large expenditures. One concerns the impact of spending. To what extent does it improve a candidate's chances for success? Another problem pertains to the donors. Who pays, and what do they get for their money? A third relates to the costs. Can expenditures be controlled without impinging on First Amendment freedoms? The next section turns to the first of these questions, the relation of expenditures to winning and losing. Subsequent sections examine the sources of contributions, attempts to regulate costs, and the impact of the regulations on presidential elections.

THE CONSEQUENCES OF SPENDING

Is spending related to electoral success? Have candidates with the largest bank rolls generally been victorious? At the presidential level, the answers seem to be yes, but it is difficult to determine the extent to which money alone has contributed to victory.

In general elections between 1860 and 1972, the winner outspent the loser twenty-one out of twenty-nine times. (See Table 2–1.) Republican candidates have spent more than their Democratic opponents in twenty-five out of the twenty-nine elections. The four times they did not, the Democrats won. This suggests that the money contributes to success and potential success attracts money.[8]

Having more funds is an advantage, but it does not guarantee victory. The fact that Nixon outspent McGovern more than two to one in 1972 does not explain McGovern's loss. It probably portended it, however, since major contributors tend to be more attracted to likely winners than to losers. Nonetheless, McGovern's $30 million was sufficient to mount an effective campaign. On the other hand, Humphrey's much narrower defeat at the hands of Nixon four years earlier was probably influenced by Humphrey's having spent less than $12 million, compared with over $25 million spent by Nixon. The closer the election, the more the disparity in funds can be a factor.

Theoretically, campaign spending should have a greater impact on the nomination process than on the general election. The need of most candidates to gain visibility, mobilize support, and develop an effective organization normally requires a large outlay of funds. Some of the biggest spenders, however, have been losers. In 1964, Nelson Rockefeller spent approximately $5 million, much of it his own money, in losing to Barry Goldwater. Four years later, an unsuccessful Rockefeller spent $8 million without entering a single primary. And in 1980, John Connally spent $13.7 million yet had only one delegate pledged to him at the time of his withdrawal—the most expensive delegate in history!

Though less striking, the 1980 Republican primaries demonstrate other examples of the high costs of losing. Representative John Anderson and Senator Howard Baker spent $7.1 million and $9 million respectively and did not win a single primary. George Bush spent $4 million less than Reagan but trailed him badly in the number of pledged delegates. In Pennsylvania alone, Bush spent $1.4 million compared with Reagan's $250,000 but received only half as many pledged delegates.

There are, of course, examples of successful candidates who spent more. John Kennedy's financial resources in 1960 not only aided his campaign in critical primaries, such as the West Virginia contest with Hubert Humphrey, but also discouraged challengers in several others, such as California and Ohio. In 1972, McGovern was able to spend $4 million on the crucial California primary, one-third of his prenomination expenses. It was McGovern's win in that primary over an unpledged slate of delegates that clinched his nomination.

In 1980 both winning candidates, Ronald Reagan and Jimmy Carter, outspent their opponents. Moreover, they outraised their opponents. One benefit of winning is the increased ability to raise money. Table 2–4 lists the spending by primary candidates in 1980.

In examining the relationship between campaign expenditures and votes received in twenty-five 1976 primary elections, Joel H. Goldstein found a mixed pattern. In fifteen of the twenty-five Republican contests, the winner outspent the loser; in contrast, in only six of the Democratic primaries did the candidate with the most votes spend the most money.[9]

Money is thus a necessary but not sufficient ingredient for success at the polls. Other factors, such as the popularity of the candidates, the extent of their partisan support, the structure and operation of their campaign organizations, and the impact of external events, also affect the results. These items will be explored in later chapters.

Table 2–4 PRENOMINATION EXPENDITURES, 1980

Republicans		Democrats	
Candidate	Expenditures	Candidate	Expenditures
Anderson	$7,148,841	Brown	$ 3,208,448
Baker	9,015,183	Carter	19,560,416
Bush	22,206,046	Kennedy	16,722,101
Connally	13,698,056	LaRouche	2,226,992
Crane	5,397,907	Total	$41,717,957
Reagan	26,746,725		
Others	1,908,208		
Total	$86,120,966		

Source: Federal Election Commission, "Presidential Pre-Nomination Campaigns," Final Report (October 1981), p. 7.

THE SOURCES OF MONEY

In addition to the high costs of campaigning and the effect that un-equal spending can have on electoral results, another critical issue is the sources of funds and the strings, if any, which are attached to giving.[10] Throughout most of America's electoral history, parties and candidates have depended on large contributors. In fact, the increase in expenditures was largely a consequence of the willingness of the rich to give.

At the end of the nineteenth century, in the midst of the industrial boom, the Republicans were able to count on the support of the Astors, Harrimans, and Vanderbilts, while the Democrats looked to financier August Belmont and inventor-industrialist Cyrus McCormick. Corporations, banks, and life insurance companies soon became prime targets of party fund raisers. The most infamous and probably the most adroit fund raiser of this period was Mark Hanna. A leading official of the Republican party, Hanna owed most of his influence to his ability to obtain substantial political contributions. He set quotas, personally assessing the amount that businesses and corporations should give. In 1896, and again in 1900, he was able to obtain contributions of $250,000 from Standard Oil. Theodore Roosevelt personally ordered the return of some of the Standard Oil money in 1904 but accepted large gifts from magnates E. H. Harriman and Henry C. Frick. Roosevelt's trust-busting activities during his Presidency led Frick to remark, "We bought the son of a bitch and then he did not stay bought."[11]

Sizable private gifts remained the principal sources of party and candidate support into the 1970s. The Republicans benefited more than the Democrats. Only in 1964 was President Lyndon B. Johnson able to raise more money from large donors than his Republican opponent, Barry Goldwater.

The reluctance of regular Republican contributors to support the Goldwater candidacy forced his organization to appeal to thousands of potential supporters through a direct mailing. The success of this effort in raising $5.8 million from approximately 651,000 people showed the potential of the mails as a fund-raising technique. Subsequently, Governor George Wallace in 1968 and Senator George McGovern in 1972 solicited the bulk of their funds in this fashion. Today, direct mail fund raising is the dominant mode of solicitation.

Despite the use of mass mailings and also party telethons to broaden the base of political contributors in the 1960s, dependence on large donors continued to grow. In 1964 over $2 million was raised in contributions of $10,000 or more. Eight years later approximately $51 million was collected in gifts of this size or larger. (See Table 2–5.)

In addition to growing more numerous, the big contributors, frequently referred to as "fat cats," contributed even greater amounts. In 1972, Chicago insurance executive W. Clement Stone and his wife contributed over $2 million to the Republicans, most of it going to Richard Nixon. Richard Mellon Scaife, heir to the Mellon fortune, gave the Nixon campaign and several other Republican candidates $1 million. The most sizable Democratic gift that year came from Stewart R. Mott, a General Motors heir, who gave $800,000. The McGovern campaign also received approximately $800,000 from political action committees of organized

Table 2–5   LARGE CONTRIBUTIONS, 1952–1972

Year	Number of Contributors		Amount
	$500+	$10,000+	$10,000 or Over*
1952	9,500	110	$ 1,936,870
1956	8,100	111	2,300,000
1960	5,300	95	1,552,009
1964	10,000	130	2,161,905
1968	15,000	424	12,187,863
1972	51,230	1,254	51,320,154

Source: Herbert E. Alexander, *Financing Politics* (Washington, D.C.: Congressional Quarterly, 1976), p. 8. Copyrighted material reprinted with permission of Congressional Quarterly Inc.
*Does not include candidates who contributed to their own campaigns.

labor even though most of the AFL-CIO's leadership did not endorse his candidacy. Donations in 1972 to both presidential campaigns exceeded $90 million, with the Republicans raising over $60 million.

The heavy-handed tactics of the Nixon fund raisers, combined with the illegality of some of the contributions in 1971 and 1972, brought into sharp focus the difficulty of maintaining a democratic selection process that was dependent on private funding.[12] Reliance on large and often anonymous contributors, the inequality of funding between parties and candidates, and the high costs of campaigning, especially in the media, all raised serious questions. Were there implicit assumptions about giving and receiving? Could elected officials be responsive to individual benefactors and to the general public at the same time? Put another way, did the need to obtain and keep large contributors affect decision making in a manner that was inconsistent with the tenets of a democratic society? Did the high cost of campaigning, in and of itself, eliminate otherwise qualified candidates from running? Were certain political parties, interest groups, or individuals consistently advantaged or disadvantaged by the distribution of funding? Had the Presidency become an office that only the wealthy could afford—or, worse still, that only those with wealthy support could seek?

CAMPAIGN FINANCE LEGISLATION

Years ago Congress first debated and attempted to resolve some of these issues through campaign finance legislation. The first such legislation was enacted in 1907. Known as the Tillman Act, it prohibited corporations from making contributions to parties or candidates. This prohibition was subsequently extended to public utilities in 1936 and to labor unions in 1944. It was not very effective, however. While money could not be given directly by corporations, utilities, and unions, there was little to prevent their officials from making personal contributions at the behest of the organization. Executives would receive bonuses with the expectation that they and their families would donate the money to certain parties and candidates. Labor unions also got around the restriction by forming political action committees. These committees solicited "voluntary" donations from members and designated candidates to receive the funds.

Legislation in the 1940s placed limits on the amount an individual could contribute to a single candidate for national office or to a political committee supporting that candidate ($5,000) and the amount the candidate's committee could spend ($3 million). These limits, however, were easily circumvented. Contributing the maximum to a number of campaign committees or, similarly, establishing a number of committees to spend the maximum amount could render the law ineffective. The inability to enforce this legislation left presidential campaigning practically unregulated until the 1970s.

In 1962, President Kennedy established a bipartisan Commission on Campaign Costs. Its recommendations included public disclosure of contributions, limits on spending, tax incentives to elicit broader giving, and supervisory committees to monitor the law. While these proposals were not immediately acted upon by Congress, they formed part of the foundation for subsequent legislation.

In 1971, Congress passed the Federal Elections Campaign Act. It sought to limit skyrocketing expenses, especially in the media, by setting ceilings on the amount of money presidential and vice presidential candidates and their families could contribute to their own campaigns and the amount that could be spent on media advertising. Procedures requiring contributions of over $100 to be publicly disclosed were also established.

A Revenue Act of the same year created tax credits and deductions to encourage contributions. For the first time, it also provided for federal subsidies for the presidential election through the establishment of a national campaign fund. Financed by an income tax check-off provision, the fund allows taxpayers to designate $1 for a special presidential election account. Since the check-off was placed in a prominent place on the income tax form, approximately 25 percent of the population have been approving the use of $1 of their taxes for the fund. In 1980, $146 million; in 1984, approximately $220 million.

Despite the passage of the funding provision in 1971, it did not go into effect until 1976. Most Republicans had opposed the legislation. In addition to conflicting with their general ideological position that the national government's role be limited, it offset the party's traditional fund-raising advantage. President Nixon was persuaded to sign the bill only after the Democratic leadership agreed to postpone the effective date of the law until after 1972, when Nixon planned to run for reelection.

There was also a short but critical delay in the effective date for the disclosure provision of the other 1971 campaign finance act. Signed by the President on February 14, 1972, it was scheduled to take effect in sixty days. This delay precipitated a frantic attempt by both parties to tap large donors who wished to remain anonymous. It is estimated that the Republicans collected a staggering $20 million, much of it pledged beforehand, during this period. Of this money, approximately $1.5 million came in the form of cash or checks that could not be easily traced.

Even after the disclosure provision went into effect, violations were numerous. Moreover, pressure on corporations, particularly by Nixon campaign officials, resulted in a long list of illegal contributions. Executives from large companies such as Gulf Oil, American, and Braniff airlines, Northrop, Greyhound, and Goodyear admitted to giving thousands of dollars of corporate funds to the Nixon campaign. In one of the most celebrated cases, the dairy industry was accused of giving more than $680,000, much of it illegally, in exchange for an increase in government support of milk prices.[13] The spending of funds on dirty tricks and other unethical and illegal activities, such as the burglary of the Democratic National Committee's Watergate headquarters, further aroused public ire and eventually resulted in new and more stringent legislation.

Congress responded by amending the 1971 act. Its new legislation, passed in 1974, included public disclosure provisions, contribution ceilings, campaign spending limits, and federal subsidies for the nomination process. A six-person commission was established to enforce the law. Two members of the commission were to be appointed by the President and four by Congress.

The law was highly controversial. Critics immediately charged a federal giveaway, a robbery of the Treasury. Opponents of the legislation also argued that the limits on contributions and spending violated the constitutionally guaranteed right to freedom of speech; that the fund provisions unfairly discriminated against third-party and independent candidates; and that appointment of four of the commissioners by Congress violated the principle of separation of powers. A suit brought by such diverse individuals and groups as a conservative Republican senator from New York, James L. Buckley, the presidential aspirant and former liberal Democratic senator from Minnesota, Eugene McCarthy, the Libertarian party, the Republican Party of Mississippi, and the New York Civil Liberties Union reached the Supreme Court one year after the legislation was enacted.

In the landmark case of *Buckley* v. *Valeo* (424 U.S. 1, 1976), the court upheld the right of Congress to regulate campaign expenditures but negated two principal provisions of the law, the overall limits on spending and the appointment by Congress of four of the six commissioners. The majority opinion contended that by placing restrictions on the amount of money an individual could spend during a campaign, the law directly and substantially restrained speech. However, the Supreme Court majority did allow limits on contributions to campaign organizations and on expenditures by those organizations if public funds were accepted.

As a consequence of the court's decision, Congress was forced to draft new legislation. In the spring of 1976, during the presidential primaries, amendments to the new campaign finance law were enacted. Public funding of the presidential election and subsidizing of the delegate selection process were continued. Similarly, the amount that could be contributed to a candidate's organization during the nomination contest was limited, and a ceiling was placed on the amount that organization could spend. The Federal Election Commission (FEC) was reconstituted with all six members to be nominated by the President, subject to the advice and consent of the Senate.

In 1979, additional amendments to the campaign finance law were enacted. Designed to reduce the reporting requirements of the law, they raised the minimum contribution and expenditure that had to be reported and decreased the number of reports that had to be filed. To encourage voluntary activities and higher turnout, the amendments also permitted state and local party committees to purchase an unlimited amount of campaign paraphernalia for candidates for national office and spend an unlimited amount on registration and get-out-the-vote activities.

The major provisions of the 1974 law with its 1976 and 1979 amendments are as follows:

Public Disclosure—All contributions of $200 or more must be identified. All expenditures of $200 or more must be reported. Campaign committees are also required to file periodic reports before the election and a final report after it.

Contribution Limits—In any election, contributions from individuals cannot exceed $1,000 to a single candidate or his organization, $20,000 to a national political party committee, and $5,000 to other political committees, with the total not to exceed $25,000 in any one year.14 Personal contributions from a candidate or his immediate family are limited to $50,000 at the prenomination stage and to $50,000 in the general election if the candidate accepts federal funds. Candidates who do not accept federal funds are not limited in what they can contribute to their own campaign. Table 2–6 summarizes the contribution limits. Individuals and political action committees can spend an unlimited amount on their own for candidates of their choice provided they do not consult or communicate in any way with the candidate's campaign organization.

Campaign Expenses—Candidates who accept public funding cannot spend more than $10 million in the primary and $20 million in the general election plus a cost-of-living increment. In 1980, this increment increased these amounts to $14.7 in the primaries and $29.44 million in the general election. In 1984 the figures will be even higher, approximately 26 million in the preconvention period and 32 million in the general election. There are also specific spending limits in the states. Based on the size of the voting-age population, these limits are also affected by the cost-of-living adjustment. In 1980, they ranged from approximately $294,400 in the smaller states to almost $4 million in the largest. Fund-raising expenses up to 20 percent of expenditures and accounting and legal fees are exempt from these spending limits. Candidates who do not accept federal funds have no limit on their expenditures. Additionally, the national parties can spend two cents per citizen of voting age in support of their presidential and vice presidential candidates. In 1980, this amounted to $4.6 million.

Matching Funds—Major party contenders who raise $5,000 in twenty states in contributions of $250 or less, a total of $100,000, are eligible

Table 2–6   CONTRIBUTION LIMITS

	To Each Candidate or Candidate Committee per Election	To National Party Committee per Calendar Year	To any Other Political Committee per Calendar Year	Total per Calendar Year
Individual may give:	$1,000	$20,000	$5,000	$25,000
Multicandidate committee* may give:	5,000	15,000	5,000	No limit
Party Committees may give	1,000 or 5,000+	No limit	5,000	No limit
Other political committees may give:	1,000	20,000	5,000	No limit

Source: Federal Election Commission, "The FEC and the Federal Campaign Finance Law" (Washington, D.C.: Government Printing Office, 1978), p. 4.

*A multicandidate committee is a political action committee with more than fifty contributors which has been registered for at least six months and, with the exception of state party committees, has made contributions to five or more federal candidates.

†Limit depends on whether or not the party committee is a multicandidate committee.

to receive matching grants during the prenomination period, which begins January 1 of the year in which the election occurs. Only the first $250 of each contribution will be matched.

Communication Notices—All authorized advertisements by candidates' organizations must state the name of the candidate or agent who authorized them. All nonauthorized advertisements must identify the person who made or financed the ad and his or her organizational affiliation, if any.

Compliance Procedures—The Federal Election Commission has authority to investigate possible violations, hold hearings, and assess certain civil penalties. Its decision may be appealed to U.S. District Courts. The Justice Department retains the authority for criminal investigation and prosecution.

THE IMPACT OF THE LAW

Congress had a number of objectives in enacting campaign finance legislation. It had hoped to reduce the dependence on large donors, discourage illicit contributions, broaden the base of public support, and curtail spiraling costs at the presidential level. In addition, the Democratic majority wanted to equalize better the funds of the Republican and Democratic nominees. Finally, the legislation was designed to buttress the two-party system.

While all these objectives have not been achieved, the new law has already had a significant impact on presidential politics. It has substantially reduced secret contributors and unexplained expenses. There have been some violations, overpayments, and improper reporting procedures, but most have been relatively minor. The most serious violation occurred in 1976 when Democratic candidate Milton Shapp, governor of Pennsylvania, was required to refund all of the $300,000 of matching funds he received when it was discovered that his workers had inflated the number of contributors in several states to meet the eligibility requirements. In 1976, and again in 1980, each of the major candidates was forced to return small amounts which had been improperly spent. Fines were also assessed for minor infractions. The Reagan campaign committee, for example, was required to pay $12,000 for not returning promptly contributions in the form of expenses paid by individuals and groups that exceeded the legal limits. In total, Reagan repaid over $250,000 to the Treasury and Carter almost $90,000.

The $1,000 limit on individual contributions, the $250 ceiling on matching grants, and the eligibility requirement to get federal funds all made the solicitation of a large number of small contributors essential during the preconvention phase. Direct mail experts who could raise this money became the new "fat cats" on whom candidates and their organizations had to depend. They play an increasingly visible and influential role.

Table 2–7 lists the revenue received by each of the major party candidates, the federal matching funds each was given, and the amount each raised from individual and group contributions during the 1980 primary campaign. Only one candidate, John Connally, chose not to accept government funds, thereby freeing himself from the spending limits. As the table indicates, individuals supplied the bulk of the funds. Of all the candidates, Carter and Connally had the highest percentage of large donors, those in the category of $750 or more.

While $1,000 is the maximum monetary contribution permitted, larger gifts in the form of goods and services are allowed. Artists and musicians, in particular, are able to generate considerable revenue for candidates they support through voluntary activities not subject to the contribution limits. In 1980 the campaign organization of Governor Jerry Brown raised almost $400,000 from two rock concerts featuring Brown's friend Linda Ronstadt and groups such as The Eagles and Chicago.[15] The

Table 2–7   PRENOMINATION REVENUES, 1980

Candidates	Net Receipts	Individual Contributions	PAC Contributions (Nonparty)	Federal Matching Funds
Republican				
Anderson	$ 7,250,709	$ 3,909,562	$ 24,495	$ 2,680,346
Baker	9,080,878	4,251,220	129,441	2,635,039
Bush	22,207,071	10,929,413	130,035	5,716,243
Connally	13,799,568	11,784,598	205,105	0
Crane	5,418,695	3,480,934	1,825	1,754,750
Reagan	28,316,966	13,885,357	285,439	7,294,458
Others	1,941,975	1,100,084	47,314	446,224
Total	$88,015,862	$49,341,168	$738,775	$20,527,060
Democrat				
Brown	$ 3,208,788	$ 1,714,108	$ 37,550	$ 892,246
Carter	19,592,143	13,000,936	460,651	5,052,806
Kennedy	16,736,948	7,760,859	232,374	3,862,555
LaRouche	2,226,922	1,557,154	8,200	526,250
Total	$41,764,801	$24,033,057	$823,654	$10,333,857

Source: Federal Election Commission, "Presidential Pre-Nomination Campaigns," Final Report (October 1981), p. 1.

Kennedy campaign organization used paintings by artist Andy Warhol as collateral for a $100,000 bank loan and auctioned other art objects to generate revenue.[16] Some candidates even pledged their own assets as security for loans.

While large donors declined in importance, many groups have actually gained in influence. Corporations and labor unions, prohibited from making direct contributions by law, have formed political action committees (PACs). Consisting of employees, stockholders, or members, these committees are funded through voluntary contributions.[17] They can affect the selection process in three ways: by giving up to $5,000 to a single candidate, by spending an unlimited amount *independently* on the candidate's behalf, and by using their organization to mobilize and register voters.

Of these methods of exerting influence, direct donations are probably the least important. Since the law prohibits presidential candidates from accepting contributions in the general election if they receive federal funds, financial gifts are limited to the nomination period. As Table 2-7 indicates, these contributions constituted only 1 percent of the total revenues in 1980. Nonetheless, the amount that has been given has increased with the proliferation of PACs. In 1976, $770,560 was donated by nonparty groups; in 1980, $1,562,429 was given. A number of Democratic candidates for their party's 1984 nomination announced that they would no longer accept contributions from special interest PACs.

There has been a much greater growth of independent expenditures. Under the law as amended in 1976, groups and individuals, while limited in the amount they can contribute, are not limited in the amount they can spend on their own in support of candidates in any election, nomination as well as general election. In 1976, approximately $250,000 was spent in this manner; in 1980, this figure was $13.7 million! Table 2-8 lists these expenditures by candidate.

As the table indicates, the expenditures were not equally divided. Ronald Reagan was the principal beneficiary. PACs were his primary backers. Topping the list was Jesse Helms's Congressional Club and the National Conservative Political Action Committee. The largest individual spender was Houston businessman Cecil R. Haden. He paid out almost $500,000 in support of Reagan's candidacy. On the liberal side, Stewart Mott and Norman Lear were the principal backers of John Anderson.

In addition to contributing money and spending it on behalf of candidates, groups can be particularly effective during the election in educating, mobilizing, and turning out voters. In 1976, labor's efforts on behalf

Table 2–8   INDEPENDENT EXPENDITURES FOR PRESIDENT IN 1980

Candidate	Expenditure	
	For	Against
Ronald Reagan (R)	$12,246,057	$47,868
John Connally (R)	288,032	
John Anderson (I)	199,438	2,635
Jimmy Carter (D)	45,869	245,611
Edward Kennedy (D)	77,189	491,161
Total	$12,856,585	$787,275

Source: U.S. Federal Election Commission, "FEC Study Shows Independent Expenditures Top $16 Million," Press Release, November 29, 1981.

of Carter were crucial in Texas and Ohio.[18] In 1980, state and local Republican party committees performed much the same function with much the same success for Reagan.

PACs have proved to be so important that presidential candidates now regularly form their own. Known as nonconnected organizations, they have been used primarily to fund organizational activities, build support, and defray travel and other expenses of the candidate in the years between elections and before the campaign actually begins.[19] Only a small portion of their budget goes into donations to others.

One of the most successful of these PACs during the 1980 election cycle was the Citizens for the Republic. Started in 1977, within a year this organization had raised $2.5 million and spent $1.9 million on operations. Most of this money was used for fund raising, travel, and other expenses of the PAC's principal speaker, Ronald Reagan. In the process of raising money, the Citizens developed a list of more than 300,000 contributors. This list was purchased for a nominal fee by the Reagan campaign committee. The PAC has continued in existence. During the first two years of the Reagan administration it raised approximately $2.5 million.

Similarly, in 1981 Democratic contenders Walter F. Mondale and Edward M. Kennedy each formed PACs to boost support for their potential candidacies. During the next two years each PAC raised over $2 million, thereby helping to defray Mondale's and Kennedy's expenses and providing money for research, travel, fund raising, and 1982 campaign contributions. The contributions to the campaigns of candidates for the Senate, the House of Representatives, and state governorships created political IOUs for the 1984 presidential campaign.

In addition to the support they receive from their own PACs, candidates and their immediate families can spend an unlimited amount of their own money prior to the primary period. That Jimmy Carter was able to sustain himself and his campaign in the early stages of his quest for the 1976 Democratic nomination gave him an edge over several other Democratic candidates such as Fred Harris and Terry Sanford, who could not do the same.[20] In their campaigns for the 1980 nomination, all of the major Republican contenders had personal finances that contributed to their capacity to mount a preprimary effort.[21] In 1984, three of the Democratic candidates had assets of over $1 million, and all but one (Senator Gary Hart) had yearly incomes of over $250,000.

Despite the loopholes that permit PACs and wealthy candidates to exert more influence, the campaign finance legislation has produced greater equity. The matching fund provision has given lesser-known candidates of the major parties a better opportunity to gain public support by enabling them to compete in more primaries. Previously, candidates without national visibility found it harder to raise the money necessary to run an effective campaign. Without such a campaign, winning the nomination became all but impossible.[22]

In addition to encouraging lesser-known candidacies, the law has increased their staying power in the campaign. It has enabled candidates to continue to seek the nomination even after disappointing showings in the early primaries. Moreover, it has required the fiction of an active candidacy right up to the convention in order to remain eligible for federal funds. This new staying power is well illustrated by the contrast between the Muskie campaign of 1972 and the Udall campaign of 1976. As the front-runner, Senator Edmund Muskie had raised over $2 million by January 31, 1972, before the primaries even began, and eventually spent over $7 million in his campaign.[23] Nonetheless, he was forced to abandon his quest for the nomination in part because of lack of funds after only five primaries (two months). Representative Morris Udall, on the other hand, was not nationally known and had not demonstrated substantial fund-raising capacity. Yet, he was able to raise over $4.5 million, including almost $2 million from the Treasury, and to compete actively in more than one-third of the states without winning one primary or controlling one state delegation other than his own. In 1980, John Anderson obtained $7.3 million from public and private sources in his quest for the Republican nomination.

By encouraging self-selection and increasing the number of candidates and their ability to run in more primaries, the Federal Election

Campaign Act also enhances the prospect of a challenge to the incumbent. Reagan raised more money than Ford in 1976, while Kennedy raised about 85 percent of Carter's total in 1980.

Once the nomination is won, the law seems to help the incumbent. Equalizing spending at the national level hurts a challenger more. Presidents make the news simply by being President; challengers have to buy time on television to present themselves as serious presidential candidates.

In 1976 the law also seemed to work to the benefit of the Democratic candidate because it eliminated the fund-raising advantage which Republican nominees have enjoyed over the years. However, in 1980 the Republicans once again benefited. Independent expenditures by PACs combined with state and local party efforts on behalf of their candidates gave the Republicans a substantial edge in fund raising and spending, an advantage that is likely to persist for some time to come.[24]

Finally, the law has affected and will continue to affect the major parties. However, its impact may be more destructive than supportive. Designed to bolster the two major parties, the law discourages candidates of other parties by requiring minor parties to obtain at least 5 percent of the presidential vote to be eligible for funds. Independent candidate John Anderson qualified in 1980, but only after the election was over. He eventually received $4.2 million, enough to pay off his debts but not enough to have mounted a vigorous campaign.

Since Anderson was not assured of federal funds, he had difficulty borrowing money. Unable to secure large bank loans, he had to depend on private contributions and loans (limited to a maximum of $1,000 per person and $5,000 per group). He raised $12.1 million, mainly through mass mailings. Ironically, having qualified in 1980, Anderson is automatically eligible for funds in 1984 according to a 1983 FEC ruling. Thus, the law, despite its intent, provides an incentive for the continuation of a third-party candidacy once that candidacy has been successfully launched in the previous election.

Finally, the law encourages major party candidates, thereby factionalizing the parties and ultimately weakening their structure. The organization of the successful candidate is not dismantled after the nomination; it is expanded, often competing with the regular party organization. This competition can undercut the position of the leadership and its capacity to fashion strong state organizations. The Democratic party is still suffering from four years of neglect during the Carter Presidency.

SUMMARY

Campaign finance became an important aspect of presidential elections by the end of the nineteenth and the beginning of the twentieth centuries. In recent years, however, it has become even more important as costs have spiraled. Expanded use of communications, particularly television, to reach the voters has been primarily responsible for the increase, although other methods of contacting voters and assessing their opinions have also added to the sharp rise in expenditures.

With few exceptions, candidates of both major parties had turned to the large contributors, the so-called "fat cats," for financial support. Their dependence on a relatively small number of large donors, combined with escalating costs, created serious problems for a democratic selection process. The 1972 presidential election, with its high expenditures, dirty tricks, and illegal campaign contributions, vividly illustrated some of these problems and generated support from Congress and the public for rectifying them.

In 1974, 1976, and 1979, Congress passed legislation designed to bring donors into the open and to prevent their undue influence on elected officials. By placing limits on contributions, controlling expenditures, and subsidizing the election, Congress hoped to make the selection process less costly and more equitable. It established a commission to oversee compliance and prosecute offenders.

The legislation has achieved some but not all of its intended goals. It has reduced the importance of large donors (except if a large donor happens to be a candidate) and has increased the importance of having a large number of small contributors during the preconvention period. It has also enhanced the significance of the political action committees. Used by presidential nominees to underwrite their preprimary costs, these PACs can also help candidates by their contributions in the primaries and by their organizing and educational efforts in the general election.

The law has not reduced expenditures in the primaries. In fact, its matching grant provision has actually encouraged major party candidacies, thereby increasing spending and also factionalism within the parties. On the other hand, the legislation has given lesser-known candidates a greater opportunity to gain visibility and to compete in more primaries than in the past. The limit on contributions, the expenditure ceilings, and the federal subsidies have contributed to equity in the prenomination period but have not achieved it.

For the general election, the campaign finance legislation had worked to equalize spending between the major party candidates. The political result of increasing equality was to deny the Republicans some of their traditional financial advantage but not to deny the incumbents some of theirs. In 1980, however, Republican party organizations at the national, state, and local levels outraised and outspent their Democratic counterparts thereby regaining their advantage.

The law has also helped major party candidates but not necessarily the major parties. It is the candidates, not the parties, who receive the bulk of the funds. Moreover, the prohibition against private contributions has made independent expenditures more important, further weakening the national parties' influence on the campaigns of their candidates. Finally, the limited funding has forced the candidates themselves to be more prudent, to exercise more central control over their finances, and to reach the largest possible audience in the most cost-effective way. Television, not grass roots organizations, directed by the national campaign organization has been the principal beneficiary in the general election campaign.

NOTES

1. Herbert E. Alexander, "Making Sense About Dollars in the 1980 Presidential Campaigns," in Michael J. Malbin (ed.), *Financing Politics in the 1980s* (Washington, D.C.: American Enterprise Institute/Chatham House, forthcoming).

2. Ibid., p. 24

3. Edward W. Chester, *Radio, Television and American Politics* (New York: Sheed & Ward, 1969), p. 21.

4. Alexander, *Financing Politics* (Washington, D.C.: Congressional Quarterly, 1976) pp. 27–28.

5. "Nielsen TV: 1969" (Chicago: A. C. Nielsen Co., 1969), p. 10.

6. Alexander, *Financing Politics*, p. 198.

7. Mary Russell, "Faced with Debts, 'New Right' Slippage, Rep. Crane Fires Campaign Manager," *Washington Post*, May 4, 1979, p. A-3.

8. The trend continued in 1980. More money was spent on behalf of Reagan than on behalf of Carter.

9. Joel H. Goldstein, "The Influence of Money on the Prenomination Stage of the Presidential Selection Process: The Case of the 1976 Election," *Presidential Studies Quarterly*, 8 (1978), 164–179.

In a study of the relationship between campaign spending and voter participation in a congressional district, Lawrence Shepard concluded: "Political attitudes appear to be substantially more responsive to changes in Republican spending than to changes in Democratic spending. This suggests that legislation aimed at reducing campaign spending will detract from Republican prospects for victory while proposals to supplement campaign spending would have the opposite tendency." Lawrence Shepard, "Does Campaign Spending Really Matter?" *Public Opinion Quarterly*, 41 (1977), 196–205.

10. This brief discussion of the sources of political contributions is based primarily on Alexander's description in *Financing Politics*, pp. 61–87. The statistics are his.

11. Henry C. Frick, as quoted in Jasper B. Shannon, *Money and Politics* (New York: Random House, 1959), p. 35.

12. In 1972 the chief fund raiser for the Nixon campaign, Maurice Stans, and Richard Nixon's private attorney, Herbert Kalmbach, collected contributions, some of them illegal, on behalf of the President. They exerted strong pressure on corporate executives despite the prohibition on corporate giving. Secret contributions totaling millions of dollars were received and three special secret funds were established to give the White House and the Committee to Reelect the President (CREEP) maximum discretion in campaign expenditures. It was from these funds that the dirty tricks of the 1972 campaign and the Watergate burglary were financed.

13. Representative Wilbur Mills, Senator Henry Jackson, and Senator Hubert Humphrey also received corporate contributions in 1972, although the amounts were small in comparison with Nixon's.

14. Foreign nationals, unless admitted to the United States for permanent residence, cannot contribute.

15. Concert-goers paid an average of $20 a ticket. Approximately half that amount was considered a contribution, eligible for federal matching funds. This increased the ticket's value to the Brown organization by about $10. After expenses, the campaign made approximately $27 a ticket.

16. Warhol contributed fifty deluxe prints of his Kennedy portrait, valued at $1,500 each, plus other works of art. Jamie Wyeth gave a lithograph edition of 300 campaign posters; each print was appraised at $800 for a total contribution of $240,000.

17. Corporations may ask for voluntary contributions from their stockholders and administrative and executive personnel without limit but may solicit employees only twice a year and only by mail. For labor unions, the provision is reversed. Members may be solicited without limit, but stockholders and executive personnel may be requested to donate only twice a year. The request must be made by mail and sent to a home address. The purpose of these provisions is to prevent coercion in obtaining contributions.

18. Michael J. Malbin, "What Should Be Done about Independent Campaign Expenditures?" *Regulation*, 6 (1982), 41–46.

19. The campaign officially begins when a candidate authorizes the establishment of an elections committee and files the authorization with the FEC. There is little incentive to do this before the period during which donations solicited by the committee are eligible for matching funds, that is, one year prior to the election year. Government funds may not be distributed until the election year itself. Walter Mondale and former Florida governor Reubin Askew were the first Democratic candidates for their party's 1984 nomination to file. Both did so on Monday, January 3, 1983.

20. Carter used his interest in a peanut warehouse business to guarantee loans that he obtained in the period January to March 1976, when federal matching funds could not be issued until Congress passed an amendment to the Campaign Finance Act.

21. Candidates are now required to file financial disclosure reports under the Ethics in Government Act. Most of the major candidates showed income in excess of $100,000 a year. Some, such as George Bush, Jimmy Carter, John Connally, and Edward Kennedy, are millionaires. All of the Republicans fall within the top 1 or 2 percent of income levels

in the United States. Fred Barbash and T. R. Reid, "Big John Connally: Richest of the Rich," *Washington Post*, May 16, 1979, p. A-6.

22. The opportunities afforded by the new law extend to everyone, not simply serious presidential contenders. Thus, Ellen McCormick, New York housewife and abortion opponent, was able to compete as a Democratic candidate in 1976, meet the eligibility requirements for federal funds, and receive almost $250,000 from the Treasury to espouse her antiabortion views.

23. Alexander, *Financing the 1972 Election* (Lexington, Mass.: D.C. Heath, 1976), pp. 129, 131.

24. Republican party committees raised four and one-half times as much money as the Democrats, contributed three times as much to their candidates, and spent more than twice as much as the Democrats in the general election. Federal Election Commission, "Press Release," February 21, 1982.

Selected Readings

Adamany, David. *Campaign Finance in America.* North Scituate, Mass.: Duxbury Press, 1972.

———. "Money, Politics and Democracy: A Review Essay," *American Political Science Review*, 71 (1977), 289–304.

Alexander, Herbert E. *Financing Politics.* Washington, D.C.: Congressional Quarterly, 1980.

———, ed. "Political Finance: Reform and Reality." *The Annals*, 425 (1976), 1–16.

Diamond, Robert A. *Dollar Politics.* Washington, D.C.: Congressional Quarterly, 1971.

Drew, Elizabeth. "A Reporter at Large: Politics and Money—II, "*New Yorker*, December 13, 1982, pp. 57–111.

Dunn, Delmer. *Financing Presidential Campaigns.* Washington, D.C.: Brookings Institution, 1972.

Goldstein, Joel. "The Influence of Money on the Prenomination Stage of the Presidential Selection Process: The Case of the 1976 Election," *Presidential Studies Quarterly*, 8 (1978), 164–179.

Heard, Alexander. *The Costs of Democracy.* Chapel Hill: University of North Carolina Press, 1960.

Malbin, Michael J. "Labor, Business, and Money—A Post-Election Analysis," *National Journal*, March 19, 1977, pp. 412–417.

———, ed. *Financing Politics in the 1980s.* Washington, D.C.: American Enterprise Institute, forthcoming.

———, ed. *Parties, Interest Groups, and Campaign Finance Laws.* Washington, D.C.: American Enterprise Institute, 1980.

———. "What Should Be Done about Independent Campaign Expenditures?" *Regulation*, 6 (1982), 41–46.

Shannon, Jasper B. *Money and Politics.* New York: Random House, 1959.

Shepard, Lawrence. "Does Campaign Spending Really Matter?" *Public Opinion Quarterly*, 41 (1977), 196–205.

Chapter 3

THE POLITICAL ENVIRONMENT

Introduction

The nature of the electorate influences the content, images, and strategies of the campaign and affects the outcome of the election—an obvious conclusion, to be sure, but one that is not always appreciated. Campaigns are not conducted in ignorance of the voters. Rather, they are calculated to appeal to the needs and desires, attitudes and opinions, associations and interactions of the electorate.

Voters do not come to the election with completely open minds. They come with preexisting views. They do not see and hear the campaign in isolation. They observe it and absorb it as part of their daily lives. In other words, their attitudes and associations affect their perceptions and influence their behavior. This is why it is important for students of presidential elections to examine the formation of political attitudes and the patterns of social interaction.

Who votes and who does not? Why do people vote for certain candidates and not others? Do campaign appeals affect voting behavior? Are the responses of the electorate predictable? Political scientists have been interested in these questions for some time. Politicians have been interested for even longer.

A great deal of social science research and political savvy have gone into finding the answers. Spurred by the development of sophisticated

51

survey techniques and methods of data analysis, political scientists, sociologists, and social psychologists have uncovered a wealth of information on how the public reacts and the electorate behaves during a campaign. They have explored psychological motivations, social influences, and political pressures that contribute to voting behavior. This chapter will examine some of their findings.

It is organized into three sections. The first discusses the partisan basis of politics. It explores the effect political attitudes have on how people evaluate the campaign and how they vote on election day. A psychological model of voting behavior is presented and then used to explain recent trends.

The second section discusses the social basis of politics. It divides the electorate into distinct and overlapping socioeconomic, ethnic, and religious groupings and then notes the relationship of these groupings to voting behavior. Particular emphasis is placed on the formation of party coalitions during the 1930s and their development since that time.

Turnout is analyzed in the third part of the chapter. Influenced by both partisan and social factors, it is also affected by the laws which govern elections and such situational variables as the closeness of the contest, interest in the campaign, and even the weather. The expansion of suffrage in the nineteenth and twentieth centuries is described in the first part of this section, and recent trends in voter turnout are discussed in the final portion.

THE PARTISAN BASIS OF POLITICS

Considerable research has been conducted on the attitudes and behavior of the American voter. Much of it has been under the direction of the Center for Political Studies at the University of Michigan. Beginning in 1952, the Center began conducting nationwide surveys during presidential elections.[1] The object of these surveys was to identify the major influences on voting behavior.

A random sample of the electorate was interviewed before and after the election. Respondents were asked a series of questions designed to reveal their attitudes toward the parties, candidates, and issues. On the basis of the answers, researchers constructed a model to explain voting behavior and presented it in a book entitled *The American Voter.*[2] Published in 1960, this very important work contained both theoretical formulations and empirical findings. Both the model and the findings were generally accepted by politicians and political scientists throughout the 1960s.

A Model of the American Voter

The model constructed by the Michigan researchers assumes that individuals are influenced by their attitudes and social relationships, in addition to the political environment in which an election occurs. In fact, it is these attitudes and relationships that condition the impact of that environment on individual voting behavior.

According to the theory, people develop attitudes early in life, largely as a consequence of interacting with their families, particularly their parents. These attitudes, in turn, tend to be reinforced by neighborhood, school, and/or religious associations. The reasons they tend to be reinforced lie in the psychological and social patterns of behavior. Psychologically, it is more pleasing to have beliefs and attitudes supported than challenged. Socially, it is more comfortable to associate with "nice," like-minded people, those with similar cultural, educational, and religious experiences. This is why the environment for most people tends to be supportive much of the time.[3]

Attitudes mature and harden over the years. Older people are less amenable to change and more set in their ways. Their behavior is more predictable.[4]

Political attitudes are no exception to this general pattern of attitude formation and maintenance. They too are developed early in life; they too are reinforced by association; they too grow in intensity over time; they too become more predictable with age.

Of all the factors that contribute to the development of a political attitude, an identification with a political party is one of the most important. It affects how people see the campaign and how they vote. Party identification operates as a conceptual mechanism. Identifiers tend to evaluate the campaign within a partisan framework. Political attitudes provide cues for interpreting the issues, for judging the candidates, and for deciding whether and how to vote. The stronger these attitudes, the more compelling the cues; conversely, the weaker the attitudes, the less likely they will affect perceptions during the campaign and influence voting.[5]

The amount of information that is known about the candidates also affects the influence of partisanship. In general, the less that is known, the more likely that people will follow their partisan inclinations when voting. Since presidential campaigns normally convey more information than other elections, the influence of party is apt to be weaker in these higher-visibility contests.

When identification with party is weak or nonexistent, other factors, such as the personalities of the candidates and their issue positions, will be correspondingly more important. In contrast to party identification, which is a long-term stabilizing factor, candidate and issue orientations are short-term, more variable influences that differ from election to election. Of the two, the image of the candidate has been more significant.

Candidate images turn on personality and policy dimensions. People tend to form general impressions about candidates on the basis of what is known about their leadership potential, decision-making capabilities, and personal traits. For an incumbent President seeking reelection, accomplishments in office provide much of the criteria for evaluation. Other characteristics, such as trustworthiness, integrity, and candor, may also be important, depending on the times. For the challenger, experience, knowledge, confidence, and assertiveness often substitute for performance, with personal qualities also considered.[6]

The candidate's position on the issues, however, seems less important than his partisanship and performance/experience. Candidates themselves contribute to this effect by fudging their own issue positions during the general election campaign so as to broaden their appeal and not alienate potential supporters. Staying in the mainstream tends to place the major party candidates close to one another on a variety of issues.

The low level of information and awareness which much of the electorate possesses also tends to downgrade the impact of issues on voting behavior. To be important, issues must stand out from campaign rhetoric. They must attract attention; they must hit home. Without personal impact, they are unlikely to be primary motivating factors in voting. To the extent that issue positions are not discernible, personality becomes the critical short-term variable.

Ironically, that portion of the electorate which can be more easily persuaded, weak partisans and independents, tends to have the least information.[7] Conversely, the most committed tend to be the most informed. They use their information to support their partisanship.

The relationship between degree of partisanship and amount of information has significant implications for a democratic society. The traditional view of a democracy holds that information and awareness are necessary in order to make a rational judgment. The capacity of citizens to obtain this information and to decide rationally is thought to be a characteristic that distinguishes democratic from nondemocratic systems. Yet, the finding that those who have the most information are also the most committed and those who lack this commitment also lack the incentive to acquire information has upset some of the assumptions of democratic theory.

Considerable debate has turned on the question: How informed and rational is the electorate when voting? One well-known political scientist, the late V. O. Key, even wrote a book dedicated to "the perverse and unorthodox argument . . . that voters are not fools."[8] Key studied the behavior of three groups of voters between 1936 and 1960: switchers, stand-patters, and new voters. He found those who switched their votes to be interested in and influenced by their own evaluation of policy, personality, and performance. In this sense, Key believed that they exercised rational judgment when voting.[9]

Others have pointed to an increasing issue awareness in recent elections as evidence that voters are making more informed and rational judgments based on their ideological preferences and policy views.[10] If correct, this would suggest that the initial model propounded by *The American Voter* may have become time-bound. But this is far from clear. Just how informed voters are and how important issues and ideology have become are matters of considerable controversy in political science today.

To summarize, *The American Voter* suggests that partisans vote habitually, not necessarily rationally or irrationally. Instead of coming to the election with open minds, most of them come with preexisting political attitudes that affect their perceptions and influence their judgment. Party identification provides a ready mechanism for evaluating the campaign and for acting in a prescribed manner on election day. Moreover, the identification of much of the electorate with political parties acts to stabilize the system. It provides a hedge against a volatile electoral response. To the extent that voters are more informed about the candidates' and parties' positions, they can and will deviate from partisan voting patterns.

Partisan Voting Patterns

The Michigan model of the American voter was based on research conducted in the 1950s. In each subsequent national election, nationwide surveys have been conducted in order to understand shifts in voting behavior. While the basic psychological explanation of voting behavior has not been changed, empirical findings point to shifts in the identification and intensity of partisan beliefs.

Two major trends stand out. First, there has been a reduction in the number of people who identify with a party, and conversely, an increase in the number of self-proclaimed independents. Second, there has been a decline in the strength of partisan identities. Each of these changes has important long- and short-term implications for American electoral politics.

Table 3–1 lists the percentages of party identifiers and independents. The table indicates that there was an 11 percent decline in the percentage of people who identify with a political party and a 13 percent increase in the number of self-proclaimed independents between 1952 and 1980. Most of the shift occurred after 1964. The table also suggests that the decline was principally in the strong partisan category. The percentage of weak partisans in 1980 was almost the same as it was in 1952.

What has happened is that partisanship has weakened among all groups. Strong partisans who feel less intensely about their political party have become weak, and some weak partisans now consider themselves independent. However, a sizable portion of the independents vote consistently for the same party. They might be referred to as independent leaners. (See Table 3–2.) Put simply, independent voting has increased far less rapidly than independent identification.[11]

According to the theory, the decline in partisanship and the growth of independents should have produced a more variable and manipulatable electorate. With weaker partisan allegiances and more independent identifiers, the candidates and issues should, in themselves, be more important influences on the vote. Both of these expectations have materialized, although they seem more related to the weakening intensity of partisan feelings than to the increasing number of self-identified independents.

Figure 3–1 indicates a dramatic rise in voting for candidates of different parties. According to Arthur H. Miller and Martin P. Wattenberg, about three times as many people divide their vote today as they did in the 1950s.[12] The increasing number of defections from partisan voting patterns has helped the Republicans more than the Democrats. Without votes from Democratic defectors, the GOP could not have won five presidential elections since 1952. The help, however, has been short-term. The Republicans have won few permanent converts—but neither have the Democrats. Both parties have suffered a decline in party identification. In 1980, 39 percent of the electorate considered themselves Democrats and only 24 percent Republicans. These percentages have been relatively constant for the last three presidential elections.

With partisanship weaker than in the past, alternative cues to voters

Table 3–1 PARTY IDENTIFICATION, 1952–1980* (IN PERCENTAGES)

Party Identification	1952	1954	1956	1958	1960	1962	1964	1966	1968	1970	1972	1974	1976	1978	1980
Strong Democrat	22	22	21	23	21	23	26	18	20	20	15	17	15	15	16
Weak Democrat	25	25	23	24	25	23	25	27	25	23	25	21	25	24	23
Independent Democrat	10	9	7	7	8	8	9	9	10	10	11	13	12	14	11
Independent Independent	5	7	9	8	8	8	8	12	11	13	13	15	14	14	12
Independent Republican	7	6	8	4	7	6	6	7	9	8	11	9	10	10	12
Weak Republican	14	14	14	16	13	16	13	15	14	15	13	14	14	13	14
Strong Republican	13	13	15	13	14	12	11	10	10	10	10	8	9	8	10
Apoliticals: Don't know	4	4	3	5	4	4	2	2	1	1	2	3	1	2	2

Source: Center for Political Studies, University of Michigan.

*The survey question was, "Generally speaking, do you usually think of yourself as a Republican, a Democrat, an Independent, or what? (If Republican or Democrat), Would you call yourself a strong (R) (D) or a not very strong (R) (D)? (If Independent), Do you think of yourself as closer to the Republican or Democratic party?"

Table 3–2   DEFECTION RATES OF PARTY IDENTIFIERS* (IN PERCENTAGES)

Party and Identification	1952	1956	1960	1964	1968	1972	1976	1980
Democrat								
Strong	17	15	9	5	11	26	9	14
Weak	39	37	28	18	38	52	25	40
Independent								
Democrat	40	33	15	11	49	44	24	55
Independent								
Republican	7	6	13	25	19	14	14	24
Republican								
Weak	6	7	13	43	12	9	22	14
Strong	1	1	2	10	3	4	3	18

Source: Warren E. Miller, "Policy Directions and Presidential Leadership: Alternative Interpretations of the 1980 Presidential Election" (with J. Merrill Shanks). *British Journal of Political Science*, Vol. 12, July 1982, pp. 299–356. Reprinted with permission.

*Entries are percentages of the appropriate category of voters who voted for a presidential candidate other than the candidate of the party with which they identified.

have become more important. Television has contributed to the focus on candidate images. Shifts in the electoral coalitions have also produced more issues that divide parties. In the 1930s, when economic concerns were dominant, ideology and partisanship dovetailed; in the late 1960s and early 1970s, when social and foreign policy issues were dominant, political attitudes and partisanship diverged.

In short, in the time since *The American Voter* was written, partisan ties have become weaker. More people feel less strongly about political parties. This, in turn, has produced more candidate voting and, to a lesser extent, more issue voting, especially at the presidential level. The increasing importance of these short-term factors has contributed to a more manipulatable and volatile electorate, one that decides later in the campaign whether and how to vote. In the 1950s the authors of *The American Voter* had discovered that a majority of voters made their voting decision *prior* to the general election campaign.[13] In 1980, approximately half the electorate decided on their choice *during* the campaign with 9 percent making their judgment on election day itself.[14]

In a study intended to be a sequel to *The American Voter*, three political scientists, Norman H. Nie, Sidney Verba, and John R. Petrocik, concluded that voting behavior has become more individualized:

> The individual voter evaluates candidates on the basis of information and impressions conveyed by the mass media, and then votes on that basis. He or she acts as an individual, not as a member of a collectivity.[15]

Figure 3–1   TRENDS IN VOTING FOR CANDIDATES OF DIFFERENT
PARTIES, 1952–1980

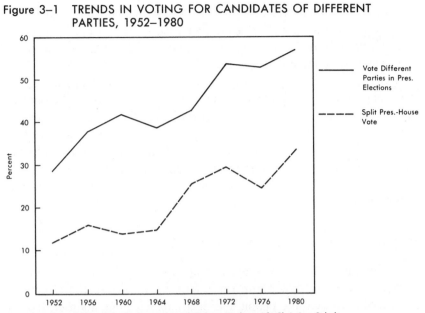

Source: Adapted from John R. Petrocik and Sidney Verba with Christine Schultz,
"Choosing the Choice and Not the Echo: A Funny Thing Happened to *The Changing
American Voter on the Way to the 1980 Election*" (paper delivered at the annual
meeting of the American Political Science Association, New York, September 3–6,
1981). Reprinted with permission of the authors.

Nie, Verba, and Petrocik do not conclude that partisanship is irrelevant.
It is still the single most important influence on voting behavior. Their
study, however, attests to its declining effect.

What explains this? Why have partisan identities weakened? The
events of the late 1960s and early 1970s, the decline in the age of the
electorate, and most particularly, the impact of television on campaigning
have all contributed.

The reaction to Vietnam and Watergate, to the credibility gaps and
political abuses of the so-called imperial Presidents, undoubtedly generated feelings of mistrust of and hostility to politicians and, particularly
among the young, less willingness to identify with a political party. Moreover, the salience of social and cultural issues rendered the traditional partisan alliances which had been built on economic ties much less relevant.

A second reason for the drop in partisan identification has been the
lowering of the voting age to eighteen and the increasing proportion of
the population who has reached that age. Over the last thirty years, the
percentage of the electorate twenty-four years of age and under has nearly
doubled. Since party identification tends to develop and harden over time,

the "youthing" of the electorate has undoubtedly contributed to the decline in partisan feelings.[16] Put another way, there has not been nearly as much growth in the number of independents among older people as there has been among younger ones.

A third factor has to do with the new mode of campaigning and the declining role of the party in that capacity. In the past, the political party came between the voter and the candidate. Political parties provided the organization, planned the campaign, and made the sales appeal. In doing so, they trumpeted their own cause. Today, much of the information comes directly from the candidate's organization via television. The party no longer mediates. It is less evident in the appeal and less important in the result.

THE SOCIAL BASIS OF POLITICS

There is another way of explaining and evaluating voting behavior. Instead of focusing directly on the political attitudes of the electorate, it is possible to examine people's associations with one another. To the extent that individuals see themselves as members of particular groups and to the extent that these groups have developed and articulated a position on the parties, candidates, or issues, the group becomes a focal point for the individual in deciding what to do. In this way, it affects perceptions of the campaign and influences voting.

While most associations, especially those that are voluntary, work to reinforce preexisting dispositions and attitudes, some do not. Instead, they create cross-pressures that counter the mind-set which at least some of the electorate brings to the campaign. Cross-pressures can increase the propensity for not voting or for voting against partisan inclinations.

Over the years certain economic, social, and geographic groupings have been evident in the coalitions that comprise the two major parties. These contemporary coalitions, which developed primarily during the New Deal period, provided the parties with a core of supporters to whom the campaigns were directed and appeals fashioned.

The Democrats, as the majority party today, have the larger of the two coalitions. It consists primarily of overlapping minorities. Catholics, Jews, blacks, and Hispanics have been particularly supportive of Democratic candidates. The Republicans, on the other hand, have been described as the minority party consisting primarily of the majority group in the country—white Anglo-Saxon Protestants.[17] Republicans also have tended to be more advantaged and prosperous. On the average, Republican identifiers have had higher incomes, more prestigious occupations, and better educational opportunities than have Democratic identifiers.

The New Deal Realignment[18]

Political coalitions develop during periods of partisan realignment. The last time this occurred was in the 1930s. Largely as a consequence of the Great Depression, the Democrats emerged as the majority party. Their coalition, held together by a common economic concern that the government play a more active role in dealing with the nation's economic problems, supported Franklin Roosevelt's New Deal program. Those who saw government involvement as a threat to the free enterprise system remained with the Republican party and opposed much of Roosevelt's domestic legislative program.

The Democrats became the majority party during this period by expanding their coalition. Since the Civil War, the Democrats had enjoyed southern support. White Protestants living in rural areas dominated the southern electorate. Blacks were largely excluded from it. Only in the election of 1928, when Al Smith, the Catholic governor of New York, ran as the Democratic candidate, was there a sizable southern popular and electoral vote for a Republican at the presidential level.

Roosevelt maintained and expanded southern support across the socioeconomic spectrum. Poor as well as wealthy southerners backed his candidacy. In each of his four presidential races, Roosevelt received well over two-thirds of the southern vote.[19]

Another group that voted Democratic prior to the 1930s was the Catholics. Living primarily in the urban centers of the North, Catholics became increasingly important to the Democrats as their numbers grew. Poor economic and social conditions, combined with the immigrant status of many Catholics, made them dependent on big-city bosses, who were able to deliver a sizable Democratic vote. In 1928 for the first time a majority of the cities in the country voted Democratic. Catholic support for Smith and the Democratic party figured prominently in this vote.

The harsh economic realities of the depression enabled Roosevelt to expand Democratic support in urban areas still further, particularly to those in the lower socioeconomic strata. Roosevelt's political coalition was differentiated along class lines. It attracted people with less education and income and those with lower-status jobs.[20]

In addition to establishing a broad-based, lower-class coalition, Roosevelt also lured black and Jewish voters from the Republican party. Blacks voted Democratic primarily for economic reasons, while Jews supported Roosevelt's liberal domestic programs and his anti-Nazi foreign policy. Neither of these groups provided the Democratic coalition of the 1930s with a large number of votes, but their long-term impact on the party and its vote has been significant.

In contrast, during the same period, the Republican party shrank. Not only were Republicans unable to attract new groups to their coalition, but they were unable to prevent the defection of some supporters, such as blacks and Jews, whose economic situation affected their partisan loyalties and influenced their vote. While the Republicans did retain the backing of a majority of business and professional people, they lost the support of much of the white Protestant working class. Republican strength remained concentrated in the Northeast, particularly in the rural areas.[21]

Contemporary Political Coalitions

The coalition that formed during the New Deal held together, for the most part, until the 1960s. During this period, blacks and Jews increased their identification with and support of the Democratic party and its candidates. Catholics, for the most part, remained Democratic, although they fluctuated more in their voting at the presidential level. Nonsouthern white Protestants continued to support the Republicans.

There were some changes, however, mainly along socioeconomic lines. Domestic prosperity contributed to the growth of a larger middle class. Had such a class identified with the Republicans for economic reasons, the Democratic majority would have been threatened. This did not occur, however. Those who gained in economic and social status did not, as a general rule, discard their partisan loyalties. The Democrats were able to hold on to the allegiance of a majority of this group and improve their position with the professional and managerial classes, which had grown substantially during this period. The Republicans continued to maintain their advantage with those in the upper socioeconomic strata. The economic improvement in the country had the effect of muting the class distinctions that were evident during the 1930s and 1940s.[22]

Finally, changes were occurring in the South. White southerners began to desert their party at the presidential level, largely over civil rights issues. In 1948, Harry Truman won 52 percent of the southern vote, compared with Roosevelt's 69 percent four years earlier. While Stevenson (in 1952) and Kennedy carried the South by reduced margins, in 1960 the southern white Protestant presidential vote went Republican.[23] If it were not for the growth of the black electorate in the South and its overwhelming support for Democratic candidates, the defection of the southern states from the Democratic camp would have been even more dramatic.

Major shifts in the national electorate began to be evident in the mid-1960s and continued into the 1970s. As a consequence of these fluctuations, the Democrats lost their dependable presidential majority but retained their advantage at the state and local levels.

Despite its minority status, the Republican party was still able to win five of the last eight presidential elections and three of the last six. Moreover, they came very close in two that they lost. Only in 1964 and 1976 did a Democratic candidate win a majority of the total presidential vote. In fact, since World War II, the Republican candidates have received 314.8 million votes for President compared with 291.6 million for Democratic candidates—a difference of more than 23 million.

The Republicans' presidential gains have not carried over into many contests for other national or for state office. During the 1960s and 1970s the Democrats controlled Congress, most state legislatures, and a majority of governorships. The Republicans were in a relatively weaker position than they had been in the 1940s and 1950s, although in 1980 they did gain control of the Senate.

The Democrats had become, in Everett Ladd's words, "the everyone party," gaining strength in most age, occupational, and social groupings.[24] The extent of Democratic dominance can be seen in Table 3–3.

Only white Protestants in the Northeast, upper-income earners, farmers, and ethnic groups from England, Scotland, and Wales considered themselves more Republican than Democratic. *In every other grouping the Democrats enjoyed an advantage.*

This is not to suggest that the Democrats had actually gained adherents in every grouping and the Republicans had lost. This did not occur. However, the electoral coalitions were changing. The distinct class basis had eroded.

One of the most significant and enduring of the shifts between the major party coalitions has been the continued defection of southern white Protestants to the Republicans at the presidential level. This shift has increased at other levels as well.[25] In 1940, Roosevelt won 80 percent of the southern white Protestant vote. Thirty-two years later George McGovern received only 14 percent.[26] Even Jimmy Carter, a southern white Protestant himself, running against a Republican President who had not done well in the South against his more conservative nomination opponent, was not able to carry the southern white Protestant vote. Were it not for his large southern black vote, Carter would have lost the South to Ford. He lost it overwhelmingly to Reagan in 1980.

Table 3–3 PARTY IDENTIFICATION OF SELECTED POPULATION
GROUPS, 1980 (IN PERCENTAGES)

Characteristic	Republican	Democrat	Independent
National total	26	43	31
Sex			
Male	27	40	33
Female	25	46	29
Race			
White	28	38	34
Southern	28	43	29
Nonsouthern	29	36	35
Nonwhite	7	80	13
Southern	7	82	11
Nonsouthern	5	82	13
Education			
College	31	34	35
High school	24	45	31
Grade school	22	55	23
Region			
East	24	44	32
Midwest	26	37	37
South	25	49	26
West	30	41	29
Age			
Total under 30	22	37	41
18–24 years	21	38	41
25–29 years	24	36	40
30–49 years	24	43	33
50 & older	31	47	22
Income (annual)			
$15,000 and over	29	38	33
$25,000 and over	33	34	33
$20,000–$24,999	27	41	32
$15,000–$19,999	22	42	36

Party identification of southerners has changed as well. Since 1952 there has been a substantial drop in Democratic party identification. The greatest loss occurred in the upper socioeconomic strata of the society. However, Republican identification increased only marginally during this period. Clearly, the Democrats' loss was not totally or even mostly the Republicans' gain (although their presidential and senatorial candidates seemed to benefit the most). Independent identifiers grew 19 percent, the same amount as the Democrats declined.[27]

Countering the decline of white southern Protestant support for the Democrats has been a corresponding decline in the backing of white

Table 3–3   PARTY IDENTIFICATION OF SELECTED POPULATION
            GROUPS, 1980 (IN PERCENTAGES) (Continued)

Characteristic	Republican	Democrat	Independent
Under $15,000	23	49	28
$10,000–$14,999	26	44	30
$ 5,000–$ 9,999	22	50	28
Under $5,000	19	56	25
Religion			
Protestant	30	42	28
Catholic	20	48	32
Jewish	12	54	34
Other	21	32	47
Occupation			
Professional and business	33	34	33
Clerical and sales	23	44	33
Manual workers	20	46	34
Skilled	23	40	37
Unskilled	17	51	32
Farmers	40	32	28
Nonlabor force	29	48	23
City size			
1,000,000 and over	21	51	28
500,000–999,999	23	42	35
50,000–499,999	25	43	32
2,500–49,999	30	40	30
Under 2,500, rural	30	39	31
Central city	19	51	30
Suburb	27	39	34
Labor union			
Labor union families	20	50	30
Non–labor union families	28	41	31

Source: "Gallup Opinion Index," December 1980, p. 65. Reprinted with permission.

northern Protestants for the Republicans 10 percent. As in the South, the decline was greatest among higher-status groups. Similarly, defecting Republicans became independents, not Democrats.[28]

One consequence of these coalition shifts has been to make the Northeast and Midwest more Democratic and the South and the Sunbelt more Republican at the presidential level and, increasingly, at the senatorial level as well. The Mountain States have also become much less Democratic. From 1960 to 1980 the Democratic vote in this region declined over 17 percent. While the decline has benefited the Republicans, it has not resulted in a Republican majority. There are still more independents in the Mountain States than there are Republicans.[29]

Another consequence of these partisan shifts has been the increasing contribution of blacks to the Democratic party. Few Republican identifiers are left among black voters, in contrast to the late 1950s, when almost 25 percent considered themselves Republican. Not only have blacks become increasingly loyal to the Democratic party, but their larger registration and turnout have increased their proportion of the total Democratic vote to more than one-fifth. In presidential elections since 1964, at least 85 percent of the black vote has gone to the Democratic candidate. (See Table 3–4.) To put it another way, in 1980 one out of every four Carter voters was black.[30]

Jewish voters have remained predominantly Democratic. They have evidenced only a small decline in their partisan sympathies but an increasingly larger swing to the Republicans in their presidential voting. Nonetheless, they have continued to give disproportionate support to the Democratic candidate. McGovern received 65 percent of the Jewish vote, Carter got 72 percent in 1976 but only 47 percent in 1980—the first election since World War II when a majority of Jews did not vote Democratic. Dissatisfaction with Carter was evident in the support Jewish voters gave Senator Edward Kennedy in the 1980 Democratic primaries—78 percent of the Jewish vote went to Kennedy as opposed to 22 percent to Carter. That dissatisfaction continued to be shown in the general election, with John Anderson receiving 14 percent of the Jewish vote and Reagan receiving 34 percent.

Whereas Jewish voters have for the most part maintained their loyalty to the Democratic coalition, Catholics have wavered more in their support. Their Democratic vote has declined from its high of 78 percent in 1960 to a low of 46 percent in 1980. In two out of the last three presidential elections, a plurality of Catholics have voted for the Republican candidate.

While Catholic allegiance to the Democratic party has weakened, a Catholic shift to Republicanism has not resulted. Rather, Catholics, like other groups in the electorate, have become more independent in their voting behavior. The Catholic vote has become more reflective of national trends.

How can the party coalitions be described today? The Democrats still receive disproportionate support from blacks, those with the lowest incomes, and those who live in the central cities. However, the relatively small size of these groups and their low turnout make them less important a part of the Democratic coalition than they were in the past. On the other hand, the larger Democratic-oriented groups (union families, southerners, and religious minorities) have weakened in their backing of Democratic candidates particularly at the presidential level. In 1980 these groups voted only slightly more Democratic than did the country as a whole.[31]

The Republicans have become more white, wealthy, and suburban, but they have not become the majority party. They have, however, improved their potential for winning an electoral majority at the national level. It is apparent that the party coalitions and the presidential vote are no longer identical.

With the social basis of parties eroding, the old coalitions have become frayed. While class, religion, and geography are still related to party identification and voting behavior, they are not as strongly related as they were in the past. Voters are less influenced by group cues. They exercise a more independent judgment on election day, a judgment that is less predictable. That is why the Republicans' chances have improved even though their coalition has not significantly expanded.

While the Republicans have been the short-run beneficiary of these trends, in the long run it is anybody's ball game. The weakening of party coalitions has led to the development of candidate-based ones. It has made campaign appeals more important. Today, it is the candidate, not the party, who takes the initiative, creates an organization, and generates an appeal. How this appeal is projected and communicated has an increasing impact on who votes and how they vote.

TURNOUT

Who votes? In one sense, this is a simple question to answer. Official election returns indicate the number of voters and the states, even the precincts, in which the votes were cast. By easy calculation, the percentage of those eligible who actually voted can be determined. In 1976, 54.3 percent of the adult population voted in the presidential election; in 1980, 53.2 percent voted. (See Table 3–5.)

For campaign strategists and political analysts, however, more information is needed. In planning a campaign, it is necessary to design and target appeals to attract specific groups of voters. In assessing the results, it is also essential to understand how particular segments of the electorate responded. By evaluating turnout on the basis of demographic characteristics and partisan attitudes, strategists and analysts alike have the information they need to make sophisticated judgments.

Voting turnout has varied widely over the years. In the first national election in 1788, only about 4 percent of the adult population participated. The presidential vote was even smaller, since most electors were designated by the state legislatures and not chosen directly by the people. The

Table 3–4   VOTE BY GROUPS IN PRESIDENTIAL ELECTIONS, 1952–1980
(IN PERCENTAGES)

	1952		1956		1960		1964	
	Steven- son	Eisen- hower	Steven- son	Eisen- hower	Ken- nedy	Nixon	John- son	Gold- water
National total	44.6	55.4	42.2	57.8	50.1	49.9	61.3	38.7
Sex								
Male	47	53	45	55	52	48	60	40
Female	42	58	39	61	49	51	62	38
Race								
White	43	57	41	59	49	51	59	41
Nonwhite	79	21	61	39	68	32	94	6
Education								
College	34	66	31	69	39	61	52	48
High school	45	55	42	58	52	48	62	38
Grade school	52	48	50	50	55	45	66	34
Occupation								
Professional								
and business	36	64	32	68	42	58	54	46
White collar	40	60	37	63	48	52	57	43
Manual	55	45	50	50	60	40	71	29
Age (years)								
Under 30	51	49	43	57	54	46	64	36
30–49	47	53	45	55	54	46	63	37
50 & older	39	61	39	61	46	54	59	41
Religion								
Protestant	37	63	37	63	38	62	55	45
Catholic	56	44	51	49	78	22	76	24
Politics								
Republican	8	92	4	96	5	95	20	80
Democrat	77	23	85	15	84	16	87	13
Independent	35	65	30	70	43	57	56	44
Region								
East	45	55	40	60	53	47	68	32
Midwest	42	58	41	59	48	52	61	39
South	51	49	49	51	51	49	52	48
West	42	58	43	57	49	51	60	40
Members of								
labor union								
families	61	39	57	43	65	35	73	27

Source: "Gallup Opinion Index," December 1980, pp. 6–7. Reprinted with permission.
*Less than 1 percent.

Table 3–4   VOTE BY GROUPS IN PRESIDENTIAL ELECTIONS, 1952–1980 (IN PERCENTAGES) (Continued)

1968			1972		1976			1980		
Hum-phrey	Nixon	Wallace	Mc-Govern	Nixon	Carter	Ford	Mc-Carthy	Carter	Reagan	Ander-son
43.0	43.4	13.6	38	62	50	48	1	41	51	7
41	43	16	37	63	53	45	1	38	53	7
45	43	12	38	62	48	51	*	44	49	6
38	47	15	32	68	46	52	1	36	56	7
85	12	3	87	13	85	15	*	86	10	2
37	54	9	37	63	42	55	2	35	53	10
42	43	15	34	66	54	46	*	43	51	5
52	33	15	49	51	58	41	1	54	42	3
34	56	10	31	69	42	56	1	33	55	10
41	47	12	36	64	50	48	2	40	51	9
50	35	15	43	57	58	41	1	48	46	5
47	38	15	48	52	53	45	1	47	41	11
44	41	15	33	67	48	49	2	38	52	8
41	47	12	36	64	52	48	*	41	54	4
35	49	16	30	70	46	53	*	39	54	6
59	33	8	48	52	57	42	1	46	47	6
9	86	5	5	95	9	91	*	8	86	5
74	12	14	67	33	82	18	*	69	26	4
31	44	25	31	69	38	57	4	29	55	14
50	43	7	42	58	51	47	1	43	47	9
44	47	9	40	60	48	50	1	41	51	7
31	36	33	29	71	54	45	*	44	52	3
44	49	7	41	59	46	51	1	35	54	9
56	29	15	46	54	63	36	1	50	43	5

Table 3–5   PARTICIPATION IN PRESIDENTIAL ELECTIONS

Year	Total Adult Population*	Total Presidential Vote	Percentage of Adult Population Voting
1824	3,964,000	363,017	9%
1840	7,381,000	2,412,698	33
1860	14,676,000	4,692,710	32
1880	25,012,000	9,219,467	37
1900	40,753,000	13,974,188	35
1920	60,581,000	26,768,613	44
1932	75,768,000	39,732,000	52.4
1940	84,728,000	49,900,000	58.9
1952	99,929,000	61,551,000	61.6
1960	109,674,000	68,838,000	62.8
1964	114,085,000	70,645,000	61.9
1968	120,285,000	73,212,000	60.9
1972	140,068,000	77,719,000	55.5
1976	150,127,000	81,556,000	54.3
1980	162,761,000	86,515,000	53.2

Source: Population figures for 1824 to 1920 are based on estimates and early census figures that appear in Neal R. Peirce, *The People's President* (New York: Simon & Schuster, 1968), p. 206. Population figures from 1932 to the present are from the U.S. Department of Commerce, Bureau of the Census, *Statistical Abstract of the United States* (Washington, D.C., 1981), p. 496.

*Restrictions based on sex, age, race, religion, and property ownership prevented a significant portion of the adult population from voting in the nineteenth and early twentieth centuries. Of those who were eligible, however, the percentage casting ballots was often quite high, particularly during the last half of the nineteenth century.

percentage of the population voting rose significantly between 1824 and 1840, leveled off through the 1800s, and then increased dramatically in the twentieth century.

Table 3–5 indicates the number and percentage of adults voting. The increasing numbers reflect the expansion of suffrage. However, while the proportion of eligible voters has increased, the percentage who actually vote has declined since 1960.

The Expansion of Suffrage

The Constitution empowered the state legislatures to determine the time, place, and manner of holding elections for national office. While it also gave Congress the authority to alter such regulations, Congress did not do so until the Civil War. Thus, the states were free to restrict suffrage and most did. In some, property ownership was a requirement to exercising the franchise; in others, a particular religious belief was necessary. In most, it was essential to be white, male, and over twenty-one.

By the 1830s, most states had eliminated property and religious restrictions. The Fifteenth Amendment, ratified in 1870, removed race and color as qualifications for voting. In theory, this enabled all black males to vote. In practice, it enfranchised those in the North and border states but not in the South. A series of institutional devices such as the poll tax, literacy test, and white primary combined effectively with social pressure to prevent blacks from voting in the South for another hundred years.

Following the Civil War, both the number of eligible voters and the percentage of actual voters increased. One political scientist estimated the rate of turnout in the 1880s to be as high as 80 percent of those eligible.[32] Close competition between the parties contributed to this higher level of participation.

In the twentieth century, the passage of the Nineteenth, Twenty-fourth, and Twenty-sixth amendments continued to expand the voting-age population. In 1920, women received the right to vote; in 1964, a poll tax was prohibited in national elections; in 1971, suffrage was extended to all citizens eighteen years of age and older. Previously, each state had established its own minimum age.

Moreover, the Supreme Court and Congress had begun to eliminate the legal and institutional barriers to voting. In 1944, the court outlawed the white primary. In the mid-1960s, Congress, by its passage of the Civil Rights Act (1964) and the Voting Rights Act (1965), banned the literacy test in federal elections for all citizens who had at least a sixth-grade education in an American school. Where less than 50 percent of the population was registered to vote, federal officials were to be sent to help facilitate registration. No longer was long and costly litigation necessary to ensure the right to vote. Amendments to the Voting Rights Act have also reduced the residence requirement for presidential elections to a maximum of thirty days.[33]

With each expansion of suffrage, the percentage of those eligible who do vote has actually declined. Since 1960, only in the South, which had a long history of discrimination, has a larger proportion of adult citizens cast ballots than in the past. Why has there been a trend toward nonvoting? In order to answer this question, the psychological and social bases of turnout must be explored.

Psychological and Social Influences on Turnout

There are a variety of motivations for voting or not voting. Interest in the election, concern over the outcome, feelings of civic responsibility, and a sense of political efficacy all contribute.[34] Naturally, the person who feels more strongly about the election is more likely to participate and vote.

As mentioned earlier in this chapter, those with more intense partisan feelings are more likely to have this interest, more likely to participate in the campaign, and more likely to vote on election day. Voting, in fact, becomes a habit. The more people have done it in the past, the more likely it is they will do it in the future.

Two political scientists, Raymond E. Wolfinger and Steven J. Rosenstone, who examined turnout in the 1972 presidential election, found that it "increases steadily with age until the mid-forties, when the peak of 74 to 76 percent is first reached. Voting rates remain at this level until about age 70, after which steady decline sets in."[35] Table 3-6 provides empirical support for the proposition that turnout increases with age, at least up to a point.

Other characteristics also related to turnout are education, income, and occupational status. As people become more educated, as they move up the socioeconomic ladder, as their jobs gain in status, they are more likely to vote. Education is the most important of these variables. It has a larger impact than any other social characteristic.[36] In 1980, for exam-

Table 3-6 VOTING TURNOUT BY POPULATION CHARACTERISTICS, 1968–1980 (IN PERCENTAGES)

	1968	1972	1976	1980
Male	69.8	64.1	59.6	59.1
Female	66.0	62.0	58.8	59.4
Age				
18–20		48.3	38.0	35.7
21–24	51.0	50.7	45.6	43.1
25–34	62.5	59.7	55.4	54.6
35–44	70.8	66.3	63.3	64.4
45–64	74.9	70.8	68.7	69.3
65 and over	65.8	63.5	62.2	65.1
Education				
8 years or less	54.5	47.4	44.1	42.6
9–11	61.3	52.0	47.2	45.6
12	72.5	65.4	59.4	58.9
More than 12	81.2	78.8	73.5	73.2
Race				
White	69.1	64.5	60.9	60.9
Black	57.6	52.1	48.7	50.5
Hispanic origin	NA	37.4	31.8	29.9

Source: U.S. Department of Commerce, Bureau of the Census, *Statistical Abstract of the United States* (Washington, D.C., 1981), pp. 499–500.

ple, less than half the whites who did not graduate from high school voted, while three-fourths of those who graduated from college did. College graduates have a higher voting participation rate than do those with less education.

The reason education is so important is that it provides the skills for processing and evaluating information, for perceiving differences between the parties, candidates, and issues, and for relating these differences to personal values and behavior. Education also increases interest in the election and concern over the outcome. Since the lesson that voting is a civic responsibility is usually learned in the classroom, schooling may also contribute to a more highly developed sense of responsibility about voting. Finally, education provides the knowledge and confidence to overcome voting hurdles—to register on time, to file absentee ballots properly, and to mark the ballot or use the voting machine correctly.[37]

Given the relationship of education to turnout, it is surprising that the rate of turnout should decline in the nation as a whole at a time when the general level of education is rising and the country is becoming more affluent.[38]

The reasons for the decline seem to be related to many of the same factors that have contributed to the decrease in partisanship and the weakening of party coalitions. These include the increasing number of younger and older voters and the growth of political cynicism and apathy in the population, particularly among the lower socioeconomic groups.

Young people tend to be more mobile than their parents. Moreover, they have not developed the habit of voting or even of identifying with a party. As a consequence, they vote with less regularity than those who are older.

Similarly, there has been an increase in the number of elderly citizens. They too tend to vote less, primarily for reasons of health. That elderly women vote less than elderly men yet outlive their male counterparts by an average of eight years also contributes to the decline in the senior citizen vote. This so-called youthing and aging of the electorate has resulted in a lower percentage of voter turnout. It does not, however, explain most of the decline.[39] All age groups have lower turnout.

Political scientist Richard Brody suggests that voters had a weaker sense of political efficacy in the 1970s than in the 1950s and 1960s. Pointing to "a substantial decline in the belief that participation is politically meaningful, that government is responsive, and that the outcome of the election is a matter of concern to the individual voter," Brody concludes, "Abstention flows from the belief—held by an increasingly large segment of the electorate—that voting simply isn't worth the effort."[40] Research on the 1980 election supports Brody's findings.[41]

To make matters worse, there seems to be a growing class bias in voting. The decline in turnout has not been evenly distributed among the population. According to a study by Thomas E. Cavanagh, it has been greater among blacks than whites and greater among those in the lowest socioeconomic groups.[42] In other words, not only do the disadvantaged participate less than their more prosperous peers, but the discrepancy in their rate of participation is increasing. It is the have-nots who are "copping out" the most, the have-nots who have adopted a "what's the use attitude," the have-nots who have the weakest sense of efficacy. And it is getting weaker. "Unless current trends are reversed," Cavanagh predicts, "the disadvantaged members of American society are likely to find themselves playing an increasingly marginal role in the American political system."[43]

SUMMARY

The electorate is not neutral. People do not come to campaigns with completely open minds. Rather, their preexisting beliefs and attitudes color their perceptions and affect their judgment.

Of these attitudes, partisanship has the strongest impact on voting behavior. It is a mechanism for placing oneself within the political world, for evaluating the campaign, and for deciding how to vote. It is also a motive for being informed, for being concerned, and for turning out on election day.

Partisan attitudes have eroded since the 1960s. The percentage of people identifying with a party and the strength of that identification have declined. One consequence has been the increasing importance of short-term factors in campaigning. Another has been the uncertainty of election outcomes, especially at the presidential level.

Since larger numbers of voters are less strongly affected by partisan cues, new importance has been placed on their perception of the images that candidates attempt to project and, to a lesser extent, on the ideological stances they take. For a candidate's image to have an impact, it must seem authentic and convey desirable attributes for the office. For a candidate's issue positions to have an effect, they must be clearly identifiable and personally meaningful to the voters.

The weakening of partisan ties has produced a presidential vote which either party can win. It has produced a vote that has less carry-over to congressional and state elections. And it has produced an electorate that is more volatile and less predictable at the presidential level.

The parties' coalitions have also shifted and, to some extent, shrunk. The Democratic party, which became the majority during the New Deal period, has lost the support of a majority of southern whites and has suffered defections from labor and minority religious grups (Catholics and Jews). But it has also maintained its support from minority racial groups (blacks and Hispanics) and cut into the northern white Protestant Republican vote. Its coalition has weakened but not disintegrated.

The Republican party is far more homogeneous than the Democratic party. Retaining the party's backing from the upper socioeconomic strata, the Republicans have gained in the South and benefited from the increased social conservatism of a growing middle class. The party has been able to win presidential elections but has not been able to broaden its electoral coalition on a long-term basis.

These trends have affected turnout as well. The decline in the percentage of the population that votes may be partially attributed to the weakening of partisan ties, to the larger proportion of the electorate that is under thirty and over seventy, and to the increasing amount of political cynicism and apathy, particularly among lower socioeconomic groups. These changes have important implications for the political system.

Both parties appear to be the losers. Not only do fewer people identify with them and feel less strongly about them, but the power of their officials has diminished. Parties still nominate the candidates but, ironically, have less influence over who is chosen; they still provide the essential labels but have less effect on who gets elected President. They still take positions but seem to have less influence on what gets enacted into law.

NOTES

1. Actually, a small interview-reinterview survey was conducted in 1948, but the results were never published. In contrast to the emphasis on political attitudes of the large-scale interview projects in the 1950s, the 1948 project had a sociological orientation.

2. Angus Campbell, Philip E. Converse, Warren E. Miller, and Donald E. Stokes, *The American Voter* (New York: John Wiley, 1960).

3. Ibid., pp. 146–152.

4. Ibid., pp. 163–165.

5. Ibid., pp. 133–136. Party identification is determined by asking the following question: "Generally speaking, do you usually think of yourself as a Republican, a Democrat, an Independent, or what?" To discern the strength of the identification, a second question is asked: "(If Republican or Democrat), Would you call yourself a strong (R)

(D) or a not very strong (R) (D)? (If Independent), Do you think of yourself as closer to the Republican or Democratic party?" In examining the concept of party identification, the University of Michigan analysts have stressed two dimensions—its direction and strength. Others, however, have criticized the Michigan model for overemphasizing party and underemphasizing other factors such as social class, political ideology, and issue positions. For a thoughtful critique see Jerrold G. Rusk, "The Michigan Election Studies: A Critical Evaluation" (paper delivered at the annual meeting of the American Political Science Association, New York, September 3–6, 1981).

6. For a more extensive discussion of desirable presidential images, see Chapter 7, pp. 000–000, and Benjamin I. Page, *Choices and Echoes in Presidential Elections* (Chicago: University of Chicago Press, 1978), pp. 232–265.

7. Campbell et al., *The American Voter*, pp. 143 and 547. Recent studies suggest that independents who lean in a partisan direction tend to be better informed than those who do not. These independent leaners have many of the characteristics of party identifiers, including loyalty to the party's candidates. They, do not, however, identify themselves as Republicans or Democrats.

8. V. O. Key, Jr., *The Responsible Electorate* (Cambridge, Mass.: Harvard University Press, 1966), p. 7.

9. The switchers, however, constituted only a small percentage of the total electorate. Stand-patters were a larger group. For them, policy preferences reinforced their partisan loyalties. The beliefs and behavior of the stand-patters confirmed the basic thesis that partisanship influences voting for most people most of the time. Ibid., p. 150.

10. See, for example, David E. RePass, "Issue Salience and Party Choice," *American Political Science Review*, 65 (1971), 389–400; John E. Jackson, "Issues, Party Choices, and Presidential Votes," *American Journal of Political Science*, 19 (1975), 161–185; Arthur H. Miller and Warren E. Miller, "Issues, Candidates and Partisan Divisions in the 1972 American Presidential Election," *British Journal of Political Science*, 5 (1975), 393–433; Arthur H. Miller, Warren E. Miller, Alden S. Raine, and Thad A. Brown, "A Majority Party in Disarray: Policy Polarization in the 1972 Election," *American Political Science Review*, 70 (1976), 753–778; Norman H. Nie, Sidney Verba, and John R. Petrocik, *The Changing American Voter* (Cambridge, Mass.: Harvard University Press, 1976), pp. 156–173; Warren E. Miller and Teresa Levitin, *Leadership and Change: The New Politics and the American Electorate* (Cambridge, Mass.: Winthrop Publishers, 1976), p. 166.

11. Hugh L. LeBlanc and Mary Beth Merrin, "Independents, Issue Partisanship and the Decline of Party," *American Politics Quarterly*, 7 (1979), 240–256.

12. Arthur H. Miller and Martin P. Wattenberg, "Policy and Performance Voting in the 1980 Election" (paper delivered at the annual meeting of the American Political Science Association, New York, September 3–6, 1981).

13. Campbell et al., *The American Voter*, p. 78.

14. Miller and Wattenberg, "Policy and Performance Voting," p. 17.

15. Nie, Verba, and Petrocik, *The Changing American Voter*, p. 347.

16. Austin Ranney, "The Political Parties: Reform and Decline," in Anthony King (ed.), *The New American Political System* (Washington, D.C.: American Enterprise Institute, 1978), p. 221.

17. For a discussion of how to measure the support of different groups in the parties' electoral coalition, see Robert Axelrod, "Where the Votes Come From: An Analysis

of Electoral Coalitions, 1952–1972," *American Political Science Review,* 66 (1972), 11–20.

18. This description of the New Deal realignment is based primarily on the discussion in Everett Carll Ladd, Jr., with Charles D. Hadley, *Transformations of the American Party System* (New York: W. W. Norton, 1974), pp. 31–87.

19. Ibid., p. 43.

20. Ibid., p. 69.

21. Ibid., pp. 55–57.

22. Ibid., pp. 93–104.

23. Ibid., p. 158.

24. Everett Carll Ladd, Jr., "The Shifting Party Coalitions, 1932–1976," in Seymour Martin Lipset (ed.), *Emerging Coalitions in American Politics* (San Francisco: Institute for Contemporary Studies, 1978), p. 83.

25. Nie, Verba, and Petrocik, *The Changing American Voter,* p. 241.

26. Ladd, "The Shifting Party Coalitions, 1932–1976," p. 92.

27. Warren E. Miller, Arthur H. Miller, and Edward J. Schneider, *American National Election Studies Data Sourcebook* (Cambridge, Mass.: Harvard University Press, 1980) p. 91.

28. Nie, Verba, and Petrocik, *The Changing American Voter,* pp. 223–226.

29. Martin P. Wattenberg and Arthur H. Miller, "Decay in Regional Party Coalitions: 1952–1980," in Seymour Martin Lipset (ed.), *Party Coalitions in the 1980s* (San Francisco: Institute for Contemporary Studies, 1981), p. 357.

30. One reason that the Mountain States are less Democratic is that they have a low percentage of blacks within their voting-age population.

31. For a more extended discussion of the composition and participation of the Democratic party coalition in 1980 see Robert Axelrod, "Communication," *American Political Science Review,* 76 (1982), 393–396.

32. V. O. Key, Jr., *Politics, Parties and Pressure Groups* (New York: Thomas Y. Crowell, 1958), p. 624.

33. Procedures, registration dates, and the permanency of registration still differ from state to state. President Carter supported and President Ford opposed a bill to facilitate registration by mail. The bill has not been passed by Congress. However, the major provisions of the Voting Rights Act were extended by legislation in 1982.

34. Campbell et al., *The American Voter,* p. 102.

35. Raymond E. Wolfinger and Steven J. Rosenstone, "Who Votes?" (paper delivered at the annual meeting of the American Political Science Association, Washington, D.C., September 1–4, 1977), p. 34.

36. Ibid., pp. 10–32.

37. Ibid., pp. 59–60.

38. In nonpresidential elections, turnout has been even lower. Clearly, the attention and excitement of the presidential campaign contribute to more participation and voting. The competitiveness of the election also affects turnout, with closer contests attracting more voters. The weather on election day is also a factor in the size of the vote.

39. For a more extended discussion of this issue see Hugh L. LeBlanc, *American Political Parties* (New York: St. Martin's Press, 1982), pp. 312–315.

40. Richard A. Brody, "The Puzzle of Political Participation in America," in King, *The New American Political System,* pp. 305–306.

41. Paul R. Abramson, John H. Aldrich, and David W. Rohde, *Change and Continuity in the 1980 Elections* (Washington, D.C.: Congressional Quarterly, 1982), p. 87.

42. Thomas E. Cavanagh, "Changes in American Voter Turnout, 1964–1976," *Political Science Quarterly*, 96 (1981), 53–65. The high participation of blacks in the 1982 Chicago and Philadelphia mayoralty primaries and elections may indicate a reversal of this trend, particularly among city dwellers.

43. Ibid., p. 63.

Selected Readings

Brody, Richard A. "The Puzzle of Political Participation in America," in Anthony King (ed.), *The New American Political System.* Washington, D.C.: American Enterprise Institute, 1978.

Campbell, Angus, Philip E. Converse, Warren E. Miller, and Donald E. Stokes. *The American Voter.* New York: John Wiley, 1960.

Cavanagh, Thomas E. "Changes in American Voter Turnout, 1964–1976," *Political Science Quarterly,* 96 (1981), 53–65.

Fishel, Jeff, ed. *Parties and Elections in an Anti-Party Age.* Bloomington: Indiana University Press, 1978.

Kirkpatrick, Jeanne J. "Changing Patterns of Electoral Competition," in Anthony King (ed.), *The New American Political System.* Washington, D.C.: American Enterprise Institute, 1978.

Ladd, Everett Carll, Jr., with Charles D. Hadley. *Transformations of the American Party System.* New York: W. W. Norton, 1975.

Lipset, Seymour Martin, ed. *Emerging Coalitions in American Politics.* San Francisco: Institute for Contemporary Studies, 1978.

———, ed. *Party Coalitions in the 1980s.* San Francisco: Institute for Contemporary Studies, 1981.

Margolis, Michael. "From Confusion to Confusion: Issues and the American Voter (1956–1972)," *American Political Science Review,* 66 (1977), 31–43.

Nie, Norman H., Sidney Verba, and John R. Petrocik. *The Changing American Voter.* Cambridge, Mass.: Harvard University Press, 1976.

Ranney, Austin. "The Political Parties: Reform and Decline," in Anthony King (ed.), *The New American Political System.* Washington, D.C.: American Enterprise Institute, 1978.

Wolfinger, Raymond E., and Steven J. Rosenstone. *Who Votes?* New Haven: Yale University Press, 1980.

PART II

THE
NOMINATION

Chapter 4

DELEGATE SELECTION

Introduction

Presidential nominees are selected by the delegates to a party's national convention. The way those delegates are chosen can influence the choice of nominees. It can also affect the influence of the state and its party leadership.

Procedures for delegate selection are determined by state law. Today, these procedures also have to conform to general guidelines and rules established by the national party. In the past, they did not. Rather, statutes passed by the state legislature reflected the needs and desires of the political leaders who controlled the state. Naturally, these laws were designed to buttress that leadership and extend its influence.

Primary elections in which the party's rank and file choose the delegates were discouraged, coopted, or even circumvented. Favorite son candidates, tapped by the leadership, prevented meaningful contests in many states. Other states held primaries but made them advisory, with the actual selection of the delegates left to caucuses, conventions, or committees which were more easily controlled by party officials. There were also impediments to potential delegates' getting on the ballot: high fees, lengthy petitions, early dates for filing. Winner-take-all provisions gave a great advantage to the organization candidate, as did rules requiring delegates to vote as a unit.

Not until the 1970s was popular participation in the selection of con-

81

vention delegates encouraged. It was the national party that took the lead by adopting a series of reforms which affected the period during which delegates could be selected, the procedures for choosing them, and ultimately, their behavior at the convention. While these rules limited the states' discretion, they did not result in uniform primaries and caucuses. Considerable variation still exists in how delegates are chosen, how the vote is apportioned, and who participates in the selection.

SELECTION PROCEDURES

Convention delegates may be elected directly. In some states just the names of the delegates appear on the ballot. In other states, both the names of the delegates and the candidates to whom they are pledged are listed. Some ballots do not even list the delegates at all. In such cases the percentage of the vote which the candidates receive determines how many delegates they get to choose. In caucuses, people are chosen directly but usually as representatives to a state meeting that will select convention delegates.

The size of the unit in which delegates may be selected also varies. Theoretically, it could be as large as the state or as small as a legislative district. In practice, Democratic party rules have established restrictions which have made congressional districts the order of the day. Republicans still permit statewide elections.

Even more critical than size is the formula for the final allocation of delegates within a district. There are a number of possibilities. One would be to elect the entire slate of delegates of the winning candidate. If the delegates are chosen directly, then another method would be to elect those with the most votes. However, this could also result in the winner taking all the delegates if those with the most votes were all for the same candidate. Under these circumstances, there would be no representation for losing candidates.

A third method would be to apportion the delegates in rough approximation to the popular vote. The problem here is how to divide the delegates equally if a large number of candidates receive small proportions of the vote. One way would be to require a minimum vote for obtaining delegates. Another would be to apportion the delegates on the basis of percentages. Each candidate who received popular votes would receive at least one delegate. A third possibility would be to give the candidate with the most votes one delegate just for winning and then divide the rest of the delegates on the basis of the proportion each candidate receives. Considerable controversy has surrounded each of these schemes.

Delegate selection rules also vary with respect to who can participate in a primary or caucus. Some states allow only registered voters to cast ballots. The parties naturally prefer this type of *closed* selection process. However, a number of states do not require registration. Primary voters simply request particular ballots. Such a system permits *cross-over* voting. It allows those who consider themselves Republican to vote Democratic and vice versa. Finally, in some states, voters are simply given all the ballots and cast whichever one they choose. This is known as an *open* primary, one which the parties strongly oppose and the Democrats have prohibited.

There are also differences in the degree to which delegates are bound to candidates at the convention. Some states require delegates to vote for the candidate to which they are pledged for at least one or two ballots or until they are released by that candidate. Others permit them to vote as they please. States have also required their delegates to vote as units, although the national parties will not enforce the unit rule. The Democrats, in fact, have banned it at their convention.

Each of these variations in the delegate selection process has important consequences. It affects who gets involved and what impact they have; who the delegates are and how they behave; and what influence the party leaders have before and during the convention. It also conditions the strategy and tactics of the candidates. Finally and ultimately, it determines the outcome of the convention: who the standard-bearers will be; what the platform says; and how much unity will prevail in the party for the general election.

Because of the magnitude of this impact, political parties have been vitally concerned with their rules for delegate selection. In fact, the Democrats have been obsessed with them for the last decade. This chapter will explore the rules and their consequences for the nomination process.

The chapter is organized into five sections. The first details the changes that have occurred from 1968 through 1980. It focuses on the procedures for delegate selection and the formulas for apportionment. The next section discusses challenges to these rules and judicial decisions on these challenges. In the third section, the effects that the reforms have had on public participation, delegate representation, and party organization are assessed. The fourth section notes the modifications to these reforms that have occurred since 1980 and points to their likely impact on the 1984 nomination. In the final section, the changes in the strategies and tactics of nomination seeking are discussed and illustrated by the game plans of the successful candidates in 1976 and 1980.

PARTY REFORMS, 1968–1980

Admonished for not being democratic in the aftermath of its tumultuous 1968 convention, the Democratic party appointed a commission, first headed by Senator George McGovern and later by Representative Donald Fraser, to study its nominating procedures and propose ways of improving them. The commission had two primary objectives: to encourage greater rank-and-file participation in party activities and to make the convention more representative of typical Democratic voters.

To achieve the first of these objectives, it recommended a series of reforms designed to tune the delegate selection process more closely to popular sentiment. The commission proposed that delegates be chosen in the calendar year of the convention. Previously, they had been selected up to two years before and thus could be out of touch with opinion in their states. It recommended that fees for entering primaries be lowered or abolished. In the past, the high costs of registration had discouraged some candidates from entering.

In nonprimary states, the commission urged that meetings for choosing the delegates be publicly announced with adequate time given for campaigning. The old system of proxy voting, whereby a state party leader would cast a large number of votes for the delegates of his choice, was to be ended. State central committees would no longer be permitted to appoint more than 10 percent of the delegates. Three-fourths of the delegates were to be chosen at levels no larger than congressional districts. The remainder were to be selected at large. The unit rule, which required delegates to vote as a bloc, was abolished. The party's national committee approved these changes.

One of the most far-reaching proposals concerned the allocation of delegates within the states. The commission recommended that they be allocated in proportion to the popular support a candidate received. Previously, Democrats had permitted winner-take-all voting.

For the next eight years the party (including three more commissions) struggled with this recommendation and methods of implementing it. In 1972 it recommended, but did not mandate, a proportional allocation system. In 1976 the party prohibited statewide primaries that awarded all the delegates to the candidate with the most votes, but it permitted delegates to be elected directly by the voters in districts within the state. This loophole resulted in some winner-take-all decisions. In 1980 the party banned loophole primaries altogether, although its Compliance Review Commission subsequently granted exemptions to two states, West Virginia and Illinois. Also in 1980 the party prohibited states from creating special districts small enough to elect a single delegate.[1]

Since the object of these changes was to make delegate selection more reflective of candidate preferences of the voters, it was also important to limit the influence of outsiders on the election of delegates. To this end the party adopted a rule in 1972 that prohibited those who were not Democrats from participating in the party's primaries. The difficulty was to determine who was a Democrat, since some states did not require or even permit registration by party.

In enforcing this rule, the party adopted a very liberal interpretation of Democratic affiliation. Identifying oneself as a Democrat at the time of voting or simply requesting a Democratic ballot was viewed as sufficient evidence of being a Democrat. This effectively permitted cross-over primaries but not open ones, although several exemptions to the open rule were granted in 1972 and again in 1976.

In addition to better translating public preferences into delegate selection, the other major objective of the party was to equalize representation on the delegations themselves. To this end the party in 1972 required that all states represent blacks, women, and youth in reasonable relationship to their presence in the state population. Failure to do so constituted a *prima facie* case of discrimination. If the delegation was challenged at the convention, the burden of proof was on the state party to prove it had not discriminated.

Considerable opposition to the application of this rule developed and it was subsequently modified after the 1972 convention. The revised rule merely required states to implement affirmative action plans. This made challenges more difficult, since the composition of the state delegation alone did not constitute sufficient evidence of discrimination to reject the delegation. In 1980, however, the rules singled out specific groups which had been subject to past discrimination (native Americans, blacks, and youth) and requested that states set goals for representation on the delegation based on their population within the state. With respect to women the party went one step further. In 1980 and thereafter, it required that each delegation be equally divided between men and women.

Also in 1980 the Democrats made one additional change to improve representation at the convention. Unhappy with the absence of elected officeholders and party leaders at its 1972 and 1976 conventions, the party wished to provide greater opportunities for them to attend. It increased the size of each state delegation by 10 percent with the proviso that these add-on delegates were to come from this group of elected officeholders and party leaders but were to be committed to candidates in the same proportion as the preferences of the elected delegates.

One consequence of these Democratic reforms was to make primaries the preferred method of delegate selection. The difficulty of satisfying the requirement for proportional voting and representation at each stage of the nominating process encouraged party officials to have primaries rather than a multistage caucus-convention system. Not only were primaries more open and more easily accessible to rank-and-file participants, but direct election made the state delegation less subject to convention challenge on the grounds of discrimination.

Moreover, primary voting became more closely tied to delegate selection than it had been in the past. The number of advisory primaries declined and binding primaries increased,[2] thereby giving the party's electorate a more direct voice in selecting the nominee.

A third consequence was not nearly as beneficial to the goals of increased participation and more equal representation. The increase in the number of primaries lengthened the process. It also enhanced the impact of the early contests in many of the smaller states. This had the effect of sealing the fate of the nomination long before the selection process was completed. As a result, voter turnout was discouraged in many of the large states that held their primaries in late April, May, and June.

From the party's perspective, other negative consequences followed from the extension of the primary season. The costs of campaigning increased; candidate fatigue and public boredom increased; divisiveness within the electoral coalition increased; even the influence of the media increased, particularly in the early critical stages of the process. Most of these consequences, though unintended, conflicted with the objectives of the reforms.

Democratic rules changes in 1980 attempted to rectify the problem, but with little success. A provision calling for a three-month period in which primaries and caucuses could be scheduled was circumvented by exemptions given to five states. The exemptions actually lengthened the process, making it the longest in U.S. electoral history. The official campaign lasted almost six months; the unofficial campaign began even before the election year.

The Republicans have been affected by Democratic rules changes as well. Pressure was created within the party to broaden public participation and improve the representation of minorities. This pressure resulted in a resolution adopted at the 1972 Republican convention urging states to provide women, youth, nationality groups, and other minorities with a greater role in the conduct of party affairs. Republicans have been affected in another way. Since the Democratic party controlled many of the state legislatures during the 1970s, some of its reforms were literally forced on the Republicans by the passage of new election laws. Finally, the Republicans have made some rules changes of their own, although they were not nearly as extensive as those of the Democrats. A Committee of Delegates and Organizations (known as the DO Committee) was appointed in 1969 and recommended that delegate selection procedures be more participatory in convention states, that more information about these procedures be promulgated to the party's electorate, and that voting by proxy at caucuses and conventions be prohibited. These recommendations, adopted in 1972, took effect in 1976.

THE LEGALITY OF PARTY RULES

For the reforms to be effective, they had to be enacted into law. Most states conformed to insure that their parties would continue to receive proper representation at the national conventions. A few did not. New Hampshire refused to move its primary date into the window period that the Democratic party had established, nor would Iowa change its caucus date. In 1976 and again in 1980, the national party recanted. Its Compliance Review Commission granted exemptions to New Hampshire, Iowa, and a number of other states.

A good deal of resistance was encountered by the party in enforcing other voting regulations. In 1972, California and Illinois each chose its delegates in a manner that did not conform to the letter and spirit of the new rules. California elected slates of delegates on a winner-take-all basis, while in Illinois the openness of the slate-making process itself was questioned. In both instances delegates selected from these states were challenged. The cases ended up in the courts.

There were two basic issues: one political and one legal. The political issue concerned which delegates would be seated, those that supported or opposed Senator McGovern. That issue was decided by the convention. McGovern's forces prevailed. The legal question concerned which institution had the higher authority, the national party or the state legislature. The Supreme Court ultimately decided in favor of the national party at least as far as its convention was concerned. In its landmark decision in the Illinois case, *Cousins* v. *Wigoda* (419 U.S. 477, 1975), the court stated that political parties were private organizations with rights of association protected by the Constitution. States could not abridge these rights unless there was a compelling constitutional reason to do so. The Supreme Court found no such compelling reason in Illinois. Therefore, while states could establish their own primary law, the party could determine the criteria for representation at its national convention.

The *Cousins* v. *Wigoda* decision provided an additional incentive for states to change their laws when they conflicted with party rules. The number of challenges declined. They were not, however, eliminated entirely. The issue of cross-over voting as practiced in the open primary continued to plague the Democrats. It was not resolved until after the party's 1980 convention, and then only as a consequence of another Supreme Court decision.

In 1978 the party prohibited open primaries. Four states had conducted this type of election in 1976. Three voluntarily changed for 1980. A fourth, Wisconsin, did not. The party's Compliance Review Commission ordered the state party to design an alternative process. In response, Wisconsin's attorney general went to court at the state level to prevent the national Democratic party from circumventing the state law. The highest court in Wisconsin sided with the attorney general. While the national Democratic party succeeded in getting the decision stayed, it had little choice but to seat the delegates who were selected in an open primary.

The issue, however, was not rendered moot by the 1980 Democratic convention, since the state court's decision would have been binding on the party for subsequent elections as well. The Democrats appealed to the United States Supreme Court and their appeal was successful. Citing the precedent of *Cousins* v. *Wigoda*, the Supreme Court concluded in the case of *Democratic Party of the U.S.* v. *La Follette* (101 S. Ct. 1010, 1981) that the state had no right to interfere with the party's delegate selection process because it had not demonstrated a compelling reason to do so. Thus, Wisconsin can still have an open primary, but the Democratic convention can refuse to seat delegates selected in it.

Taken together, the two decisions acknowledge the party's power to specify and enforce rules for participation at its nominating convention. Whether these rules are made mandatory or advisory is up to the national party to determine. The Democrats have required state parties to conform; the Republicans have not.

While the procedures for choosing convention delegates have not engendered major political or legal controversies within the Republican party, the formula for apportioning the delegates has. The Republicans determine the size of each delegation on the basis of three criteria: statehood (6 delegates), House districts (3 per district), and support for Republican candidates elected within the previous four years (1 for a Republican governor, 1 for each Republican senator, 1 for a Republican majority of House members, and a bonus of 4.5 delegates plus 60 percent of the electoral vote if the state voted for the Republican presidential candidate in the last election).

The plan effectively discriminates against the larger states in two ways. In the first place, many of the bonus delegates are awarded to a state without regard to its size. Thus, the voting strength of the larger states at the convention is proportionately reduced by the bonuses, while that of the smaller states is increased. To illustrate, Alaska had its delegation doubled in 1972, while California's was increased by only 6.7 percent, both as a result of bonuses. Second, since the larger states are more competitive, they are less likely to be awarded bonus delegates on a recurring basis. Particularly hard hit are the states in the Northeast and Midwest, such as New York, Pennsylvania, and Ohio. By voting for Carter in 1976, these states lost their bonuses and had their 1980 delegations reduced.

The Ripon Society, a liberal Republican organization, has continually challenged the constitutionality of this apportionment rule, but it has not been successful. The first of these challenges, initiated in the form of a lawsuit, was declared moot by the court when delays forced the decision after the 1972 Republican convention. A second court case, begun in 1975, challenged the formula on the grounds that it violated the Supreme Court's "one person-one vote" rule. It was rejected when the U.S. Court of Appeals of the District of Columbia ruled against the Ripon Society and the Supreme Court refused to intervene. In 1980 the Society again contested the rules, but to no avail.

The bonus plan has worked to the advantage of conservative candidates seeking the Republican nomination. In 1976 and 1980 it helped Ronald Reagan. It has also increased the size of Republican conventions.

The Democratic apportionment formula has also been subject to controversy. Under the plan used since 1968 and modified in 1976, the Democrats have allotted 50 percent of each state delegation on the basis of its electoral vote and 50 percent on the basis of its average Democratic vote in the last three presidential elections. The rule for apportionment was challenged in 1971 on the grounds that it did not conform to the "one person–one vote" principle, but the Court of Appeals asserted that it did not violate the equal protection clause of the Fourteenth Amendment. The Democratic formula results in even larger conventions than the Republican. Table 4–1 lists the apportionment of Republican and Democrat convention delegates for 1980 and 1984.

THE IMPACT OF THE RULES CHANGES

The new rules produced some of their desired effects. They opened up the nomination process by allowing more people to participate. They increased minority representation at the conventions. But they also decreased the influence of state party leaders over the selection of delegates and ultimately lessened the influence of party leaders in the presidential electoral process.

Table 4-1   DELEGATE APPORTIONMENT IN 1980 AND 1984

Democratic Party			Republican Party		
State	1980	1984	State	1980	1984
Alabama	45	62	Alabama	27	38
Alaska	11	14	Alaska	19	18
Arizona	29	39	Arizona	28	32
Arkansas	33	42	Arkansas	19	29
California	306	345	California	168	176
Colorado	40	51	Colorado	31	35
Connecticut	54	60	Connecticut	35	35
Delaware	14	18	Delaware	12	19
District of Columbia	19	19	District of Columbia	14	14
Florida	100	143	Florida	51	82
Georgia	63	82	Georgia	36	37
Hawaii	19	27	Hawaii	14	14
Idaho	17	22	Idaho	21	21
Illinois	179	194	Illinois	102	93
Indiana	80	88	Indiana	54	52
Iowa	50	58	Iowa	37	37
Kansas	37	44	Kansas	32	32
Kentucky	50	63	Kentucky	27	37*
Louisiana	51	68	Louisiana	31	41*
Maine	22	27	Maine	21	20
Maryland	59	74	Maryland	30	31
Massachusetts	111	116	Massachusetts	42	52
Michigan	141	155	Michigan	82	77
Minnesota	75	86	Minnesota	34	32
Mississippi	32	43	Mississippi	22	30*
Missouri	77	86	Missouri	37	47
Montana	19	25	Montana	20	20
Nebraska	24	30	Nebraska	25	24

Turnout

In 1980 over 32 million people voted in presidential primaries compared with approximately 12 million in 1968, 22 million in 1972, and 29 million in 1976. Overall, approximately 21 percent of the voting-age population participated in the 1980 primaries and approximately 7 percent in the caucuses.

Turnout varied considerably from state to state. In New Hampshire, for example, 82 percent of the registered Democrats voted in their party's primary compared with 57.5 percent of the Democrats in California and 27 percent in New York. In contrast, caucus turnout among the Demo-

Table 4-1   DELEGATE APPORTIONMENT IN 1980 AND 1984 (Continued)

Democratic Party			Republican Party		
State	1980	1984	State	1980	1984
Nevada	12	20	Nevada	17	22
New Hampshire	19	22	New Hampshire	22	22
New Jersey	113	122	New Jersey	66	64
New Mexico	20	28	New Mexico	22	24
New York	282	285	New York	123	136
North Carolina	69	88	North Carolina	40	53
North Dakota	14	18	North Dakota	17	18
Ohio	161	175	Ohio	77	89
Oklahoma	42	53	Oklahoma	34	35
Oregon	39	50	Oregon	29	32
Pennsylvania	185	195	Pennsylvania	83	98
Rhode Island	23	27	Puerto Rico	14	14
South Carolina	37	48	Rhode Island	13	14
South Dakota	19	19	South Carolina	25	35
Tennessee	55	76	South Dakota	22	19
Texas	152	200	Tennessee	32	46
Utah	20	27	Texas	80	109
Vermont	12	17	Utah	21	26
Virginia	64	78	Vermont	19	19
Washington	58	70	Virginia	51	50
West Virginia	35	44	Virgin Islands	4	4
Wisconsin	75	89	Washington	37	43
Wyoming	11	15	West Virginia	18	19
Democrats Abroad	4	5	Wisconsin	34	46
Guam	4	7	Wyoming	19	18
Latin America	4	5	Guam	4	4
Puerto Rico	41	53	Totals	1,994	2,234
Virgin Islands	4	6			
Totals	3,331	3,923			

*May be increased by 1 if a Republican governor is elected in 1983.

crats ranged from a high of 18 percent in Iowa to only 1 percent in Delaware.[3]

While turnout in presidential primaries has increased since 1968, it is still below what it was between 1948 and 1968. In a study of eleven states holding competitive presidential primaries during this earlier period, Austin Ranney found an average of 39 percent voting in the primaries and 69 percent voting in the general election.[4]

In his study, Ranney also noted that primary voters came disproportionately from the well-educated, upper economic strata of society. Despite the objectives of the reforms, demographic differences between the electorates in the primaries and general election have persisted. Surveys commissioned by the Democratic party in 1976 and 1980 found that primary voters had more education and higher incomes than the average Democratic voter in the general election.[5] The surveys also indicated that minorities were underrepresented in the primaries. Income differences, however, have narrowed. In short, participants in the preconvention process do not mirror the demography of the voting-age population.

Representation

As a consequence of the reforms, the demographic representation of certain groups at the conventions increased. Prior to 1972, the delegates were predominantly white, male, and well educated. Mostly professionals whose income and social status placed them considerably above the national mean, they were expected to pay their own way to the convention. Large financial contributors, as well as elected officeholders and party officials, were frequently in attendance.

In 1972 the demographic profile of convention delegates began to change. The proportion of women rose substantially. Youth and minority representation, especially in Democratic delegations, also increased.

A slight reversal of these trends occurred in 1976. As Table 4–2 indicates, the percentage of minorities, women, and those under thirty declined in both parties from their 1972 high. The easing of Democratic party guidelines for delegate representation in 1976 may have been partially responsible for the drop. In 1980, however, the Democratic percentages increased while the Republicans' remained constant.

Despite the changes in delegate composition, the delegates' income and educational levels remained well above the national average. In 1980 the median income of the Democratic delegates was $37,000; the national figure was $17,000. Further, 65 percent of the Democratic delegates had

Table 4–2 THE DEMOGRAPHY OF THE DELEGATES, 1968–1980

| | National Convention Delegates | | | | | | | | Public | |
| | 1968 | | 1972 | | 1976 | | 1980 | | 1980 | |
	Dem.	Rep.	Dem.	Rep.	Dem.	Rep.	Dem.	Rep.	Dem.	Rep.
Women	13%	16%	40%	29%	33%	31%	49%	29%	56%	53%
Blacks	5	2	15	4	11	3	15	3	19	4
Under thirty	3	4	22	8	15	7	11	5	27	27
Median age (years)	(49)	(49)	(42)		(43)	(48)	(44)	(49)	(43)	(45)
Lawyers	28	22	12		16	15	13	15		
Teachers	8	2	11		12	4	15	15		
Union members			16		21	3	27	4	29*	18*
Attended first convention	67	66	83	78	80	78	87	84		
College graduate	19		21		21	27	20	26	11	18
Postgraduate	44	34	36		43	38	45	39		
Protestant			42		47	73	47	72	63	74
Catholic			26		34	18	37	22	29	21
Jewish			9		9	3	8	3	4	1
Liberal					40	3	46	2	21	13
Moderate					47	45	42	36	44	40
Conservative					8	48	6	58	26	41

Source: CBS News Delegate Surveys, 1968 through 1980. Characteristics of the public are average values from seven CBS News/*New York Times* polls, 1980. Reprinted from Warren J. Mitofsky and Martin Plissner, "The Making of the Delegates, 1968–1980," *Public Opinion*, III (1980), 43. © 1980, American Enterprise Institute for Public Policy Research, Washington, D.C. 20036.

*Households with a union member.

attended college, in sharp contrast to 16 percent of the party's rank and file.[6] Similarly, the educational and income levels of Republican delegates was substantially above the national average. Clearly, the 1980 convention delegates enjoyed a much higher standard of living and much greater educational opportunities than most Americans.

Another significant change in the composition of the conventions was an increase in first-time participants and a decline in party officials. In 1972, 83 percent of the Democrats and 78 percent of the Republicans were attending their first convention. By 1980, these figures rose to 87 percent and 84 percent respectively.

Congressional representation dropped dramatically in Democratic conventions. Table 4–3 indicates the magnitude of the decline between 1968 and 1980.

The percentage of delegates who held major positions within the state also decreased during the 1970s. However, in 1980 this trend was reversed. For the Democrats, the 10 percent addition to each state delegation increased the participation of elected officeholders and party officials at the state and local levels. CBS News estimated that 64 percent of the Democratic delegates in 1980 held elected office, an increase of 7 percent from the previous convention.[7]

It is more difficult to determine the extent to which ideological and issue perceptions of recent delegates differed from those of their predecessors and from the electorate as a whole. One study of the 1968 convention delegates, which predictably found differences between Republicans and Democrats, also discerned intraparty differences between delegates se-

Table 4–3   REPRESENTATION OF MAJOR ELECTED OFFICALS AT NATIONAL CONVENTIONS, 1968–1980* (IN PERCENTAGES)

	1968	1972	1976	1980
Democrats				
Governors	96	57	44	74
U.S. Senators	61	28	18	14
U.S. Representatives	32	12	14	14
Republicans				
Governors	92	80	69	68
U.S. Senators	58	50	59	63
U.S. Representatives	31	19	36	40

Source: Hugh L. LeBlanc, *American Political Parties* (New York: St. Martin's Press, 1982), p. 220. LeBlanc derived the data in this table from Warren J. Mitofsky and Martin Plissner, "The Making of the Delegates, 1968–1980," *Public Opinion* (1980), p. 43. Reprinted with permission
*Figures represent the percentages of Democratic or Republican officeholders from each group who served as delegates.

lected in primaries and those from nonprimary states.[8] These intraparty differences, however, were not evident in later years.

In general, convention delegates have been found to be more issue and ideology conscious than their party's rank and file. Moreover, they have tended to display a greater degree of ideological consistency in their attitudes than other party sympathizers. Republican delegates have been found to be more conservative than Republicans as a whole. In fact, in 1956, Herbert McClosky claimed that Republican delegates were so conservative that most Republican party identifiers were actually closer to the Democratic delegates' positions on a range of issues than they were to those of the Republican delegates.[9] In 1972, Jeanne Kirkpatrick discovered that the pattern was reversed. Democratic rank-and-file party identifiers had beliefs that conformed more closely to those of the Republican delegates than to the Democratic delegates'.[10] Subsequently, the views of Democratic delegates have moderated somewhat although they are still more liberal than the average Democratic voter's.

Surveys of the ideological perspectives of convention delegates in 1976 and 1980 reveal clear distinctions between Republicans and Democrats. (See Table 4–2.) Most of the delegates who considered themselves conservative were Republicans. Most of those who considered themselves liberal were Democrats. Moreover, the issue stands of the delegates confirm their ideological cleavage. Republican and Democratic delegates consistently took conservative and liberal positions, respectively, on a range of policy matters.[11] If these positions were plotted on an ideological continuum, they would be more consistent (or ideologically pure) than the electorate they represented and much more consistent (or pure) than the public as a whole.

Changes in the preconvention process seem to have contributed to the purity of these perspectives. The selection of more activists who have less of a tie to the party regardless of the candidate seems to have resulted in more delegates who could be described as issue purists and fewer who might be termed partisan pragmatists. If compromise is made more difficult as a consequence, this development could have ominous consequences for party unity and for the electability of the nominees.

In short, despite the reforms, there continue to be differences between the ideological and demographic characteristics of convention delegates and the electorate as a whole. Convention delegates reflect some demographic characteristics of their party's rank and file more accurately than in the past, but this does not necessarily make them more ideologically representative.[12] In fact, delegates have tended to exaggerate the differences among the beliefs and attitudes of the respective electorates. Whether this makes contemporary conventions more or less representative is difficult to say. One thing is clear: it is difficult to achieve electoral representation, reward party activism, and maintain an open selection process at the same time.

Party Organization

While increasing turnout and improving representation were two desired effects of the reforms, weakening the state party structures was not. Yet this too seems to have been a consequence of the rules changes. By promoting internal democracy, the reforms devitalized party organizations. Nomination seeking became a self-selection process. When combined with government subsidies during the primaries, the reforms seemed to encourage the proliferation of candidates. This proliferation, in turn, led to the creation of separate electoral organizations to seek delegate support. Composed largely of activists devoted to the election of a particular candidate, these organizations rivaled the regular party organization in the general election and posed additional problems for it when the election was over.

Contributing to the difficulties of state party organizations was the weakened position of their leadership. No longer able to control their state's delegation, much less guarantee themselves and their supporters a place in it, party leaders had to compete with the supporters of the successful candidate for influence over the campaign and, if successful, for recognition by the new administration. Winning candidates who did not owe their victory to the regular party organization had less reason to depend on it once the election was over and, conversely, more reason to try to take it over.

Winners and Losers

Rules changes are never neutral. They usually benefit one group at the expense of another. Similarly, they tend to help certain candidates and hurt others. The reforms adopted by the Democratic party were no exception.

Clearly, the discrimination provision in 1972, the requirement for affirmative action in 1976 and thereafter, and the rule requiring an equal number of men and women in state delegations in 1980 has helped gain representation for women, youth, and minorities. These changes also have reduced the proportion of white, male, and older delegates who attend. For candidates seeking the party's nomination, this has necessitated that slates of delegates supporting a candidate be demographically balanced to insure that a multitude of groups are included. However, the selection of 25 percent of the delegates at the state level has eased the problem of achieving affirmative action goals because delegates can be chosen to insure that racial, ethnic, sex, and age groups are properly represented.

The openness of the process and the greater participation by the party's rank and file have helped amateurs become delegates and, conversely, have reduced the number of party leaders and public officials at the convention. Recent candidates have depended less on the energies and endorsements of party leaders and more on the organizing capacities of their own state campaign groups.

The outlawing of winner-take-all primaries by the Democratic party and the opening of the caucus process have had an even greater impact on power within the party. In the past, the biggest states, particularly in the Northeast and Midwest, had the largest bloc of votes at Democratic conventions. Under the current apportionment formula, the ten most populous states control 54 percent of the convention delegates. This has given these states disproportionate influence in selecting the nominee and designing the party's platform. The new rules that prescribe proportional voting in primaries and multistage voting in convention states fragment these delegations. This fragmentation decreases the clout of the larger, more competitive states and increases that of the more homogeneous ones—the middle-sized states in the South and Southwest. The proliferation of primaries and the elongation of the prenomination process has also benefited certain states at the expense of others. The early contests, most of which occur in the smaller states, have received disproportionate attention from the candidates and media alike.

Obviously, candidates have had to adjust their strategies accordingly. Instead of concentrating all or most of their resources in the bigger states, they now have to begin earlier, run in more states, and campaign for a longer period. This has aggravated problems of organization and finance and has contributed to the influence of the media on the outcome of the election.

In addition to changing the geographic emphasis, the reforms have decreased the advantage of the front-runners and increased the opportunities for a successful challenge by a lesser-known candidate. The result has been that more people have seriously sought their party's nomination and this, in turn, has led to the splintering of the primary vote.[13]

REFORMING THE REFORMS: THE HUNT COMMISSION

Dissatisfaction with some of these consequences—the poor representation of elected leaders, the proliferation of primaries, the length of the nominating season, and the perfunctory nature of the convention itself—led the Democratic party once again to reexamine its rules for delegate selection. In 1981 a commission, headed by Governor James B. Hunt, Jr., of North Carolina, was established for this purpose. Meeting during the winter of 1981–1982, the commission, composed of a cross-section of party officials and interest group representatives, proposed a series of rules changes to rectify the negative effects of the reforms. These changes were approved by the party's national committee in March 1982.

The new reforms fall into three categories: those that affect the representation of officeholders and party officials; those that affect the allocation of delegates to the candidates; and those that affect the behavior of delegates at the convention.

As noted previously, for some time the party had been unhappy with the decreasing number of its elected officials who attended the convention as delegates. The absence of these officials, it was said, contributed to the lack of support which the nominees received during the campaign and after the election. Carter's difficulties, in particular, were cited as evidence of the need for closer cooperation between party leaders and the presidential standard-bearer.

The commission believed that a greater representation of these leaders would have both a moderating and unifying effect on the party. It would

1. bring seasoned and sensitive judgment to the selection of a nominee and to the conduct of other party business;
2. create stronger ties between the party and its officeholders, promoting a unified campaign strategy and teamwork in government;
3. strengthen the party's ties to its constituencies and its broad mainstream appeal.[14]

Finally, it would reward those who held office and might be candidates for reelection.

The problem was how to accomplish this objective without discouraging grass roots participation and without reducing the number of delegates chosen in the primaries or caucuses. The commission recommended the allocation of additional delegates. Reserved for party and elected officials, these new slots were to be apportioned on the basis of the size of the state and the number of Democratice officeholders. Party caucuses in the Senate and the House were to select up to three-fifths of their members as delegates. The remainder were to come from state officials and party leaders, with priority given to governors and large city mayors.

In all, 561 delegates were added. They constitute 14 percent of all the delegates in 1984. And they are all to be unpledged.

After some debate the rule that state delegations be equally divided between men and women was retained. In effect, this will mean that women will constitute a majority of the pledged delegates at the 1984 convention, since the large bulk of the unpledged elected and party officials will be male. Youth, however, were dropped from the list of groups specially targeted by the party for affirmative action, and Asian-Pacifics were added.[15]

The commission also specified that the 10 percent bonus which had been created four years earlier to give better representation to state party leaders was to be continued. This second group of add-on delegates, chosen by the elected delegates of the state, was to be pledged.

Population shifts have also affected the apportionment, with the southern states being the principal beneficiaries. In all, the apportionment changes will enlarge the 1984 convention to 3,923 delegates, making it approximately 16 percent larger than it was in 1980. (See Table 4.1.) They will also provide many more unpledged delegates. At the very least, this should make convention decisions less predictable than they have been in the past. In a close contest, the unpledged delegates could hold the balance of power.

Increasing the number of unpledged delegates was also designed to alleviate another problem—locking up the nomination before most states had held their caucuses or primaries. The impact of the early contests in determining the nominee had encouraged states to move up the date on which they selected their delegates. In 1972, 38 percent of the delegates were chosen by the second week in May; in 1980, this figure was 55 percent.

The Hunt Commission sought to moderate the effect of the smaller, early caucuses and primaries in another way. It continued the so-called "window period," which specified that delegate selection occur between the second Tuesdays of March and June. Only Iowa and New Hampshire were given special permission to hold their contests earlier but not as much earlier as in past years. Originally, the commision specified that they could do so only fifteen and seven days, respectively, before the window opened. However, when neighboring Vermont decided to hold a non-binding presidential popularity vote on the day of its town meetings in early March, New Hampshire and Iowa threatened to move their contests one week earlier. The party's Compliance Review Commission opposed the move.

Front-loading remains a problem, however, with more than a dozen states scheduling their primaries and the first round of their caucuses during the first week the window officially opens. By the end of March 1984 almost 50 percent of the Democratic delegates will have been selected.

The tighter time frame reduces the importance of Iowa and New Hampshire. It tends to favor candidates with larger organizations, more money, and greater name recognition. With fewer days between the Iowa caucus, the New Hampshire primary, and the other contests, candidates will have to mount simultaneous campaigns in several states, and the media, particularly at the local level, will have to cover them.

Another change, and one that is likely to have an even greater effect on the selection of the party's nominee, was the decision to modify the formula by which delegates were allocated to the candidate. The rule that had been in effect undercompensated the winner in districts in which there were an equal number of delegates. A win by less than 20 percent resulted in an even split of delegates. This hurt Kennedy more than Carter in 1980. His popular vote in the large, competitive states did not translate into a delegate count of similar proportions.

The 1980 allocation rule had discouraged candidates from investing resources in districts in which they could reach the minimum necessary to gain delegates but not win enough votes to dominate clearly. Candidates tended to write off close contests rather than put much time, effort, and money into them.

To prevent these discrepancies from reoccurring, the commission proposed three modifications to its so-called "fair reflection rule" for 1984. First, it increased the minimum percentage of the vote needed to win delegates.[16] This change will make it more difficult for minor candidates to siphon delegate support from the front-runners.

A second and more important adjustment permits states to award a bonus of one delegate to the plurality winner of districts that elect three or more delegates *before* the rest of the delegates are apportioned. This "winner-take-more" system rewards the popular vote leader and enlarges his margin of victory. It thereby provides an incentive for the candidates to devote greater resources to evenly contested districts.

The third change is just as significant. It once again permits the "loophole primaries," those in which individual delegates within districts are elected directly by the voters. Such primaries also work to the advantage of the popular vote leader, who could conceivably get *all* the delegates on the basis of only a plurality of the votes (as few as 35 or 45 percent depending on the number of other candidates running in the district). Losing candidates, on the other hand, could be shut out even though their delegates receive a substantial portion of the vote.

In 1976, thirteen states held loophole primaries; in 1980, only two conducted them. In 1984, more states will do so. The incentive for the states is that loophole primaries produce more cohesive voting blocs, which will tend to increase their influence at the convention.

What are the consequences of these changes likely to be? For one thing, the clout of the smaller states who hold earlier caucuses and primaries is likely to be reduced. Winning these contests will still bring media attention and financial support, but the bandwagon, which victories in the past had generated, is likely to build more slowly. Conversely, the larger states are likely to have a larger impact. Their voting power, measured in terms of blocs of delegates, should be enhanced by loophole and winner-take-more primaries. Party professionals are also likely to be beneficiaries. With their representation increased, they should exercise greater sway over convention deliberations and could even determine the nominee in a close contest. In any event, Democratic aspirants for the nomination will have to take these changes into account in designing their strategies for 1984.

CAMPAIGNING FOR DELEGATES

The rules changes, new finance laws, and television coverage have all affected nomination seeking. In the past, entering primaries was optional for leading candidates and required only for those who did not enjoy party support or national recognition. Today, it is essential for everyone, even an incumbent President. No longer can a front-runner safely sit on the sidelines and wait for the call. The winds of a draft may be hard to resist but, more often than not, it is the candidate who is manning the bellows.

In the past, candidates carefully chose the primaries they would enter and concentrated their efforts where they thought they would run best. Today, they have less discretion. By allocating delegates on the basis of a proportional primary vote or multistage convention system, the nomination process now provides incentives for campaigning in a larger number of states. This change has resulted in a proliferation of presidential candidates.

Strategy and tactics have also changed. The success of the McGovern and Carter preconvention campaigns and the near-success of the Reagan challenge in 1976 have provided new answers to the old questions: when to declare, where to run, how to organize, what to claim, and how to win. Prior to 1972, it was considered wise to wait for an opportune moment in the spring of the presidential election year before announcing one's candidacy. Adlai Stevenson did not announce his intentions until the Democratic convention. John F. Kennedy made his announcement two months before the New Hampshire primary. It was considered wise to restrict primary efforts and obtain the backing of the state party leaders and work through their organizations. The successful candidates were those who could unify the party. They took few chances. The object of their campaign was to maintain a winning image.

Much of this conventional wisdom is no longer valid. Today, it is necessary, especially for lesser-known candidates, to plan early. Whether or not candidates choose to make a formal public declaration, they must create an organization, devise a strategy, and raise money well in advance of the first caucuses and primaries. These needs prompted George McGovern to announce his candidacy for the 1972 presidential nomination in January 1971, almost a year and a half before the Democratic convention, and Jimmy Carter to begin his quest in 1974, two years before the 1976 Democratic convention. By the end of 1979, Republican George Bush had already spent 328 days on the road and traveled some 350,000 miles.

It is now common practice to begin campaigning three to four years before the nomination. In the winter of 1981, Walter Mondale and Edward Kennedy had already created candidate-oriented PACs and had filed them with the FEC in accordance with the provisions of the law. Most of the other hopefuls had established some type of exploratory committee, been to the early primary states several times, and set up some organizational headquarters for their efforts. Mondale and Kennedy, who had the largest staffs, had already developed in-depth organizations in several states that were scheduled to hold their nomination contests early in the year.

It is now even customary to withdraw early. Kennedy surprised political pundits by announcing on December 1, 1982, that he would not seek the Democratic nomination in 1984 because of family matters; Morris Udall did the same three months later. Had they not stepped down, both would have remained the focus of media attention and been evaluated as if they were candidates.

Doing well in the initial primaries and caucuses and qualifying for matching grants are the principal public aims of most candidates. The early primaries are particularly important for lesser-known aspirants, less for the number of delegates they can win than for the amount of publicity they can generate. New Hampshire, traditionally the first state to hold a presidential primary, produces a lot of media coverage. For the last thirty years, it has ranked first in the amount of attention it has received.[17] Naturally, the candidate who does surprisingly well in this primary will benefit enormously. Eugene McCarthy in 1968, George McGovern in 1972, and Jimmy Carter in 1976 all gained visibility and credibility from their New Hampshire performances, even though none had a majority of the vote and only Carter had a plurality. Winning 28 percent of the presidential preference vote in 1976, Carter scored an overwhelming media victory.

The initial round of the Iowa caucuses, held before the New Hampshire primary, has also received extensive attention in recent years.[18] Covered as if it were a primary because it is the first "official" contest, the caucus has assumed importance far beyond the number of delegates who are actually involved. Both Carter in 1976 and Bush in 1980 received great boosts from their narrow victories in the state. In 1976, Carter got 27.6 percent of the vote, the most of any candidate, although an unpledged slate of electors received 37 percent. Carter eventually ended up with more than 50 percent of the delegates. His media victory was much more spectacular. According to Thomas E. Patterson, Carter received 726 lines in *Time* and *Newsweek,* compared with an average of 30 for the other candidates.[19]

George Bush scored a similar triumph in 1980. A straw poll of the participants at the Republican caucuses in Iowa gave him a 6 percent lead over Ronald Reagan but a huge bonanza from the media. He quadrupled his coverage.[20] Bush quickly moved from having less than 10 percent support among the Republican rank and file to being a serious contender for the GOP nomination with 28 percent backing—almost as much as Reagan had at the time.[21] In short, early victories help establish front-runner status and provide an important psychological boost. Being declared a winner improves one's standing in the polls and makes raising money easier. It may also contribute to later primary success.

The media can have a negative effect as well. In Bush's case, his upset of Reagan in Iowa and a subsequent victory in Puerto Rico enhanced expectations of his performance in later contests, particularly in

New Hampshire. When he lost that state to Reagan, his defeat was magnified by his two earlier wins. Had he not been declared winner of the first round, his New Hampshire performance would not have been nearly as newsworthy.

Moreover, according to Michael Robinson and Margaret A. Sheehan, the media treat front-runners more harshly than challengers. There is more investigative reporting and more implicit criticism of their candidacies. Being a front-runner not only guarantees greater coverage, but it also guarantees greater scrutiny.[22]

The fund-raising advantages of early candidacies and primary victories are significant. Limits on individual contributions require that a broad base of contributors be established as quickly as possible in order to provide a source of revenue for the early primaries and to qualify for government matching funds. Direct mail fund raising is the technique most frequently employed to establish this base of contributors. It is a costly method, and the rewards are slow in coming, but the payoffs can be great. Table 4–4 indicates how candidates can use prospective mailings to raise large sums for their campaign.

There are various direct mail techniques. Fund raisers for George Bush utilized a more personalized approach in contrast to the mass sales appeal of other Republican candidates. Instead of mailing one letter to hundreds of thousands of people, the Bush campaign mailed scores of highly personalized letters—typewriter quality, typed envelope, signed with a signature machine rather than printed—to small "high ticket" lists such as graduates of Andover preparatory school and Yale University, Bush's alma maters. The relative sophistication of these mailings increased their per-unit cost but it also increased their return. Instead of receiving the standard contribution of $25, Bush got an average donation of $149. He raised a total of $4 million at a cost of $850,000 utilizing this approach. Put another way, for every 21 cents the Bush campaign invested, it recovered $1. As a result, Bush was the only candidate besides Jimmy Carter who did not suffer a cash flow problem during the 1980 preconvention period.

Whatever the type of direct mail campaign that is employed, a sufficient amount of time must be allotted to sift and appeal to potential donors. That is why fund-raising efforts must begin early if they are to reap long-range benefits for the campaign. It also explains why being eligible for matching funds as soon as possible is so important. The additional revenue provided by the government subsidies can help defray the sizable start-up costs of direct mail as well as the initial operating expenditures

Table 4-4 How to Raise $2 Million by Direct Mail

	"House List"	Bank Balance
1. Raise $200,000 for first mailing.	0	$ 200,000
2. Use that to pay for 800,000 letters at 25 cents per letter	0	0
3. Get a response rate of 1%, meaning 8,000 first-time donors giving an average of $25. The mailing returns $200,000.	8,000	$ 200,000
4. Use $196,000 and mail 784,000 letters at 25 cents per letter. One percent response yields $196,000 and adds 7,840 donors. Use balance of $4,000 to mail to 8,000 donors from first mailing.	8,000	0
5. Net profit of $29,600 derived from mailing of 8,000-name house list. Recover $196,000, adding 7,840 names to house file.	15,840	$ 233,600
6. Take the whole sum and prospect again. Mail 934,400 letters at 25 cents per letter. One percent response will yield $233,600 and 9,340 new donors.	15,840	$ 233,600
7. Mail house file of 25,180. Invest 75 cents per letter, request upgraded donation. Fifteen percent response at $35 will yield $132,195	25,180	$ 346,910
8. Do another mass mailing of 1,445,459 letters at 24 cents each. One percent response will yield 14,454 new donors. At $25, costs are recovered	25,180	$ 346,910
9. Mail donors only. At 67 cents per letter and a response of 18% with an average of $32, a net income of $201,736 will be received and added to the recovered cost of the promotional mailing.	39,634	$ 548,646
10. Take $250,000 of your net money and do another prospect mailing to 1,000,000 prospects. Add 10,000 names to your list and recover $250,000.	49,634	$ 548,646
11. Mail house file every 30 days. Segment $100-plus donors for special treatment. Mail after election, too. Seven donor mailings will cost approximately $175,000. At minimum 15% response and average of $35, a net income of $1,662,500 will be received.	49,634 × 7	$2,210,646

Source: Odell, Roper and Associates Inc. Reprinted with permission.

of the campaign. Government matching funds also increase candidates' borrowing power, and, equally important, enhance their credibility.[23] Today, candidates demonstrate their popular support by qualifying early. Walter Mondale was the first of the 1984 Democratic aspirants to qualify, doing so on January 6, 1983. It took his committee just 48 hours to raise more than double the requisite amount. Other Democratic qualifiers quickly followed.

Another important and difficult task is determining how the money raised can be most effectively allocated. Costs have increased far more rapidly than has the government's cost-of-living adjustment. Transportation expenses continue to rise. In 1980, plane fares alone had jumped more than 50 percent from the previous nomination period, and food and hotel accommodations were also more costly. Television production charges increased by as much as 100 percent while the costs for air time on the major networks were considerably higher than in 1976. Even fund raising was much more expensive. Compounding these higher costs were the limits imposed by the government on candidates who accept matching funds.

The early caucuses and primaries in small states posed particular problems. A variety of techniques were utilized to stay within the relatively low spending limits in Iowa and New Hampshire. Campaign workers slept and, if possible, ate in neighboring states. Some were even paid from out-of-state budgets. Candidates and their staffs took interstate flights with stop-overs in the critical states so that the air fares would not be subject to the state ceilings. Nonetheless, Carter and Kennedy exceeded the limits in Iowa and New Hampshire as did Reagan in New Hampshire.

To overcome this problem, John Connally went a step further. Believing that he could not defeat Ronald Reagan if he could not outspend him, Connally refused federal matching funds so as not to be bound by the spending limits. He hoped that if he won these early contests he would be able to raise sufficient funds through private donations.

Later primaries in larger states proved to be less of a problem. For one thing, spending ceilings were higher. Moreover, candidates had to be increasingly concerned about a countervailing problem, staying within the overall spending limits for the primary period. As it was, Reagan and Carter almost "maxed-out" (that is, used most of their permissible expenditures) before the primaries ended; at the beginning of May, each had less than $3 million left.

In general, the campaign finance law has benefited the better-known candidates, who were able to raise more money and who also could use their reputations to build organizations and attract volunteers. Lesser-known candidates have succeeded financially only if they have been able to do well in the early primaries and caucuses.

An early candidacy serves the additional purpose of providing time to develop an organization in those primaries and caucuses in which an active campaign is contemplated. In the past, getting the endorsements of state party leaders and using their organizations to run campaigns in their states was regarded as the surest and easiest course of action. An effective state organization could be expected to turn out the faithful.

The rules changes, however, have weakened the ability of state party leaders to deliver the vote. This, along with the need to run in many primaries during a fairly short period of time, has required the creation of separate candidate organizations. The Republicans have generally established separate units within each state, while the Democrats have usually opted for more centralized structures that hopscotch from state to state. These organizations are often large and costly, numbering several hundred paid staffers and thousands of volunteers.

In order to mobilize primary voters, such organizations must operate telephone banks, engage in door-to-door canvassing, and circulate campaign literature. To create the impression of public support and to generate excitement, they must also assemble crowds and, in states without primaries, get sympathetic individuals to participate in caucuses. Eugene McCarthy and George McGovern recruited thousands of college students to help them in their primary efforts. In 1976, Carter's "peanut brigade," a group of Georgians who followed their candidate from state to state, was particularly effective in canvassing and organizing in the early primaries.

Targeting appeals to special audiences is particularly important. Candidates tend to concentrate on the local press—making themselves available to reporters and editors, timing speeches and announcements to receive maximum press coverage, buying advertisements to be broadcast on the radio during rush hours and on television during the evening's prime time. Financial factors limit their use of the national media. In 1980, only John Connally purchased time on the major networks. Most candidates dealt directly with local affiliates.

In addition to broadcasting commercial messages, candidates must anticipate the slant the news media is likely to take and adjust their comments accordingly. Since the media tend to evaluate primaries on the basis of established expectations, candidates consistently tend to underpredict their vote. They wish to claim success on election night before the cameras, regardless of whether they actually win the popular preference vote or get the most delegates. Eugene McCarthy's ability to do this was a key factor in his primary challenge first of Lyndon Johnson and then of Robert Kennedy in 1968. McCarthy contested nine primaries and won two but minimized the impact of his seven losses using this low prediction posture.

The Carter campaign in 1976 purposely kept its predictions low. In the words of campaign manager Hamilton Jordan:

> It has already been established in the minds of the national press that Mo Udall is going to do well in New Hampshire. He has established that expectation. If he does not win in New Hampshire, I think now by the measuring criteria that the press is going to apply, he will have underperformed. Well, we'd never talk about winning in New Hampshire. We never talk about winning anywhere. We talk about doing well.[24]

Other criteria which the media use to evaluate the performance of candidates include their standing in the public opinion polls, their previous primary performances, and the amount of effort they have put into a particular campaign. Which of these criteria are emphasized affects how the results are interpreted. In general, media analysts opt for the unexpected. What makes news are items that are surprising, not predictable.

There have also been changes in the candidates' appeals. The reforms have provided greater incentive to be specific about policies during the nomination phase. Since party leaders can no longer be counted on to deliver the vote, candidates must forge their own winning coalitions. This requires an appeal to specific groups within the party. The appeal is normally couched in terms of a promise or position to which the group is likely to be sympathetic.

McGovern in 1972, Udall in 1976, Kennedy in 1980, and Cranston in 1984 designed their campaigns for the liberal wing of the Democratic party. Similarly, Reagan made an issue-oriented appeal to Republican conservatives in 1976 and again in 1980. In contrast, Ford and Carter in 1976 and Bush and Carter in 1980 and Glenn in 1984 adopted a middle-of-the-road approach. They stressed stylistic issues, especially to their opponents' constituencies, and emphasized consensus issues to their own supporters. To illustrate, in 1980 Bush stressed his broad national experience; Reagan emphasized his ideological and policy perspectives; Kennedy and Connally pointed to their leadership skills; Anderson differentiated his policy positions from those of the other Republican contenders; Carter focused on his personal qualities as President and his role as a peacemaker.

In addition to deciding to run early, creating an effective organization, and targeting the appeal, it is important for candidates to enter many more primary and convention campaigns than in the past. Candidates, especially front-runners, used to take few chances. Even the McGovern campaign, generally regarded as a genuine grass roots effort, operated on the assumption that primaries which had been regarded as important in the past would continue to be so in 1972. By concentrating his primary efforts in New Hampshire, Wisconsin, and California, McGovern benefited not only from the attention given to these contests in the media but also from the significance placed on their results by reporters. The Carter campaign of 1976 brought these assumptions into question. It operated on the premise that victories or even respectable showings in the early primaries could produce sufficient momentum for a convention victory, an assumption which turned out to be correct.

Finally, because candidates must run in many elections at or about the same time, mount cost-effective media campaigns in several states, and create and target appeals to as many potential supporters as possible, polling is absolutely essential. The use of polls by candidates is fairly recent. Thomas E. Dewey was the first to have private polling data available to him when he tried unsuccessfully to obtain the Republican nomination in 1940. John F. Kennedy was the first candidate to engage a pollster in his quest for the nomination. Preconvention surveys conducted by Louis Harris in 1960 indicated that Hubert Humphrey, Kennedy's principal rival, was vulnerable in West Virginia and Wisconsin. On the basis of this information, the Kennedy campaign decided to concentrate time, effort, and money in these Protestant states. Victories in both helped demonstrate Kennedy's broad appeal, thereby improving his changes for the nomination enormously.

Today, all major presidential candidates commission polls. These private surveys are important for several reasons. They provide information about the beliefs and attitudes of voters, their perceptions of the candidates, and the kinds of appeals that are apt to be most effective. Armed with this information, candidates can design appropriate strategies. Periodic polling permits them to monitor these strategies over the course of the campaign, tuning their appeals more precisely to targeted groups within the electorate.

Poll results are also used to build momentum, increase morale, raise money, and affect media coverage. By indicating who can win and who should be taken seriously, polls affect the amount of attention candidates receive. In general, the more coverage they have, particularly during the early months, the more volunteers they can attract and the more money they can raise.

The benefits of appearing to be popular and electable suggest why candidates have also used their private polls for promotional purposes. Releasing favorable surveys is a standard stratagem.[25] Nelson Rockefeller, in fact, tied his quest for the Republican nomination in 1968 to poll data. Since he did not enter the primaries, Rockefeller's aim was to convince Republican delegates that he, not Richard Nixon, would be the strongest candidate. Private surveys conducted for Rockefeller in nine large states, five important congressional districts, and the nation as a whole one month before the Republican convention indicated that he would do better against potential Democratic candidates than Nixon. Unfortunately for Rockefeller, the final Gallup preconvention poll, fielded two days after President Eisenhower endorsed Nixon, did not support these findings. The Gallup results undercut the credibility of Rockfeller's polls as well as another national survey poll that had Rockefeller in the lead and thus effectively ended his chances for the nomination.

While polls directly affect a candidate's strategy and tactics, their impact on the general public is less direct. Despite the fear of many politicians, there is little empirical data to suggest that polls create a bandwagon effect. What they provide, however, is visibility and credibility, both of which are particularly important in the early campaigning.

There is some evidence of a relationship between a candidate's standing in the polls, success in the primaries, and winning the nomination. Table 4–5 indicates how the poll leaders have done. What it does not indicate, however, is whether the public opinion leaders won because they were more popular or whether they were more popular initially because they were better known and ultimately because they looked like winners.

All of these factors—timing, finance, organization, and communications—affect the quest for delegates. They help shape the candidates' strategies for the nomination. Generally speaking there are two successful contemporary prototypes, one for the lesser-known aspirant, the other for the front-runner. In 1976, Carter effectively utilized the first of these strategies. In 1980 he adopted the second. His campaigns illustrate the major decisions which candidates make, given their status, when seeking delegates for their party's nomination.

The Non–Front-Runner Strategy

The Carter strategy in 1976 was to run hard and fast at the outset. Stress was placed on the early primaries. Since Carter had a name recognition problem, a major objective of his early campaign was to attract the

Table 4–5   PUBLIC OPINION AND THE NOMINATION

Year and Party		Gallup Poll after First Primary	Final Gallup Poll before Convention	Party Nominee
1940	D	Roosevelt	Roosevelt	Roosevelt*
	R	Dewey	Willkie	Willkie
1944	D	Roosevelt	Roosevelt	Roosevelt*
	R	Dewey	Dewey	Dewey
1948	D	Truman	Truman	Truman*
	R	Stassen	Dewey	Dewey
1952	D	Kefauver	Kefauver	Stevenson
	R	Eisenhower	Eisenhower	Eisenhower*
1956	D	Stevenson	Stevenson	Stevenson
	R	Eisenhower	Eisenhower	Eisenhower*
1960	D	J. Kennedy	Kennedy	Kennedy*
	R	Nixon	Nixon	Nixon
1964	D	—	Johnson	Johnson*
	R	Lodge	Goldwater & Nixon (tie)	Goldwater
1968	D	R. Kennedy	Humphrey	Humphrey
	R	Nixon	Nixon	Nixon*
1972	D	Humphrey	McGovern	McGovern
	R	—	Nixon	Nixon*
1976	D	Humphrey	Carter	Carter*
	R	Ford	Ford	Ford
1980	D	Carter	Carter	Carter
	R	Reagan	Reagan	Reagan*

Source: *The Gallup Poll, Public Opinion 1935–1971*, Vol. 1–3 (New York: Random House, 1972); *Gallup Opinion Index* (Princeton, N.J.: Gallup International, 1971–1980). Reprinted with permission. *Indicates general election winner.

media. Once his credibility was established, Carter hoped to expand his organization into as many states as possible.

Hamilton Jordan, Carter's campaign manager, designed the basic game plan two years before the election. He described the early preconvention strategy as follows:

> The prospect of a crowded field coupled with the new proportional representation rule does not permit much flexibility in the early primaries. No serious candidate will have the luxury of picking or choosing among the early primaries. To pursue such a strategy would cost that candidate delegate votes and increase the possibility of being lost in the crowd. I think that we have to assume that everybody will be running in the first five or six primaries.
>
> A crowded field enhances the possiblity of several inconclusive primaries with four or five candidates separated by only a few percentage points. Such

a muddled picture will not continue for long as the press will begin to make "winners" of some and "losers" of others. The intense press coverage which naturally focuses on the early primaries plus the decent time intervals which separate the March and mid-April primaries dictate a serious effort in all of the first five primaries. Our "public" strategy would probably be that Florida was the first and real test of the Carter campaign and that New Hampshire would just be a warm-up. In fact, a strong, surprise showing in New Hampshire should be our goal which would have tremendous impact on successive primaries.[26]

The goal was achieved. Dubbed the person to beat after his victories in the Iowa caucus and New Hampshire primary, Carter's defeat of George Wallace in Florida enabled him to overcome a disappointing fourth place in Massachusetts a week earlier and become the acknowledged front-runner.

The efficiency of the Carter organization, the effectiveness of his personal style of campaigning, and the lack of strong opposition helped Carter to win eight of the next nine primaries. These victories gave him approximately 35 percent of the delegates selected by early May, more than double that of his nearest competitor. Although Carter lost ten out of the last seventeen primaries, he was able to continue to build a delegate lead over the field. By the end of the primaries, his nomination had become a foregone conclusion.

Four years earlier, a similar strategy had failed. Edmund Muskie, the Democratic front-runner, had entered the early primaries, lost his lead in the public opinion polls, and was finally forced to withdraw from active candidacy after his sixth primary. A variety of factors explain why Carter's strategy worked and Muskie's did not. The times were different. A larger number (and percentage) of delegates were chosen in the primaries in 1976 than in 1972. Additionally, more were selected in proportion to the popular presidential vote. Thus, even though Carter lost primaries, he continued to win delegates.

The Carter effort in 1976 became the model for George Bush in 1980. Concentrating his efforts in Iowa and New Hampshire, Bush built in-depth organizations in both states, campaigned vigorously, and used the media to increase name recall. His first visit to Iowa was made eleven months before the caucus. While there, he attended coffee klatches, spoke to local groups, and was available to the media. In all, he made twenty-one trips to the state over the course of the year. By the time other candidates arrived, Bush was known and his organization was in place.

His efforts paid off. Bush's victory in Iowa elevated him overnight to the status of a major contender. Without this initial victory (or another important early one), it is unlikely that his campaign would have gotten off the ground.

Bush's subsequent problems were twofold. He was unable to meet the heightened expectations, and he was unable to eliminate other moderate Republican candidates soon enough to become *the* alternative to Reagan. His lackluster style of campaigning and de-emphasis of substantive issues contributed to his difficulties.

New Hampshire burst the Bush bubble. His narrow win over John Anderson in Massachusetts the following week did little to invigorate his campaign. He was expected to do better. Moreover, Anderson's strong showing impressed the media. In subsequent weeks, Anderson was presented as the new Republican alternative. It was not until April that Bush was able to resurrect his claim to being the only viable alternative to Reagan. By then it was too late.

For lesser known aspirants, the non–front-runner strategy offers an opportunity to increase their recognition by the public and, at the same time, to demonstrate their effectiveness as candidates. A win, no matter how slight, confounds the odds, surprises the media, embarrasses the front-runner, and enervates the non–front-runner's candidacy. Media coverage expands; fund raising is made easier; volunteers join the organization; even endorsements become more likely. In the 1984 campaign all of the Democratic candidates except for Walter Mondale and John Glenn plan to follow this route to the nomination.

The Front-Runner Strategy

Carter devised a new stratagem for 1980, based on the continuation of certain basic assumptions but a change in his status and situation. In 1980, as in 1976, he assumed the need to emphasize the early contests, to run simultaneously in a variety of states, and to make a broad-gauged appeal to a significant portion of the Democratic coalition. He also deemed it essential to have a solid financial and organizational base in place at the outset.

Now that he was an incumbent President, not a relatively unknown southern governor, and was running against a formidable opponent, Senator Edward Kennedy, not an array of untested candidates, Carter had to meet a new campaign expectation—that he would be renominated. Any prospective challenge to his candidacy, any perceived weakness, could be expected to receive considerable media attention. As a consequence, the

President had to anticipate such a challenge publicly in order to deflect its impact.[27] In seeking renomination, Carter also had to adopt a strategy that maximized the political clout of his office and, at the same time, minimized public expectations of his performance as President.

The Carter strategy was designed by Hamilton Jordan in January 1979. Jordan, the architect of Carter's successful quest for the Presidency four years earlier, proposed an early start in developing an organization, raising money, and articulating an appeal. His object was to nip the Kennedy challenge in the bud or, failing that, to blunt its effect. As Jordan saw it, the nomination would be decided in the early caucuses and primaries:

> It is absolutely essential that we win the early contests and establish momentum. If we win the early contests, it is difficult to see how anyone could defeat us for the nomination. Conversely, if we lose the early contest(s), it is difficult to see how we could recoup and win the nomination.[28]

One way to improve the President's chances was to try to influence the scheduling of primaries and caucuses. It was to Carter's advantage to have those in which he expected to do well at the beginning and those in which he expected to do poorly sandwiched between more favorable contests. The Carter organization succeeded in advancing the dates of several southern primaries and in delaying the date of at least one northern one, Connecticut, for about a month. Most attempts to influence the scheduling of primaries were made in 1979, before the Kennedy organization was operating.

In addition to the organizing efforts which began in August 1979 and continued throughout the fall, much attention was also given by the Carter organization to budgetary matters. By the end of the year over $3 million had been raised. Cost-cutting measures were also introduced early and maintained throughout the campaign. This was in sharp contrast to the Kennedy campaign, which literally spent itself into debt.[29]

A key element of Carter's strategy was the allocation of a large proportion of financial resources for the early contests. Funds were even set aside for a nonbinding straw vote in Florida in November 1979; it was feared that a loss to Senator Kennedy there would encourage the draft-Kennedy movement. This strategy helped Carter take an early lead, which buttressed the campaign later on when it was faced with severe expenditure problems.

Throughout the nomination process the President used the powers of his office to maximize his political support. Grants and appointments were timed to enhance endorsements of Carter by leading state and local officials.[30] White House personnel with campaign experience took extended leaves of absence to work in the primaries and caucuses, and cabinet members campaigned around the country as surrogates for the President.[31] Throughout, Carter exuded confidence. This was also part of the strategy. "If Kennedy runs, I'll whip his ass," Carter told a group of visiting members of Congress during the summer of 1979. White House officials urged the legislators to make the President's remarks public, which they did.[32]

The initial thrusts of the Carter strategy were helped by events in Iran and Afghanistan as the crises rallied Americans around their leader. These developments also provided a convenient rationalization for a "Rose Garden" strategy—that is, staying in the White House because of the demands of the job. (Ford adopted a similar strategy during his 1976 campaign.) By remaining in the White House, a President accentuates the differences between himself and the other candidates. He also continues in the public eye by exercising the duties of office and at the same time avoids the pitfalls of campaigning. The strategy, however, did not prevent Carter from making hundreds of phone calls from the White House in his own behalf, receiving numerous visitors, giving many interviews, holding news conferences, and making announcements.

Superior organizations in Florida and Iowa helped the President score impressive victories in both states. These, in turn, contributed to his win in the first real primary, New Hampshire. A victory in the nonbinding Vermont primary helped reduce the significance of Kennedy's home-state triumph in Massachusetts, which occurred on the same day. Victories in Alabama, Florida, Georgia, and Illinois put the President comfortably ahead. Buttressed by the rule that allocated delegates in proportion to the popular vote, Carter had for all intents and purposes secured the nomination by the end of April. In terms of pledged delegates, he was well ahead of his standing four years earlier. Table 4–6 traces Carter's acquisition of delegates in 1976 and 1980.

On the Republican side, Reagan adopted a strategy that was similar to Carter's—at least initially. He ran as if he were the incumbent. Ignoring other candidates within the party, Reagan even refused to debate, on the grounds that it would be divisive. He made few campaign appearances in Iowa, the first caucus state, and had little television advertising.

The Reagan plan was designed in 1979. Confident of winning the nomination, Reagan and his strategists saw the prenomination period as

Table 4–6   CARTER'S ACQUISITION OF DELEGATES, 1976 AND 1980

	1976		1980	
	Cumulative number	As percentage of total needed to win*	Cumulative number	As percentage of total needed to win†
March				
1			10	0.6
6, 8	36	2.3	44	2.6
13, 15	70	4.6	225	13.5
20, 22	123	8.1	441	24.6
27, 29	167	11.0	552	33.1
April				
3, 5	167	11.0	623	37.3
10, 12	232	15.4	662	39.7
17, 19	258	17.1	706	42.3
24, 26	264	17.5	869	52.1
May				
1, 3	333	22.1	940	56.4
8, 10	552	36.6	1,120	67.2
15, 17	565	37.5	1,166	69.9
22, 24	717	47.6	1,223	73.4
29, 31	876	58.2	1,308	78.5
June				
5, 7	895	59.4	1,632	97.9
12, 14	1,115	74.0	1,644	98.6

Source: Nelson Polsby, "The Democratic Nomination," in Austin Ranney (ed.), *The American Elections of 1980* (Washington D.C.: American Enterprise Institute, 1981), p. 48. Polsby utilizes data from the *National Journal* in his count. © 1981, American Enterprise Institute for Public Policy Research, Washington, D.C. 20036.
*N = 1,505.
†N = 1,666.

a time for building a solid coalition and issue agenda for the general election. After his loss in Iowa, Reagan adjusted his strategy accordingly. He began to campaign more actively, debate other Republicans, run television commercials, and build strong field organizations. On the eve of his victory in New Hampshire, he fired John Sears, his campaign manager, and replaced him with a group of loyal aides, most of whom had worked with him in California.

Like Carter, Reagan spent a disproportionate amount of his money in the early primaries and caucuses. Before the first vote was cast in New Hampshire, he had expended 74 percent of the permissible amount.[33] Concentrating in the Northeast, where he had been weakest in 1976, Reagan built an early lead. Given his support in the South and West, this proved to be an effective strategy. By the end of March, he had succeeded in becoming the odds-on favorite for the nomination. His large delegate lead discouraged former President Ford, who toyed with the idea of entering the contest, from doing so.

Democratic contenders Walter Mondale and John Glenn began their campaigns for the 1984 nomination with strategies that resembled Carter's and Reagan's in 1980. Each planned a broad-based campaign to take advantage of their high name recognition. The initial strategies of both candidates, designed well before the preconvention period got underway, called for campaigns in all fifty states with emphasis to be placed on potential areas of strength. For Glenn, seven states which had early caucuses and primaries were targeted: Iowa, New Hampshire, Florida, Georgia, Alabama, Mississippi, and Illinois. Four others—Pennsylvania, Missouri, Michigan, and Texas—were to be added as the campaign progressed. Mondale also planned to concentrate on the states which held the early contests. A key ingredient of his original game plan was to gain the support of major groups within the Democratic party, particularly organized labor and educators. In contrast, Glenn's strategy proposed that he mount a national appeal to mainstream Democrats rather than to specific interests within the party's electoral coalition.

Strategists for both Mondale and Glenn tried to influence the delegate selection process to maximize their strengths. Mondale's proponents lobbied to convert primaries to caucuses to take advantage of their large organization and the political IOUs the former Vice President had collected. Glenn's advisers in turn wished to keep the primaries moving or maintain those in which the senator anticipated he would do well toward the beginning of the window period. The Ohio primary was scheduled one month earlier than in 1980 to help its native son.

A Note on the 1980 Kennedy Campaign

Senator Edward Kennedy did not adopt a typical front-runner or non–front-runner strategy. At the outset he sought to capitalize on the popularity of his candidacy. Endorsements by national and local leaders and grass roots efforts in a number of states were intended to demonstrate the extent of his public support and provide momentum for a series of wins in the early caucuses and primaries.

Unfortunately for Kennedy, his campaign got off to a late and shaky start. Kennedy did not decide to run until the fall of 1979, after he had filmed a lengthy television interview with Roger Mudd of CBS. He had no organization in place and little money raised, in sharp contrast to Carter at that point in time. Moreover, his start-up costs were extremely high.

Money was unwisely spent on a luxurious private plane for the senator, on an expensive remodeling of his national campaign headquarters (an empty showroom for a Cadillac dealership), and on high salaries for his senior campaign staff. Tensions between his Washington and field organizations further aggravated the situation.

Kennedy contributed to his own difficulties. He appeared uncertain and hesitant in the early television interview with Mudd. Soon after the American hostages were seized in Iran, he made a statement critical of the Shah, for which he was roundly censured. Soon after his defeat in a straw poll in Florida, he pointed to Iowa as the first "real" contest, thereby heightening expectations of his performance. His sizable defeat thus became more difficult to excuse or explain. New Hampshire also proved to be an embarrassment. After he lost in a New England state, his capacity to win at all was seriously questioned. Kennedy's victory the following week in his home state, Massachusetts, was more than offset by the defeats he suffered in Florida and in Vermont's nonbinding presidential preference vote.

The Kennedy campaign never recovered from these early setbacks. Its lack of money required that resources be concentrated in the large industrial states, forced the concession of much of the South and West, and made pro-Kennedy committees in other states raise their own funds for the campaign. Moreover, Kennedy's stringent criticism of Carter seemed to reinforce the negative personal image stemming in large part from his accident at Chappaquiddick and his subsequent marital difficulties. The press treated him harshly at the beginning of the campaign. His issue appeal placed him solidly in the liberal camp, alienating party moderates. Even the proportional voting rule worked to his disadvantage. His popular vote exceeded his delegate support. While he was able to generate an emotional outpouring of support at the Democratic convention, he was never really in contention for the nomination after the Illinois primary.

SUMMARY

The delegate selection process has changed dramatically since 1968. Originally dominated by state party leaders, it has become more open to the party's rank and file as a consequence of the reforms initiated by the Democratic party. These reforms, designed to broaden the base of public participation and increase the representation of the party's electorate at its nominating convention, have led to a greater number of primaries and more delegates selected in them. Turnout has been improved, but the power of state party leaders has been weakened. A proliferation of candidates and candidate organizations has resulted.

The delegates selected for the last three conventions were demographically more representative than those of previous eras. They included larger percentages of women, minorities, and youth, but, with the exception of Democratic women beginning in 1980, they were still less than the proportion of these groups in the electorate and, generally, in the party as a whole. Party professionals, particularly members of Congress, continue to be underrepresented. The Democrats have attempted to alleviate this situation by adding additional slots to each state's delegation to be filled by national and state elected and party officials. Attitudinally, the delegates remain more ideologically conscious and consistent in their views than rank-and-file partisan supporters.

The process of seeking delegates has also been affected by the reforms. Primaries have become more important. They can no longer be avoided by front-runners, even incumbent Presidents. The days of the power brokers are over. There is greater public participation, yet the electorate remains extremely volatile. Name recognition is important, and the media have a tremendous impact.

Given the more broadly based mode of delegate selection, it is now necessary for all candidates to develop a preconvention strategy that maximizes their public appeal. In recent years two basic strategies have emerged which have been successful. Both are predicated on certain fundamental assumptions:

1. Sufficient time and energy must be devoted to personal campaigning in the prenomination and early nomination periods. Only an incumbent can remain in the Rose Garden, and even he can remain there too long.
2. A strong, in-depth organization for the initial caucuses and primaries must be built. It is not possible to win by media alone. Television advertising is important, but it is organization that mobilizes the vote.
3. A firm financial base must be established early and a spending strategy devised. All caucuses and primaries are not equal; the first ones are more important and, hence, require greater resources.
4. The order of events and the rules of the game must be understood and, if possible, manipulated. Magnifying victories and minimizing defeats usually require that strong states be isolated and weak ones paired with strong ones.

The strategies differ primarily in how the candidates mobilize the resources needed to win.

For the non–front-runner the initial goal is to establish credibility as a viable candidate. Publicly announcing one's intentions, establishing a campaign headquarters, qualifying for matching funds, and obtaining political endorsements are necessary but not sufficient. At the outset, the key is recognition. Over the long haul, it is momentum. Recognition is bestowed by the media on those who do well in the early primaries and caucuses; momentum is achieved by a series of prenomination victories. Together they compensate for what the non–front-runner lacks in reputation and popular appeal. That is why non–front-runners must concentrate their time, efforts, and resources in the first few contests. They have no choice. Winning will provide them with opportunities; losing will confirm their secondary status.

For the front-runners, the task is different. They have to maintain their credibility, not establish it. This provides them with a little more flexibility at the outset. Their candidacy may be announced later, although their organization must still be in place early. Particular primaries and caucuses may be targeted, but the first ones still have to be contested. A broad-based campaign can be planned, but the major resources still have to be spent early.

The principal advantages of the front-runners are greater name recognition and a larger resource base. Status and position make it easier to raise money, establish an organization, and obtain endorsements. This enhances the front-runner's potential but does not guarantee success. It is still possible to lose but it usually takes longer. A single defeat can be overcome, but it is more difficult to survive a string of setbacks.

In the end, it is the ability to generate a broad-based public appeal that is likely to be decisive. Only one person in each party can amass a majority of the delegates, and that is the individual who can build a broad coalition. While specific groups may be targeted, if the overall constituency is too narrow, the nomination cannot be won. That is why candidates tend to broaden and moderate their appeal over the course of the prenomination process.

NOTES

1. The party held to its previous rule that candidates had to receive at least 15 percent of the vote in order to obtain delegates. Carter supporters had attempted to increase the percentage needed in order to discourage minority candidates from running.

2. Some states hold a presidential preference vote with a separate election of convention delegates by a state convention. Others connect the presidential vote and delegate selection on an at-large or district basis. By voting for a particular candidate and/or dele-

gates pledged to that candidate, voters may register their presidential choice and delegate selection at the same time and by the same vote. The number of these primaries has increased as a consequence of the rules changes. A third alternative is to cast separate votes for President and convention delegates.

3. Elaine Kamarck, "Openness, Participation and Party Building: Reforms for a Stronger Democratic Party" (paper prepared for the Hunt Commission of the Democratic Party, 1981), pp. 2–4.

4. Austin Ranney, *Participation in American Presidential Nominations, 1976* (Washington, D.C.: American Enterprise Institute, 1977), p. 24.

5. Commission on Presidential Nomination and Party Structure, *Openness, Participation and Party Building: Reforms for a Stronger Democratic Party* (Washington, D.C.: Democratic National Committee, 1978), pp. 11–12.

6. "Demographic Representation at the National Convention" (paper prepared for the Hunt Commission of the Democratic Party, 1981), p. 3.

7. "The Role of Elected and Party Officials in the National Convention" (paper prepared for the Hunt Commission of the Democratic Party, 1981), p. 2.

8. John W. Soule and James W. Clarke, "Issue Conflict and Consensus: A Comparative Study of Democratic and Republican Delegates to the 1968 National Conventions," *Journal of Politics,* 33 (1971), 77–85.

9. Herbert McCloskey et al., "Issue Conflict and Consensus among Party Leaders and Followers," *American Political Science Review,* 54 (1960), 406–427.

10. Jeanne Kirkpatrick, "Representation in the American National Conventions: The Case of 1972," *British Journal of Political Science,* 5 (1975), 313–322.

11. Warren J. Mitofsky and Martin Plissner, "The Making of the Delegates, 1968–1980," *Public Opinion,* 3 (1980), 40–42; John S. Jackson, Barbara Brown, and David Bositis, "Herbert McCloskey and Friends Revisited, 1980 Democratic and Republican Party Elites Compared to the Mass Public," *American Politics Quarterly,* 10 (1982), 165–178.

12. Jackson, Brown, and Bositis, "Herbert McCloskey Revisited," 165–178; Kamarck, *Openness, Participation and Party Building,* p. 6.

13. The 1972 Pennsylvania primary provides a clear and dramatic example of how the rules affect the results. Hubert Humphrey was the popular choice in the state, receiving almost 500,000 votes (35 percent of the total). Operating under a district system—one delegate per legislative district—he got 93 delegates, 51 percent of the total. Had the primary been winner-take-all, Humphrey would have won all of Pennsylvania's 182 delegates. Had the delegates been awarded on the basis of each candidate's proportion of the popular vote, he would have received 66. James I. Lengle and Byron Shafer, "Primary Rules, Political Power, and Social Change," *American Political Science Review,* 70 (1976), 28.

14. "The Role of Elected and Party Officials," p. 2.

15. In addition to women, those who remained included blacks, Hispanics, and native Americans.

16. The commission established a set formula for the threshold in primary states (100 percent divided by the number being nominated), but in no case was it to exceed 25 percent. For the caucuses, it was a straight 20 percent over the course of the preconvention period.

17. Michael J. Robinson and Margaret A. Sheehan, *Over the Wire and on TV: CBS and UPI in Campaign '80* (New York: Russell Sage Foundation, 1983), p. 174.

18. In examining the coverage given the Iowa caucus by CBS News during the last three nominations, Robinson and Sheehan found that in 1972, "the Iowa caucuses merited only three items on [Evening News]; in 1976, half a dozen; in 1980, a score." Ibid., p. 175.

19. Thomas E. Patterson, "Press Coverage and Candidate Success in Presidential Primaries: The 1976 Democratic Race" (paper delivered at the annual meeting of the American Political Science Association, Washington, D.C., September 1–4, 1977), p. 5.

20. Robinson and Sheehan, *Over the Wire and on TV,* p. 80.

21. Thomas E. Patterson, "Television and Election Strategy," in Gerald Benjamin (ed.), *The Communications Revolution in Politics* (New York: Academy of Political Science, 1982), p. 26.

22. Robinson and Sheehan, p. 243.

23. Terry Sanford, former North Carolina governor and Democratic candidate for President in 1976, found this out the hard way. Planning to concentrate his initial fund raising in his home state, Sanford hoped to develop campaign organizations in other states and to build into them a fund-raising capability. In his study of 1976 campaign organizations, F. Christopher Arterton found that Sanford's plan ran counter to the perception of the press that eligibility for matching funds was a criterion for evaluating the success of early candidates. F. Christopher Arterton, "Campaign Organizations Face the Mass Media in the 1976 Presidential Nomination Process" (paper delivered at the annual meeting of the American Political Science Association, Washington, D.C., September 1–4, 1977), p. 6.

24. Hamilton Jordan, quoted in Arterton, "Campaign Organizations Face the Mass Media," p. 23.

25. This tactic can border on the unethical if conclusions based on unrepresentative samples are presented or if parts of surveys that distort the general findings are released. This occurred in 1967 after the publication of Gallup and Harris polls of New Hampshire voters showed President Johnson running behind several Republican contenders. A private poll, commissioned by the Democratic National Committee, was leaked to columnist Drew Pearson. The poll had Johnson still in the lead. What was not immediately apparent was that the poll consisted of a relatively small sample of people taken in only one county of the state, a Democratic county. When these facts became known, the poll lost its significance as a barometer of New Hampshire opinion.

26. Hamilton Jordan, "Memorandum to Jimmy Carter, August 4, 1974," in Martin Schram, *Running for President, 1976* (New York: Stein & Day, 1977), pp. 379–380.

27. The description of Carter's strategy is based on Martin Schram, "The President's Campaign," *Washington Post,* June 8, 1980, p. A-16.

28. Hamilton Jordan, quoted ibid.

29. From March to December 1979 the Carter campaign spent $2.8 million; the Kennedy campaign spent that amount in its first two months! Martin Schram, "Making the Opponent the Issue," *Washington Post,* June 9, 1980, p. A-8.

30. Grants to New Hampshire and Iowa increased significantly before their respective primary and caucus. A $2.2 million grant to establish a nonprofit shoe center in Philadelphia was announced approximately two weeks before the critical Pennsylvania primary. Cities of those elected officials who supported the President did well during this period. Detroit, for example, received $12 million in housing grants and money for 1,600 inner-city jobs. Its mayor, Coleman Young, was a strong backer of President Carter. On the other hand, Chicago, whose mayor switched to Kennedy, was hurt.

31. Iowa was a favorite "vacation" spot for busy White House aides who took leave in January 1980 to work for President Carter.

32. Schram, "The President's Campaign," p. A-16.

33. Richard Wirthlin, quoted in Jonathan Moore (ed.), *The Campaign for President—1980 in Retrospect* (Cambridge, Mass.: Ballinger, 1981), p. 113.

Selected Readings

Aldrich, John H. *Before the Convention.* Chicago: University of Chicago Press, 1980.

Cavala, William. "Changing the Rules Changes the Game: Party Reform and the 1972 California Delegation to the Democratic National Convention," *American Political Science Review,* 68 (1974), 27–42.

Congressional Quarterly. *Presidential Elections Since 1789.* Washington, D.C.: Congressional Quarterly, 1979.

Davis, James W. *Presidential Primaries: Road to the White House.* New York: Thomas Y. Crowell, 1967.

Epstein, Leon D. "Political Science and Presidential Nominations," *Political Science Quarterly,* 93 (1978), 177–195.

Fleishman, Joel L., ed. *The Future of American Political Parties.* Englewood Cliffs, N.J.: Prentice-Hall, 1982.

Jackson, John S., Barbara Brown, and David Bositis. "Herbert McCloskey and Friends Revisited, 1980 Democratic and Republican Party Elites Compared to the Mass Public," *American Politics Quarterly,* 10 (1982), 158–180.

Keech, William R., and Donald R. Matthews. *The Party's Choice.* Washington, D.C.: Brookings Institution, 1976.

Kirkpatrick, Jeanne J. *The New Presidential Elite: Men and Women in National Politics.* New York: Russell Sage Foundation, 1976.

Lengle, James, and Byron Shafer. "Primary Rules, Political Power, and Social Change," *American Political Science Review,* 70 (1976), 25–40.

Mitofsky, Warren J., and Martin Plissner, "The Making of the Delegates, 1968–1980," *Public Opinion,* 3 (1980), 37–43.

Nakamura, R. T., "Beyond Purism and Professionalism: Styles of Convention Delegate Fellowship," *American Journal of Political Science,* 24 (1980), 207–232.

Polsby, Nelson W. *The Consequences of Party Reform.* New York: Oxford University Press, 1983.

Ranney, Austin. *Participation in American Presidential Nominations, 1976.* Washington, D.C.: American Enterprise Institute, 1977.

———. "Turnout and Representation in Presidential Primary Elections," *American Political Science Review,* 66 (1972), 21–37.

Report of the Commission on Presidential Nomination. Washington, D.C.: Democratic National Committee, 1982.

Chapter 5

THE
CONVENTION

Introduction

Theoretically, national conventions perform four basic functions. As the party's supreme governing body, they determine its rules and regulations; they choose its presidential and vice presidential nominees; they decide on its platform; and they provide a forum for unifying the party and for launching its presidential campaign. In practice, however, conventions often ratify previously made decisions. The choice of a presidential candidate is frequently a foregone conclusion and the selection of his running mate is, in reality, the presidential nominee's. Similarly, drafts of party platforms are formulated prior to the convention and are either accepted by the delegates with little or no change or shape the character of the debate at the convention.

A variety of factors have reduced the convention's decision-making capabilities. The way in which most of the delegates are selected enhances the prospects that they will be publicly committed to a candidate and that their votes for the nominee will be known long before they are cast. In fact, the major television networks, news magazines, and newspapers regularly conduct delegate counts during the preconvention stage of the nomination process and forecast the results.

The broadcasting of conventions has also detracted from the delegates' ability to bargain and cajole. It is difficult to compromise before a television camera, especially during prime time. Public exposure has forced negotiations off the convention floor and even out of committee rooms.

Size is another factor that has affected the proceedings. Conventions used to be relatively small. In 1860, 303 delegates nominated Democrat Stephen Douglas while 466 chose Republican Abraham Lincoln. Today, the participants run into the thousands. Table 5–1 lists the number of delegate votes at Democratic and Republican conventions since 1940. When alternates and delegates who possess fractional votes are included, the numbers grow even more. In 1984 the Republicans, swelled by the bonus given states that went for the GOP in 1980, will have at least 2,234 delegates and as many alternates, while the Democrats, augmented by the add-on delegates of elected and party officials, will have 3,923 delegates. The Democrats, however, have reduced the number of alternates from 2,053 to 1,310.

Because of the large number of delegates, divisions within the party have been magnified. There is more pressure from minorities to be heard. These pressures, in turn, have produced the need for more efficient organizations, both within the groups desiring recognition and by party officials and candidate representatives seeking to maintain order and to create a unifying image. For the party leaders and the prospective nominee, the task has become one of orchestration, and the goal is to conduct a huge pep rally replete with ritual and pomp—a made-for-television production.

Table 5–1 DELEGATE VOTES AT NOMINATING CONVENTIONS, 1940–1984*

Year	Republicans	Democrats
1940	1,000	1,100
1944	1,059	1,176
1948	1,094	1,234
1952	1,206	1,230
1956	1,323	1,372
1960	1,331	1,521
1964	1,308	2,316
1968	1,333	2,622
1972	1,348	3,016
1976	2,259	3,008
1980	1,994	3,331
1984	2,234†	3,923

Source: Richard C. Bain and Judith H. Parris, *Convention Decisions and Voting Records,* 2nd ed. (Washington, D.C.: Brookings Institution, 1973), Appendix C. Copyright © 1973 by the Brookings Institution. Updated by author.

*The magic number, the number of votes needed for nomination, equals one more than half.

†Does not include additional votes that may result from the election of Republican governors in 1983.

This chapter explores some of these aspects of modern conventions. The first section describes the formal organization. It discusses the choice of a city, the selection of officers and speakers, and the agenda for the meeting. The following section focuses on the staging—specifically, how the media have covered conventions and how the parties have reacted to that coverage. Illustrations from recent conventions are used to highlight the drama and trauma of television reporting.

Subsequent portions of the chapter deal with the politics of choice—namely, procedural and substantive issues and presidential and vice presidential selection. The third section examines rules fights, credentials challenges, and platform debates as barometers of the party's cohesiveness. These disputes indicate the relative strength of different groups within the party and the importance they attach to prizes other than the nomination. They also provide a perspective on the inner workings of the party, sometimes forecasting the presidential vote and/or the amount of support the nominee can expect in the election.

The fourth section of the chapter explores the selection of the presidential candidates. It looks at candidate organizations as they strive to win the nomination and then unify the party. Lastly, it examines the characteristics of the nominees as described in the light of recent conventions.

ORGANIZATION AND AGENDA

Preliminary decisions on the convention are made by the party's national committee, usually on the recommendation of its chairman and the appropriate convention committees. An incumbent President normally exercises considerable influence over the choice of a convention city. The site of the meeting, the apportionment of delegates, the rules by which they are selected, and the officers and major speakers must be determined well in advance.

The site is usually chosen at least one year ahead. In the past, the location of the city and its accessibility by railroad were important considerations in determining where to hold the meeting. Chicago's central geographic position has made it the most popular site, hosting fourteen Republican and ten Democratic conventions. Today, air transportation has extended the range of options to almost any city in the continental United States. However, other factors, such as the size of the convention hall, its suitability for television, the number of hotel rooms and transportation facilities available, the political atmosphere of the city, and its desire to host the meeting limit the actual choices to only a few.

The size of modern conventions requires huge halls to seat the delegates and alternates and to accommodate the thousands of others who wish to attend.[1] In 1980 the Democratic convention in New York's Madison Square Garden attracted an estimated 25,000 people to a basketball/hockey arena that normally holds about 18,000. The Republicans were far less crowded in the Joe Louis arena in Detroit than the Democrats were in Madison Square Garden in New York. On the other hand, the inadequate number of hotel rooms in the Motor City forced some delegates to stay in Canada and commute across the border. For 1984 each party will need 22,000 to 24,000 hotel rooms for delegates, alternates, and other attendees and a convention hall sufficient to seat over 25,000 people.

Having adequate press and broadcasting facilities has also been considered essential, although the mass media, particularly television, have not influenced the choice of a convention city nearly as much as they have affected the scheduling of events. Still, one of the reasons the Democrats rejected Philadelphia in 1980 was the construction of its convention hall. The low ceiling and numerous pillars would have impaired television coverage. Security has also become a major concern. The 1968 demonstrations at the Democratic convention in Chicago have led leaders of both parties to take elaborate precautions to prevent potentially disruptive activities.

The cost of preparing the physical facilities for conventions can be extremely high. While cities cannot pay the parties directly for hosting a convention, the FEC has permitted the national committees to accept services in kind from them. Thus, in 1976 New York City spent $1.4 million in converting Madison Square Garden from a sports palace to a convention hall. New York also assumed the bulk of the cost for added security during the convention. These services, which can exceed several million dollars, supplement the amount which the law provides to the major parties for holding their conventions. In 1980 the federal subsidy was $4.5 million; in 1984 it should be approximately $6 million. For their services, host cities can expect to benefit many times over from the money which the delegates spend on hotel rooms, food, and other commodities.

The political atmosphere has also been important in selecting a convention site. Parties and their prospective nominees prefer to launch their campaign among supporters. Being nominated in Chicago in 1860 helped Lincoln almost as much as it hurt Humphrey 108 years later. Cities can have symbolic significance as well. The choice of Detroit for the 1980 Republican convention was designed to emphasize the party's determination to broaden its appeal, particularly to labor, minorities, and ethnic groups. In the words of party chairman William Brock:

> We had very, very carefully worked to break several Republican stereo-types—by holding the Convention in Detroit for one thing. . . .Detroit offered minority opportunities, blue collar, labor unions, and primarily the economic mix of issues that we had determined . . . were going to be the definitive issues.[2]

The Democrats ruled out such cities as Atlanta and Chicago in 1980 because their states had not ratified the Equal Rights Amendment (ERA). The party eliminated non-ERA states in 1984 also, even though the date for approving the amendment had expired.

The apportionment of delegates is another decision that must be made prior to the convention. The Republicans normally approve their apportionment formula at their previous convention, while the Democrats allow their national committee to make the decision. The increase in the size of Democratic delegations for the 1984 Democratic convention was approved in 1983 by the Democratic National Committee. Additional changes in party rules were approved by the committee during the previous year.

Other preconvention decisions include the selection of convention officials and speakers: the temporary and permanent chairmen of the convention, the heads of the principal committees, and the keynote speaker. These selections, made at the suggestion of the chairman of the national committee after consultation with party leaders, are rarely challenged by the convention. Both the Democrats and the Republicans traditionally have turned to members of Congress to fill most of these positions.

Over the years, a standard agenda has been followed by both parties. (See Table 5–2.) The first day is devoted to speeches. Short addresses by party officials and state and local leaders begin the meeting, while the main event is the keynote address. Given during prime viewing hours to a large home and convention audience, the objective of the keynote address is to unify the delegates despite the divisions that may have occurred during the preconvention period. To do this, the speech ritually trumpets the achievements of the party, eulogizing its heroes and severely criticizing the opposition for its ill-conceived programs, inept leadership, and general inability to cope with the nation's problems.

The keynoter for the party that does not control the White House sounds a litany of past failures and suggests in a not-so-subtle way that

Table 5–2   AGENDA OF NATIONAL NOMINATING CONVENTIONS

First Day
Opening ceremonies (prayer, Pledge of Allegiance, National Anthem) Welcoming speeches (governor of host state and mayor of host city) Election of convention officers Treasurer's report (treasurer of the national committee) Chairman's report (chairman of the national committee) Keynote address

Second Day
Opening ceremonies Credentials Committee report* Rules Committee report* Platform Committee report*

Third Day
Opening ceremonies Nominations of presidential candidates Roll call for presidential nomination

Fourth Day

Opening ceremonies
Nominations of vice presidential candidates
Roll call for vice presidential nomination
Acceptance speeches:
  Vice presidential nominee
  Presidential nominee
Adjournment

*These reports are often interspersed with short speeches by party and public officials.

the country needs new leadership. Naturally, the keynoter for the party in office reverses the blame and praise. Noting the accomplishments of the administration and its unfinished business, the speaker urges a continuation of the party's effective leadership.[3]

On the second day, the committee reports are presented by the chairmen of the committees.[4] Often the product of lengthy negotiations, they represent the majority's consensus. In order for a minority to present its views to the convention, a certain percentage of the committee in question must concur in the minority report. For their 1980 convention, the Democrats raised this figure from 10 to 25 percent of the full committee, thereby making challenges more difficult and providing more inducement for the minority to compromise during the committee's deliberations.

The third day is devoted to the presidential nomination and balloting. In an evenly divided convention, this is clearly the most exciting period. Much ritual has surrounded the nomination itself. In early conventions, it was customary for a delegate simply to rise and place the name of a candidate in nomination without a formal speech. Gradually, the practice of making a nomination became more elaborate. Speeches were lengthened. Ritual required that the virtues of the candidate first be extolled and his name not be mentioned until the very end. Presumably, after hearing all of the virtues, the delegates would be anxiously awaiting the identity of their new leader. Today, with public speculation beginning months before and the selection often a foregone conclusion by the time of the convention, the practice of withholding the name has been abandoned. The achievements of the nominee are still repeated, however.

Demonstrations normally follow the nomination. The advent of television, however, has changed the character of these demonstrations. No longer spontaneous, they are now carefully staged to create the impression of significant support.[5] Signs and posters almost magically appear in the hands of supporters as they march around the floor after the candidate's name has been placed in nomination. Here's how Myra MacPherson described the scene at the 1976 Republican convention when Ronald Reagan was nominated.

> Reaganites in a last-gasp show, drowned Kemper Arena in bellowing klaxon horns that sounded, as one person observed, like the "hum of a thousand killer bees." They snaked through the aisles and tossed nerf Frisbees and threw confetti and thundered "Reagan" cheers. What had been so carefully staged finally became spontaneous, and floor leaders could not shut them up. Ford delegates agonized in the TV lights.[6]

Since 1972, the Democrats have tried to ban demonstrations. Their convention procedures designate a specific amount of time for nominating and seconding speeches. The time during which demonstrations occur is deducted from this amount.

Once all nominations have been made, the balloting begins. The secretary of the convention calls the roll of states in alphabetical order, with the chairman of each delegation announcing the vote. A poll of the delegation may be requested by any member.

Vice presidential selection, followed by the nominees' acceptance speeches, are the final order of business. They occur on the last day of the convention. In their early years, nominating conventions evidenced some difficulty in getting candidates to accept the vice presidential nomination. Because of the low esteem in which the office was held, a number of prominent individuals, including Henry Clay and Daniel Webster, actually refused it. In Webster's words, "I do not propose to be buried until I am really dead and in my coffin."[7]

Today, the Vice Presidency is coveted but still not publicly sought. Its increased significance, especially as a stepping stone to the Presidency, has generated a desire to win the nomination. Yet, it is almost impossible to run for it directly. There are no vice presidential primaries and no government matching funds for vice presidential candidates. Only one "vote" really counts—the presidential nominee's.

In choosing the vice presidential candidate, the convention normally accepts the recommendation of its presidential standard-bearer, although in recent years there have been a sprinkling of protest votes for others.[8] The most serious of these protests occurred during the 1968 conventions, when Governor George Romney of Michigan (Republican) and Georgia legislator Julian Bond (Democrat) received a number of votes.[9] At twenty-eight, Bond was not old enough to serve had he been nominated and subsequently elected.

Only once in recent history has the convention had to make more than a pro forma decision. In 1956, Democrat Adlai Stevenson professed to have no personal preference. He allowed the convention to choose between Estes Kefauver and John Kennedy. The convention chose Kefauver, the most popular Democrat in the public opinion polls at the time of his nomination.

Since the choice of a vice presidential nominee is usually not difficult or particularly controversial, a great deal of time is not set aside for it. Moreover, the decision is frequently made on the afternoon of the last day in order to leave the prime viewing hours for the acceptance speeches of the vice presidential and presidential nominees. These speeches are the crowning event of the convention. They are the time for displays of enthusiasm and unity. They mark the beginning of the party's campaign.

The custom of giving acceptance speeches was begun in 1932 by Franklin Roosevelt. Prior to that time, conventions designated committees to inform the presidential and vice presidential nominees of their decisions. Journeying to the candidate's home, the committees would announce the selection in a public ceremony. The nominee, in turn, would accept in a speech stating his positions on the major issues of the day. The last major party candidate to be told of the nomination in this fashion was Republican Wendell Willkie in 1940.

Today, acceptance speeches can be occasions for great oratory: they are both a call to the faithful and an address to the country. Harry Truman's speech to the Democratic convention in 1948 is frequently cited as one that helped to fire up the party. It greatly aided his candidacy. Truman chided the Republicans for obstructing and ultimately rejecting many of his legislative proposals and then adopting a party platform that called for some of the same social and economic goals. He then electrified the Democratic convention by challenging the Republicans to live up to their convention promises and pass legislation to achieve these goals in a special session of Congress which he announced he was calling. When the Republican-controlled Congress failed to enact the legislation, Truman was able to pin a "do-nothing" label on the Republicans and make that the basic theme of his successful presidential campaign.

Gerald Ford's address to a divided Republican convention in 1976 was also a high point in his campaign for the Presidency. Not an eloquent speaker or debater, Ford excited the convention by his remarks. Cameras caught the enthusiasm of the delegates for advertisements which were later shown throughout the campaign. Similarly, Ronald Reagan's address in 1980 marked the emotional culmination of his long quest for the nomination. His speech, carefully synchronized to emphasize the themes in the Republican platform, set the tone for his presidential campaign. Jimmy Carter's 1980 acceptance speech did not. Unlike his 1976 address, which aroused a Carter-dominated convention, his 1980 remarks did not generate nearly the enthusiasm that Senator Kennedy's speech did before the same convention two days earlier.[10]

Acceptance speeches are political appeals to the nation. They are important because of the large numbers of television viewers. Candidates attempt to tailor their presentations accordingly. Teleprompters are now standard fare; voices are modulated for the television audience rather than amplified for the convention hall; key words are used to highlight basic themes. Drama is created whenever possible. Take the final words of Reagan's 1980 acceptance speech as described by reporter Tom Shales:

> "I'll confess that I've been a little afraid to suggest what I'm going to suggest," Reagan said with a nervous gulp and glistening eyes as he neared the end of his 44-minute prime-time speech. "I'm more afraid not to." Pause. "Can we begin our crusade joined together in a moment of silent prayer?"
>
> Certainly no one shouted "No."
>
> And so Reagan, his eyes growing mistier, quickly surveyed the hall

and then humbly bowed his head, and the only sound that could be heard was the roar of the air conditioning in Detroit's Joe Louis Arena. After about 15 spellbinding seconds, Reagan ended his speech with "God bless America," and a demonstration ensued.

He never made a movie with a better finish than that.[11]

DRAMA AND STAGING

Television broadcasting of national conventions began in 1952. Almost immediately, a sizable audience was attracted. According to the Nielsen ratings, 20 to 30 percent of the potential audience watched the conventions between 1952 and 1968, with the number swelling during the most significant events.[12] In 1972 an estimated 115 million people saw some part of the conventions on one of the three major networks.[13] In 1980 this figure was close to 150 million, although at any one time only about half the viewing audience was tuned in. The major networks provided almost continuous prime-time coverage.

Watching the conventions can affect viewers' opinions and attitudes. In the short run, the convention almost always boosts the popularity of the nominees. The boost, however, is usually temporary. Several months afterward, the impact is more difficult to ascertain.

Political scientists have suggested three major effects of conventions on voters: (1) they heighten interest, thereby increasing turnout; (2) they arouse latent feelings, thereby raising partisan awareness; (3) they color perceptions, thereby affecting personal judgments of the candidates and their issue stands.[14] Studies have also shown that convention watchers tend to make their voting decisions earlier in the campaign.

Politicians assume that the more unified the convention, the more favorable its impact. This assumption has persuaded party leaders to take television coverage into account when planning, staging, and scheduling national party conventions. The choice of a convention site, the decoration of the hall, the selection of speakers, and the instructions to the delegates (see Figure 5–1) are all made with television in mind. More often than not, this attempt to create the proper visual effect has resulted in pure theater.

Movie stars regularly make appearances. Color guards, marching bands, and an orchestra amuse the delegates and television audiences alike. Films about the party and its recent presidents are shown. Entertaining while they inform, the films provide an additional benefit for the

Figure 5–1   TELEVISION WARNING TO DELEGATES

As a Delegate or an Alternate Delegate to the 1952 Democratic National Convention or a Guest at the Convention . . .

Y O U

WILL BE ON

TELEVISION !

140,000,000 eyes will watch our convention.

70,000,000 people will watch us nominate the next President and Vice President of the United States.

Eight Television cameras will be covering every inch of Convention Hall, inside and outside. They can cover every person in the Hall. They'll pick up everything of interest – and everything out of the ordinary.

Even if you're in a crowd, the eye of Television can project a closeup picture of Y O U to those 70,000,000 people watching. You probably won't even know the camera is on Y O U !

Empty seats will give a very bad impression. Television starts covering **Convention** Hall thirty minutes before each session.

BE ON TIME for each session.

Television will be watching Y O U !

Source: Reprinted from the 1976 Democratic National Convention Program.

party: the darkened hall makes it more difficult for the networks to interview the delegates. The newspeople are forced to carry the movie on their
networks or talk from the quiet of anchor booths. This minimizes the divisiveness which a variety of opinions can present and the turmoil which
thousands of people milling about on the convention floor can create.

Conventions have also become faster paced than in the past. Te-
dious reports and roll calls have been reduced. There are fewer candidates
placed in nomination, and the speeches themselves are shorter. The
length of the meetings has also been reduced. In 1952 the Democratic
and Republican conventions each had ten sessions which lasted over forty
hours. By 1968 the number of sessions had been cut to five and the number of hours to less than thirty for the Democrats and twenty-five for the
Republicans. Afternoon sessions, when held, no longer receive gavel-
to-gavel television coverage.

In 1972, Republican party leaders even went so far as to prepare
and follow a script that indicated who was to do what and when. Summaries of the script were given to the networks to help them with their coverage. Experienced consultants are regularly hired by convention officials
to advise them on all aspects of the production.

Timing is perhaps the most critical element. Major addresses
are scheduled during prime viewing hours in order to maximize the size
of the audience. A 10:30 P.M. Eastern Daylight Savings Time acceptance speech is considered ideal. Most nominees try to give their address
about this time. In 1972, however, a debate over party rules and the
nomination of several candidates for the Democratic vice presidential
nomination delayed McGovern's speech until 2:48 A.M., prime time
only in Hawaii and Guam. As a result, his audience was substantially
smaller than usual.

While major unifying events are timed to increase the number of
viewers, potentially disruptive and discordant situations are scheduled to
minimize them. Raucous debates, likely to convey the image of a divided
party, are delayed if possible until after prime time. In the 1964 Republican convention, for example, when Goldwater partisans got wind of a series of minority platform amendments favored by Nelson Rockefeller and
George Romney, they arranged to have the majority report read in its
entirety in order to postpone the amendments until the early morning
hours in the East, when most potential supporters of the minority position
would not be watching. In the 1964 Democratic convention, President
Johnson rescheduled a movie paying tribute to President John Kennedy
until after the vice presidential nomination to preclude any bandwagon

for Robert Kennedy, who was to introduce the film. In 1980, Carter agreed to several platform changes in order to avoid a divisive floor fight.

While party officials try to present a united front favoring their nominee and platform, television does not. In order to generate and maintain viewer interest, television tends to emphasize variety, maximize suspense, and exaggerate conflict. This has meant less focus on the official proceedings and more on other activities.

As an action medium, television is constantly scanning the convention for dramatic events and human interest stories. Delegates are pictured talking, eating, sleeping, parading, even watching television. Interviews with prominent individuals, rank-and-file delegates, and family and friends of the prospective nominee are conducted. To provide a balanced presentation, supporters and opponents are frequently juxtaposed. To maintain the audience's attention, the interviews are kept short, usually focusing on reactions to actual or potential problems. This creates the impression of division, making the convention seem more fractured to the viewer than to the participant.[15]

A variety of factors heightens this discordant effect: the simultaneous picturing of multiple events, the compactness of the interviews, the crowd of delegates pressed together or milling around the hall. When compared with the calm of the anchor booth, the floor appears to be a sea of confusion.[16]

Presidential nominees and their organizations try to moderate the negative effect of this coverage in a variety of ways. They make top campaign officials and members of the candidate's family available for interviews. They create photo opportunities for the press. They release personal information about the candidate and private polls to present his chances in the most favorable light.

Where there is little discord, they may even try to create tension as a device to hold the audience. The most frequent unresolved question is, who will be the vice presidential nominee? Unless an incumbent President and Vice President are seeking renomination, the vice presidential recommendation of the presidential nominee is usually not revealed until the morning of the nomination itself. Lyndon Johnson went so far as to ask the two most likely candidates to join him in Washington during the convention to heighten the drama. In order to avoid tipping off the press, presidential candidates have not made in-depth inquiries about their running mates. This had serious repercussions in 1972, when Thomas Eagleton, the Democratic vice presidential nominee, was forced to leave the ticket after his history of mental depression became known. George

McGovern was not aware of Eagleton's past illness when he picked him.

In 1980 the vice presidential charade reached new heights. Throughout the first three days of the Republican convention, network correspondents speculated on who Reagan's running mate would be. On the second day of the convention, unbeknown to the public, officials of the Reagan organization approached former President Ford, who expressed interest in the nomination. As private talks were being conducted, Ford indicated his willingness to consider the Vice Presidency during a television interview. This immediately fueled public speculation and turned the media focus from the convention to the Reagan-Ford negotiations. When these negotiations failed, Reagan ended the speculation himself by coming to the convention to generate support for his second choice, George Bush.

The media tend to play up various other contests, such as credentials and platform disputes. While some of these have had a major impact on convention decisions, such as the fight over the composition of the California delegation at the 1972 Democratic convention, others have not. Despite the publicity given to the challenges of the regular Democratic delegation from Mississippi in 1964 and the South Carolina delegation in 1972, neither had a tangible effect on the outcome of the convention, although both had symbolic significance. Similarly, the tight control exercised over the 1964 Republican convention by Goldwater supporters and over the 1968 Democratic convention by those sympathetic to Hubert Humphrey gave the platform debates of those years the character of media events.

Even more controversial than television coverage *in* recent conventions has been the major networks' coverage *outside* the conventions. Television's reporting of the 1968 Chicago demonstrations in particular generated considerable public and party criticism. Not only were the networks charged with overemphasizing the disruptions to the detriment of their convention coverage, but they were seen as helping to incite the demonstrators by the mere presence of their live cameras in the streets.

Claiming that the events were newsworthy and certainly not of their own creation, the networks responded by denying that the demonstrations received disproportionate coverage. CBS News reported that it had devoted only thirty-two minutes to these events out of more than thirty-eight hours of total convention coverage.[17] Nonetheless, the combination of outside disturbances and inside conflict led to the association in the public mind of turmoil and division with the Democratic party in 1968.

Beginning in 1972, Democratic party leaders tried to minimize this potentially discordant effect by exercising more control over the press. They reduced the number of press passes and restricted the major networks to four camera crews on the floor at any one time. However, in 1972 and 1980 there was still considerable controversy, though not in 1976. In the future, television can be expected to continue to emphasize conflict in its coverage of national conventions, while party leaders will try to present as much unity as their skill (and the division of delegates) will permit.

RULES, CREDENTIALS, AND PLATFORMS

Adopting the Rules

Obviously there can be a real basis for controversy at national conventions. Since the presidential nominations have usually not been in doubt recently, the rules, credentials, and/or platform become the subjects for debate and often for division. All three can have a major impact on what the convention decides and how it appears to the public.

Rules govern the manner in which the convention is conducted. They are interpreted by the chairman of the convention, with the convention itself having ultimate authority. The rules committee can propose changes, but they must be approved by the delegates.

In formulating the rules, there is a natural tension between the desire of the minority for extended debate and easy floor challenges and the interest of the majority, especially the leadership, in an efficiently run convention that has a cohesive effect on party members and presents a unifying image to the electorate. A humorous incident at the 1956 Republican convention illustrates this tension. In the nomination for Vice President, Richard Nixon was expected to be the unanimous choice. A movement to dump him from the ticket led by perennial candidate Harold Stassen had failed. When the roll of states was called for nominations, a delegate from Nebraska grabbed the microphone and said he had a nomination to make. "Who?" said a surprised Joseph Martin, chairman of the convention. "Joe Smith," the delegate replied. Martin did not permit the name of Joe Smith to be placed in nomination, although the Democrats were later to argue that any Joe Smith would have been better than Nixon.

For the most part, convention rules have not caused much wrangling. Those that have generated the most controversy have concerned voting for the party's nominees. Until 1936 the Democrats operated under a rule that required a two-thirds vote for winning the nomination.

James K. Polk's selection in 1844 was a consequence of Martin Van Buren's failure to obtain the support of two-thirds of the convention, although he had a majority. The two-thirds rule in effect permitted a minority, such as delegates from the South, to veto a person they opposed.

The Democratic party also enforced the unit rule, a requirement that some states adopted to maximize their voting strength. The rule obligated all members of a delegation to vote for the delegation majority's position regardless of their own views. Beginning in 1968, the Democratic convention refused to enforce unit voting any longer. The elimination of this winner-take-all principle obviously reduced the probability that state delegations would vote as units and ultimately weakened the power of state party leaders. The Republicans never sanctioned or prohibited unit voting. When the Mississippi delegation decided to vote as a unit at the 1976 convention to enhance its influence and perhaps tip the balance to Ford, there was little Reagan could do or party officials would do.

Among the recent rules controversies that have divided the Republican party, two stand out. In 1952, Eisenhower supporters challenged the credentials of a sizable number of Taft delegates from southern states. Before deciding on the challenges, however, the convention adopted a "fair play" amendment that prohibited contested delegates from voting on any question, including their own credentials. This rule, which effectively prevented many Taft delegates from voting, swung the challenges and eventually the nomination to Eisenhower.

The other recent dispute that became a precursor of the presidential vote occurred during the 1976 Republican convention, when the Reagan organization proposed a rules change that would have required Ford to indicate his choice for Vice President before the vote for President, as Reagan had done. Ford's supporters strongly opposed and subsequently beat this amendment. As a consequence, there was no way for Reagan to shake the remaining delegates loose from Ford's coalition. Ford won the presidential vote 1,187 to 1,070, almost the identical margin of his rules victory.

An even more acrimonious division over party rules occurred in 1980 at the Democratic convention. At issue was a proposed requirement that delegates vote for the candidate to whom they were publicly pledged at the time they were chosen to attend the convention. Trailing Carter by about 600 delegates, Kennedy, who had previously supported the requirement, urged an open convention in which delegates could vote their consciences rather than merely exercise their commitments. This would have required rejection of the pledged delegate rule. Naturally, the Carter organization favored the rule and strenuously lobbied for it, successfully. By a vote of 1,936.4 to 1,390.6 the convention accepted the binding rule, thereby assuring President Carter's renomination.[18] The Democrats subsequently repealed this rule for 1984, requiring instead that delegates reflect in good conscience the sentiments of those who elected them.[19]

Challenging Credentials

Disputes over credentials have been more frequent and, in general, have had greater impact on conventions. Approximately 7 percent of all Republican delegates and 3.5 percent of all Democratic delegates were challenged between 1872 and 1956.[20] In 1912 and again in 1952, these challenges affected the outcome of the Republican convention. William Howard Taft's victory over Theodore Roosevelt in 1912 and Eisenhower's over Robert Taft in 1952 resulted from convention decisions to seat certain delegates and reject others.

In both cases, grass roots challenges to old-line party leaders generated competing delegate claims. The convention in 1912 rejected these challenges and seated the regular party delegates, producing a walkout by Roosevelt's supporters and giving the nomination to Taft. In 1952 the delegates denied the nomination to his son. By deciding to prevent challenged delegates from voting until their credentials were accepted, the convention neutralized Taft's advantage and eventually tilted the vote toward Eisenhower.

Recent Democratic conventions have also witnessed credentials fights. In 1968, delegates from fifteen states were challenged largely on the grounds that state leaders had wrongfully excluded rank-and-file party members from caucuses and conventions. In 1972, challenges were based on allegations that certain delegations did not possess sufficient minority representation or were chosen in a manner that did not conform to party rules.

The California challenge at the 1972 Democratic convention illustrates the second of these complaints. McGovern had won the primary and, according to California law, was entitled to all the delegates. The credentials committee, however, decided that the state's delegates should be divided in proportion to the popular vote because Democratic rules clearly preferred proportional voting. McGovern forces challenged this ruling and won on the convention floor, thereby making his nomination all but certain. There have been no serious delegate challenges at either convention since 1972.

Drafting the Platform

Traditionally, the platform has been the focus of much public attention during the convention. In recent years, it has been the subject of considerable controversy. The Democrats, in particular, have found themselves divided over a variety of policy proposals. Far from unifying the party, Democratic platform debates in 1968 and 1972 have exacerbated the divisions within the party.

Two often conflicting aims lie at the heart of the platform-drafting process. One has to do with winning the election and the other with pleasing the party's coalition. In order to maximize the vote, platforms cannot alienate. They must permit people to see what they want to see. This is accomplished by increasing the level of vagueness and ambiguity on the most controversial and emotionally charged issues. When appealing to the party's coalition, on the other hand, traditional images must be evoked and "bread and butter" positions stressed. A laundry list of promises is normally presented with something for everyone.

The tension resulting from "the electoral incentives to fudge and the coalition incentives to deliver"[21] has caused real problems for platform drafters and has resulted in documents that contain rhetoric, self-praise, and unrealistic goals. This, in turn, has led to the criticism that platforms are substantially meaningless and politically unimportant, that they bind and guide no one. There may be some truth to this criticism, but it also overstates the case.

While platforms contain rhetoric and self-praise, they also consist of goals and proposals that differentiate them from one another. In an examination of the Democratic and Republican platforms between 1944 and 1976, Gerald Pomper found that most of the differences were evident in the planks made by one party but not by the other.[22] (See Table 5–3.) Over these years the Republicans emphasized defense and general governmental matters, while the Democrats stressed economic issues, particularly those of labor and social welfare.

Party platforms are appeals to broad constituencies. As the minority party, the Republicans have sought to extend their electoral base by appealing to independents and Democrats on the basis of national issues which tend to affect the society as a whole. In contrast, the Democrats have designed their platforms to appeal to many of the groups that comprise their majority coalition. They have tended to emphasize domestic issues, such as those that involve social and economic policies.

The 1980 platforms reflected these differences. The Republicans

Table 5–3   SIMILARITY AND CONFLICT IN PLATFORM PLEDGES*

	(N)	One-Party Pledge Only	Bipartisan Pledges	Conflicting Pledges
Election Year				
1944	(102)	70%	28%	2%
1948	(124)	51	42	7
1952	(205)	52	29	19
1956	(302)	61	34	5
1960	(464)	51	39	10
1964	(202)	70	19	11
1968	(457)	77	16	7
1972	(698)	83	13	5
1976	(640)	76	17	7
Policy Topic				
Foreign	(509)	60	34	6
Defense	(166)	74	22	4
Economics	(397)	76	15	9
Labor	(180)	65	17	18
Agriculture	(243)	66	27	7
Resources	(338)	69	22	9
Welfare	(696)	71	19	10
Government	(441)	78	18	4
Civil rights	(225)	63	35	2
All pledges	(3,194)	69%	23%	8%
N Total	3,194	2,218	731	245

Source: Gerald Pomper, with Susan S. Lederman, *Elections in America*, 2nd ed. (New York: Longman, 1980), p. 169.
*Rows add up horizontally to 100 percent for the three columns.

stressed defense and foreign policy issues. In advocating a policy of "peace through strength," they urged increased defense expenditures, opposition to Soviet expansionism, and new guidelines for providing foreign aid. While the Democrats also favored greater military spending, the focus of their platform was domestic: a $12 billion jobs program, national health insurance, and educational support for the disadvantaged—all programs which the Republicans opposed.

The parties also differed significantly on social issues. The Democrats supported the Equal Rights Amendment; the Republicans did not. The Democrats took a strong pro-choice stand on abortion; the Republicans wanted a constitutional amendment banning abortion. The Democrats continued to support busing as a last resort to achieve racial integration in schools; the Republicans strongly opposed forced busing for any reason.

Platform differences are important. Despite the conventional wisdom that platforms are forgotten once the convention is over and the campaign concluded, elected officials of both parties have a relatively good record of meeting their pledges. Approximately three-quarters of party platforms are rhetoric. About one-fourth contain fairly specific promises. Of these, Pomper found that almost 75 percent of them have been kept.[23] Other political scientists have also calculated high percentages of convention and campaign pledges that have been redeemed.[24]

One reason that so many of the convention promises have been acted upon is that elected officials participate in the drafting of platforms; in fact, they hold many of the key committee positions. For the party in power the incumbent President usually takes the lead, exercising the most influence when seeking reelection. For the party out of power, members of Congress, mainly the leadership, tend to exercise the greater influence.

In contrast, some candidates for the nomination may not display much personal interest in the platform-drafting process but will designate representatives to look out for their concerns. Chester Bowles, chairman of the 1960 Democratic platform committee, commented that John Kennedy paid only scant attention to the platform draft.[25] His brother Edward, however, was deeply involved in platform disputes at the 1980 Democratic convention.

The platform chairman normally exercises considerable influence. Appointed by the chairman of the national committee, he, in turn, chooses the staff, invites the testimony of witnesses, negotiates disputes, and generally oversees the process. The staff is usually responsible for the first draft of the platform. Approximately one week before the convention, members of the platform committee formally meet to hold hearings, examine and "mark up" the draft, and present a final report to the convention. This report has frequently been submitted as a whole to preclude amendments. The entire process has traditionally been designed to minimize outside pressures and maximize the leadership's control. Between 1944 and 1960, conventions made few significant changes in their platform committee's reports.

The exception during this period was in 1948. A major dispute arose over the civil rights section of the Democratic platform. Delegates from the southern states offered three amendments designed to promote a states' rights position. The convention rejected them and instead adopted a proposal that further strengthened the party's commitment to civil rights. This led to a walkout of delegates from several southern states.[26]

Beginning in 1964 and continuing through 1980, the acquiescence which had greeted earlier party platforms has been replaced by acrimonious debate. While the majority has continued to carry the day, minority proposals now receive attention on the floor (and in the media). These proposals often reveal deep differences within the parties.

In 1964, Republicans Nelson Rockefeller and George Romney proposed platform amendments that condemned extremism and urged a stronger civil rights position. Goldwater partisans soundly defeated these challenges. The 1968 Democratic convention witnessed an emotional four-hour debate on United States policy in Vietnam. While the convention voted to sustain the majority position, which had the approval of President Johnson, the discussion reinforced the image of a divided party to millions of home viewers.

In 1980 a major debate over economic and social issues again divided the Democrats. Delegates supporting Senator Edward Kennedy sought to amend the platform's economic planks, while feminists and other ERA and pro-choice sympathizers favored the minority reports of the platform committee. Considerable negotiation between Carter and Kennedy factions preceded the final resolution of the dispute.

Although Carter enjoyed the backing of a majority of the delegates, he was forced to compromise on several key issues. Failure to have done so would have left the convention divided and would have seriously impaired his chances for reelection.[27] As it was, the debate had a damaging impact on his candidacy. The compromise which helped resolve the issues permitted Kennedy to address the convention during prime time. In exchange Kennedy agreed to support the President in the general election.

A variety of factors have contributed to the increasing number of platform disputes. The development of caucus groups within the party, such as women, blacks, and Hispanics, has generated additional demands on the platform and pressures to open the process further. These groups have become better organized, have been more adept at bargaining, and have gotten many of their policy objectives incorporated in the platforms.

Changes in the selection process seem to have produced more issue-oriented delegates who are less dependent on and loyal to party leadership. These issue activists tend to gravitate to the platform committee and, specifically, to the subcommittee considering "their" issues. This has tended to exaggerate rather than minimize the policy differences among the delegates. Television has also magnified the problem by providing publicity for platform challenges.

As a consequence, the platform-drafting process has become both more open and more divisive in recent years. The Republicans have suffered less than the Democrats. As the more homogeneous and smaller of the two parties, they have been subjected to fewer and less intense pressures from organized interest groups. The Democrats, on the other hand, have had to contend with larger and more cohesive caucus groups. Their disputes have tended to be more numerous and more prolonged than the Republicans' and more likely to be decided on the convention floor.

PLATFORM DRAFTING IN 1980*

The Republican Experience

Officially, the drafting process began in January 1980 with the first of ten public hearings which the Republican National Committee held to solicit ideas for its platform. In actuality, the hearings had little effect because most were held even before a platform committee was constituted. The committee, chaired by Senator John Tower and staffed by personnel from congressional committees and the Republican National Committee, began meeting in the spring of the year. It was organized on the basis of six policy subcommittees, each headed by a member of Congress.

The platform was put together in the following way: Each subcommittee prepared a draft within its own policy area. These drafts were reviewed by the congressional leadership of the full committee and eventually by the committee itself.

Although the sessions were open to the public, most of them received little media attention because of two factors: the lack of major discord on most important policy issues and the impediments placed in the way of press coverage. Drafts of the proposed planks and amendments were not distributed to journalists, making it difficult for them to follow the debate. Only in the area of human resources were drafts available. As a result, the divisions over the ERA and abortion were emphasized in the media.

While representatives of the Reagan campaign attended the deliberations and expressed the candidate's views, they did not attempt to impose a platform on the delegates. Rather, they sought one that would be acceptable to the mainstream of the party. The final document engendered practically no debate. It incorporated the major themes of the Reagan campaign.

The Democratic Experience

With a Democratic President running for reelection, the initial draft of the Democratic platform was prepared in close consultation with the White House. The result—a document that lauded the administration's accomplishments, criticized the policies of its Republican predecessors, and promised specific programs for the various components of the party—was presented to the platform committee when it began its deliberations in June. The committee, chaired by Governor Richard W. Riley of South Carolina, included supporters of Carter and Kennedy as well as representatives of most of the caucus and interest groups.

Democratic procedures called for a subcommittee to prepare a complete draft based on the 1976 platform and on proposals from the candidates. The preliminary White House draft enlarged by several noncontroversial amendments was reported to the full committee, which then divided into five task forces to consider the individual planks. Much controversy followed.

Under party rules a majority of the committee could determine the provisions reported to the convention. However, minority reports could be filed if supported by at least 25 percent of the delegates. Carter's delegates comprised the majority on most issues, but Kennedy had sufficient support to force convention consideration of his key proposals. In all, twenty-three minority reports were attached to the final document. They took seventeen hours to debate and delayed the adoption of the platform until the third day of the convention.

---

*This description of the platform-drafting process in 1980 is based primarily on the discussion contained in Michael J. Malbin, "The Conventions, Platforms, and Issue Activists," in Austin Ranney (ed.), *The American Elections of 1980* (Washington, D.C.: American Enterprise Institute, 1981), pp. 100–127.

PRESIDENTIAL AND VICE PRESIDENTIAL SELECTION

Strategies and Tactics

There are a number of prizes at nominating conventions. The platform contains some of them. Credentials, rules, and procedures can also be important, but the big prize is the presidential nomination. When that is in doubt, all the efforts of the leading contenders must be directed at obtaining the required number of votes. When it is not in doubt, the leading contenders can concentrate on uniting the party and converting the convention into a huge campaign rally for themselves. In 1976 the Reagan organization focused its attention on winning the nomination; in 1980 it sought to present a united front. In contrast, Carter sought to mollify disaffected delegates in 1976 and 1980. Every candidate naturally tries to broaden his base of support.

The key to success, regardless of the objective, is organization. Recent conventions have seen the operation of highly structured and efficient candidate organizations. Designed to maximize the flow of information and extend political influence, these organizations usually have elaborate communication systems connecting floor supporters to a command center outside the convention hall. Key staff members at the command center monitor reports, articulate positions, and make strategic decisions. The Kennedy organization in 1960 is considered the prototype of these modern convention operations.

Prior to the Democratic convention, Kennedy's aides had compiled data on the delegates that included their role within the state party, their issue positions, and their preferences for President. Even their religion and their relationship (if any) to the Kennedys were noted. This information was updated throughout the convention. People on the floor were assigned to observe and report on each state delegation. A small group of Kennedy's top aides synthesized these reports and prepared a daily summary for the candidate. They also coordinated the floor activities. A separate telephone system was even installed, with walkie-talkies held in reserve in case the phones failed. They did not.[28]

Most campaign organizations since 1960 have been cut from the same mold. Tight-knit operations with an elaborate floor structure and communications system, they have consisted of "whips" divided by state and connected by a special telephone hookup to the campaign headquarters normally located in a trailer outside the convention hall.

Organizations can make a difference. In 1976, Ford's was far superior to Reagan's. Political scientist F. Christopher Arterton describes the Ford system as follows:

> The Convention floor was divided into zones each coordinated by a floor leader wearing a red hat for easy visual identification. In communicating upward, each floor leader had phones tied to the Ford trailer. The chain reached downward into the delegations through assistants responsible for

the states in their zone. These assistants could communicate either with the Ford leader in their states or with designated coordinators ("whips") of four to eight delegates. Thus, wavering delegates might be contacted by one of three separate means: by the operatives from the primary floor structure of zones, by a designated Ford "delegation monitor," coordinated by phone on the old geographical desk system, or, by a backup system of eight "floaters" roving the floor, wearing yellow hats, and using walkie-talkies to connect them with the trailer. The Ford committee went so far in their preparations as to have repairmen standing by to replace sabotaged phonelines.[29]

Reagan, on the other hand, designated a few individuals to speak for him on issues that arose and used the geographic leaders of the preconvention period to pass the word on the floor. It was thought that little coaxing of Reagan delegates would be necessary. Leaders of the Reagan organization believed that supporters of the former California governor could be counted on to follow his lead.

Having a weak floor organization, however, placed Reagan at a strategic disadvantage when the need for mobile and rapid decision making occurred, such as when the Mississippi delegation caucused on the floor before a crucial vote. Arterton reports that Reagan's key coordinators had to fight their way through crowded aisles to get to the delegation.[30] Reagan learned his lesson. In 1980 his convention organization was smooth and efficient. It effectively controlled activities on the floor and at the podium.

In addition to having an effective organization, candidates should also have a general strategy, the contours of which are shaped by the aspirant's status at the time of the convention. The object for leading candidates is to maintain the momentum, win on the first ballot, and prepare for the general election. For those who are behind, the goal is to challenge the certainty of the initial balloting, despite public predictions to the contrary, and demonstrate the ability to win the nomination and the election.

Front-runners must avoid taking unnecessary risks. Ford followed this strategy in 1976 and Carter did the same in 1980. Both compromised on key platform planks but held their ground on rules challenges that could have jeopardized their nomination.

Sometimes it is necessary for front-runners to show their strength. They must be careful not to flaunt it, however, and accentuate divisions created by the primaries and caucuses. Once the nomination is assured, the object of front-runners is to unify the faithful and present a united front for the general election. To do this requires reaching out to disaffected members of the party. Reagan's behavior at the 1980 Republican convention is illustrative. He met with women unhappy with the party's stance on the ERA, appeased moderates by his selection of George Bush as his running mate, and appealed to Democrats and independents by references to Franklin Roosevelt and to nonpartisan themes in his acceptance speech.

For the non–front-runner there are two immediate needs: to indicate the vulnerability of the front-runner and to emphasize his own capacity to win the nomination. Two tactics have been employed by challengers to accomplish these ends. One is to release polls showing the strength of the non–front-runner and the weakness of the convention leader in the general election. The objective here is to play on the delegates' desire to nominate a winner. The Rockefeller campaign planned such a move for the 1968 Republican convention. By not entering the primaries, Rockefeller hoped to demonstrate his popularity by pointing to public opinion polls that showed him to be a stronger candidate than Nixon. His stratagem failed when the final Gallup Poll showed Nixon to be the more popular Republican.

A second tactic, one that has been used in recent conventions, is to create an issue prior to the presidential balloting and win on it. If the issue affects rules which affect the vote—so much the better. Reagan in 1976 and Kennedy in 1980 tried this ploy without success. Their defeats on key votes confirmed their status as also-rans but did not end their campaigns.

With the nomination out of reach, the non–front-runners then concentrated on the platform. Each had a variety of motives: to influence the party and its nominee, to save face, to position themselves for the next battle in four years. For the most part, the front-runners did not accept these platform challenges, choosing instead to concede policy positions in order to obtain their opponents' backing in the forthcoming campaign.

The Presidential Consensus

The voting for President is usually anticlimactic. Since 1924, when the Democrats took 103 ballots to nominate John W. Davis, there have only been four conventions (two Democratic and two Republican) in which more than one ballot has been needed. (See Tables 5–4 and 5–5.) In 1932 the Democrats held four roll calls before the required two-thirds

Table 5–4   DEMOCRATIC PARTY CONVENTIONS AND NOMINEES, 1832–1980

Year	City	Dates	Presidential Nominee	Vice Presidential Nominee	No. of Pres. Ballots
1832	Baltimore	May 21–23	Andrew Jackson	Martin Van Buren	1
1835	Baltimore	May 20–22	Martin Van Buren	Richard M. Johnson	1
1840	Baltimore	May 5–6	Martin Van Buren	*	1
1844	Baltimore	May 27–29	James K. Polk	George M. Dallas	9
1848	Baltimore	May 22–25	Lewis Cass	William O. Butler	4
1852	Baltimore	June 1–5	Franklin Pierce	William R. King	49
1856	Cincinnati	June 2–6	James Buchanan	John C. Breckinridge	17
1860	Charleston	April 23–May 3	Deadlocked		57
1860	Baltimore	June 18–23	Stephen A. Douglas	Benjamin Fitzpatrick Herschel V. Johnson†	2
1864	Chicago	August 29–31	George B. McClellan	George H. Pendleton	1
1868	New York	July 4–9	Horatio Seymour	Francis P. Blair	22
1872	Baltimore	July 9–10	Horace Greeley	Benjamin G. Brown	1
1876	St. Louis	June 27–29	Samuel J. Tilden	Thomas A. Hendricks	2
1880	Cincinnati	June 22–24	Winfield S. Hancock	William H. English	2
1884	Chicago	July 8–11	Grover Cleveland	Thomas A. Hendricks	2
1888	St. Louis	June 5–7	Grover Cleveland	Allen G. Thurman	1
1892	Chicago	June 21–23	Grover Cleveland	Adlai E. Stevenson	1
1896	Chicago	July 7–11	William J. Bryan	Arthur Sewall	5
1900	Kansas City	July 4–6	William J. Bryan	Adlai E. Stevenson	1
1904	St. Louis	July 6–9	Alton B. Parker	Henry G. Davis	1
1908	Denver	July 7–10	William J. Bryan	John W. Kern	1

Year	City	Dates	Presidential nominee	Vice Presidential nominee	Ballots
1912	Baltimore	June 25–July 2	Woodrow Wilson	Thomas R. Marshall	46
1916	St. Louis	June 14–16	Woodrow Wilson	Thomas R. Marshall	1
1920	San Francisco	June 28–July 6	James M. Cox	Franklin D. Roosevelt	43
1924	New York	June 24–July 9	John W. Davis	Charles W. Bryan	103
1928	Houston	June 26–29	Alfred E. Smith	Joseph T. Robinson	1
1932	Chicago	June 27–July 2	Franklin D. Roosevelt	John N. Garner	4
1936	Philadelphia	June 23–27	Franklin D. Roosevelt	John N. Garner	Acclamation
1940	Chicago	July 15–18	Franklin D. Roosevelt	Henry A. Wallace	1
1944	Chicago	July 19–21	Franklin D. Roosevelt	Harry S. Truman	1
1948	Philadelphia	July 12–14	Harry S. Truman	Alben W. Barkley	1
1952	Chicago	July 21–26	Adlai E. Stevenson	John J. Sparkman	3
1956	Chicago	August 13–17	Adlai E. Stevenson	Estes Kefauver	1
1960	Los Angeles	July 11–15	John F. Kennedy	Lyndon B. Johnson	1
1964	Atlantic City	August 24–27	Lyndon B. Johnson	Hubert H. Humphrey	Acclamation
1968	Chicago	August 26–29	Hubert H. Humphrey	Edmund S. Muskie	1
1972	Miami Beach	July 10–13	George McGovern	Thomas F. Eagleton‡	1
				R. Sargent Shriver‡	
1976	New York	July 12–15	Jimmy Carter	Walter F. Mondale	1
1980	New York	August 11–14	Jimmy Carter	Walter F. Mondale	1
1984	San Francisco	July 16–19			

Source: Updated from *National Party Conventions, 1831–72* (Washington, D.C.: Congressional Quarterly, 1976), pp. 8–9. Copyrighted material reprinted with permission of Congressional Quarterly Inc.

*The 1840 Democratic convention did not nominate a candidate for Vice President.

†The 1860 Democratic convention nominated Benjamin Fitzpatrick, who declined shortly after the convention adjourned. On June 25 the Democratic National Committee selected Herschel V. Johnson as the party's candidate for Vice President.

‡The 1972 Democratic convention nominated Thomas F. Eagleton, who withdrew from the ticket on July 31. On August 8 the Democratic National Committee selected R. Sargent Shriver as the party's candidate for Vice President.

Table 5–5   REPUBLICAN PARTY CONVENTIONS AND NOMINEES, 1856–1980

Year	City	Dates	Presidential Nominee	Vice Presidential Nominee	No. of Pres. Ballots
1856	Philadelphia	June 17–19	John C. Fremont	William L. Dayton	2
1860	Chicago	May 16–18	Abraham Lincoln	Hannibal Hamlin	3
1864	Baltimore	June 7–8	Abraham Lincoln	Andrew Johnson	1
1868	Chicago	May 20–21	Ulysses S. Grant	Schuyler Colfax	1
1872	Philadelphia	June 5–6	Ulysses S. Grant	Henry Wilson	1
1876	Cincinnati	June 14–16	Rutherford B. Hayes	William A. Wheeler	7
1880	Chicago	June 2–8	James A. Garfield	Chester A. Arthur	36
1884	Chicago	June 3–6	James G. Blaine	John A. Logan	4
1888	Chicago	June 19–25	Benjamin Harrison	Levi P. Morton	8
1892	Minneapolis	June 7–10	Benjamin Harrison	Whitelaw Reid	1
1896	St. Louis	June 16–18	William McKinley	Garret A. Hobart	1
1900	Philadelphia	June 19–21	William McKinley	Theodore Roosevelt	1
1904	Chicago	June 21–23	Theodore Roosevelt	Charles W. Fairbanks	1
1908	Chicago	June 16–19	William H. Taft	James S. Sherman	1
1912	Chicago	June 18–22	William H. Taft	James S. Sherman	1
				Nicholas Murray Butler*	

Year	City	Dates	Presidential nominee	Vice presidential nominee	
1916	Chicago	June 7–10	Charles E. Hughes	Charles W. Fairbanks	3
1920	Chicago	June 8–12	Warren G. Harding	Calvin Coolidge	10
1924	Cleveland	June 10–12	Calvin Coolidge	Charles G. Dawes	1
1928	Kansas City	June 12–15	Herbert Hoover	Charles Curtis	1
1932	Chicago	June 14–16	Herbert Hoover	Charles Curtis	1
1936	Cleveland	June 9–12	Alfred M. Landon	Frank Knox	1
1940	Philadelphia	June 24–28	Wendell L. Willkie	Charles L. McNary	6
1944	Chicago	June 26–28	Thomas E. Dewey	John W. Bricker	1
1948	Philadelphia	June 21–25	Thomas E. Dewey	Earl Warren	3
1952	Chicago	July 7–11	Dwight D. Eisenhower	Richard M. Nixon	1
1956	San Francisco	August 20–23	Dwight D. Eisenhower	Richard M. Nixon	1
1960	Chicago	July 25–28	Richard M. Nixon	Henry Cabot Lodge	1
1964	San Francisco	July 13–16	Barry Goldwater	William E. Miller	1
1968	Miami Beach	August 5–8	Richard M. Nixon	Spiro T. Agnew	1
1972	Miami Beach	August 21–23	Richard M. Nixon	Spiro T. Agnew	1
1976	Kansas City	August 16–19	Gerald R. Ford	Robert J. Dole	1
1980	Detroit	July 14–18	Ronald Reagan	George Bush	1
1984	Dallas	August 20–23			

Source: Updated from *National Party Conventions, 1831–72* (Washington, D.C.: Congressional Quarterly, 1976), pp. 8–9. Copyrighted material reprinted with permission of Congressional Quarterly Inc.

*The 1912 Republican convention nominated James S. Sherman, who died on October 30. The Republican National Committee subsequently selected Nicholas Murray Butler to receive the Republican electoral votes for Vice President.

agreed on Franklin Roosevelt. After the Democrats had abolished their two-thirds rule, they needed more than one ballot only once—in 1952, when three were required to nominate Adlai Stevenson. In 1940, Republican Wendell Willkie was selected on the eighth ballot, breaking a deadlock among Thomas Dewey, Arthur Vandenberg, and himself. Eight years later, Dewey was nominated on the third ballot.

What explains the one-ballot phenomenon? For one thing, the desire to support the winner helps generate a bandwagon effect. The bandwagon attracts candidate-oriented delegates who are more likely to submerge their ideological and issue preferences in order to be on the victorious side. They estimate who will win and then vote accordingly.

Estimates may be based on hunches, on inside information, or, increasingly, on public polls of how the delegates will vote. Three political scientists have even gone so far as to devise a formula for predicting the convention winner based on these surveys. It works like this: take the candidate's support in the most recent poll or convention ballot (S_1), subtract the support from the next to last poll or convention ballot (S_2), and divide that figure $(S_1 - S_2)$ by the minimum proportion of the vote needed to win the nomination (Q) minus the support the candidate began with (S_1). The result is what they call a Gain-Deficit ratio (R). Thus,

$$R = \frac{(S_1 - S_2)}{(Q - S_1)}.$$

If R exceeds .360, then the candidate who has attained this critical value should win.[31]

When tested, this formula was successful in predicting the outcome of nine of eleven majority rule conventions before 1952 and all of them after 1952.[32] Moreover, these predictions could be made even before all the delegates were chosen. The authors found that when 80 percent were selected, the outcome of the convention was predictable.[33]

Unsuccessful candidates can usually read the handwriting on the wall. They tend to withdraw before the balloting begins. This enhances the prospects of a first-round decision and makes the tally not necessarily indicative of the actual competition for the nomination. Not only does the level of competition decrease as the convention nears but most nomination processes have not been all that competitive.

Two political scientists, William R. Keech and Donald R. Matthews, have categorized presidential nominations as consensual, semiconsensual, and nonconsensual.[34] Consensual nominations have occurred in nine of the last twenty-five conventions. The successful nominee, in five cases an incumbent President, has faced little or no opposition within his party. He was the party's most popular nominee in the preprimary and postprimary periods. Examples include Johnson in 1964, Nixon in 1972, and Reagan in 1980. Each was the overwhelming choice of his party's rank and file. The delegates simply ratified their selection. Their convention took on the aura of a coronation.

In semiconsensual nominations, there is a provisional leader, supported by most factions of the party, who survives the preconvention process to win the nomination. Adlai Stevenson (1956), John Kennedy (1960), and Richard Nixon (1968) are examples of semiconsensual candidates. In cases of a semiconsensus, the delegates unite behind the nominee. The convention is a family reunion.

The absence of a preconvention leader characterizes nonconsensual nominations. A number of candidates actively compete to be their party's standard-bearer. The winner is the person who gains a majority of the delegates. Barry Goldwater (1964), Hubert Humphrey (1968), George McGovern (1972), Gerald Ford (1976), and Jimmy Carter (1980) are recent examples. The convention never really coalesces. It is like a large town meeting. Some delegates leave happy, others grumble. The nominee usually loses the election.

Jimmy Carter's nomination in 1976 does not exactly fit this pattern. No consensus was present at the beginning of that nomination process, but one did emerge by the end. This suggests that primaries can *build* as well as destroy party unity, that they can create a consensus when none exists.[35]

Characteristics of the Nominee

The nomination of a one-term southern governor by the Democrats in 1976 and the nomination of a former movie actor and ex–California governor by the Republicans in 1980 also indicate that changes in the preconvention process may have affected the kind of people chosen by their parties. In theory, many are qualified. The Constitution prescribes only three formal criteria for the Presidency: a minimum age of thirty-five, a fourteen-year residence in the United States, and native-born status. Naturalized citizens are not eligible for the office.

In practice, a number of informal qualifications limit the pool of potential nominees. Successful candidates have usually been well known prior to the delegate selection process. Most have had promising political careers and have held high government positions. Of all the positions from which to seek the presidential nomination, the Presidency is clearly the best. Only five incumbent Presidents (three of whom were Vice Presidents who succeeded to the office) failed in their quest for the nomination. It should be noted, however, that several others were persuaded to retire rather than face tough challenges. An incumbent President's influence over his party, especially prior to 1972, his record as President (which his party cannot easily disavow), and the prominence of his office all contribute to his renomination potential.

Over the years, there have been a variety of other paths to the White House. When the congressional caucus system was in operation, the position of secretary of state within the administration was regarded as a stepping stone to the nomination if the incumbent chose not to seek another term. When national conventions replaced the congressional caucus, the Senate became the incubator for most successful presidential candidates. After the Civil War, governors emerged as the most likely contenders, particularly for the party that did not control the White House. Governors of large states in particular possessed a political base, a prestigious executive position, and leverage by virtue of their control over their delegations.

The position of governors as potential candidates weakened with the development of national television networks in the 1950s. With most state houses not located in major population centers, governors did not get as much exposure as Washington-based officials. Lacking national media coverage in an age of television and national political experience at the time the role of government in Washington was expanding, most governors also did not possess the staffing resources which the White House and Senate provided. It is no wonder that between 1960 and 1972 all party nominees came from the upper legislative chamber or the White House. The nominations of Carter in 1976 and Reagan in 1980 have broken this trend. Yet while the rules changes and finance legislation have once again increased the opportunities for governors, they have not reduced the advantage which a national reputation and Washington experience can provide as an apprenticeship for the Presidency.

There are other informal criteria, although they have less to do with qualifications for office than with public prejudices. Only white males have ever been nominated by either of the major parties.[36] Until 1960, no Catholic had been elected, although Governor Al Smith of New York was nominated by the Democrats in 1928. Nor has there been a candidate without a northern European heritage, a surprising commentary on a country that has regarded itself as a melting pot.

Personal matters, such as health and family life, can also be factors. After George Wallace was crippled by a would-be assassin's bullet, even his own supporters began to question his ability to withstand the rigors of the office. Senator Thomas Eagleton was forced to withdraw as the Democratic vice presidential nominee in 1972 when his past psychological illness became public. Today, presidential and vice presidential candidates are expected to release medical reports on their health.

Family ties have also affected nominations and elections. There have been only two bachelors elected President, James Buchanan and Grover Cleveland.[37] During the 1884 campaign, Cleveland was accused of fathering an illegitimate child. He was taunted by his opponents: "Ma, Ma, Where's my Pa?/Gone to the White House/Ha! Ha! Ha!" Cleveland admitted responsibility for the child, even though he was not certain he was the father.

Until 1980 no divorcé had ever been elected. However, Andrew Jackson married a divorced woman, or at least a woman he thought was divorced. As it turned out, she had not been granted the final court papers legally dissolving her previous marriage. When this information was revealed during the 1828 campaign, Jackson's opponents asked rhetorically, "Do we want a whore in the White House?"[38] Jackson and Cleveland both won.

In more recent times, candidates have been hurt by marital problems and allegations of sexual misconduct. The dissolution of Nelson Rockefeller's marriage and his subsequent remarriage seriously damaged his presidential aspirations in 1964. During the critical California primary against Barry Goldwater, Rockefeller's second wife gave birth, thereby calling attention to the remarriage and prompting much anti-Rockefeller feeling. "We need a leader, not a lover" was the slogan of Goldwater partisans in California. That Adlai Stevenson was also divorced did not improve his chances. Senator Edward Kennedy's marital problems and the Chappaquiddick incident were serious detriments to his presidential candidacy in 1980 and contributed to his decision not to seek his party's nomination in 1984.[39] Reagan's election in 1980, however, suggests that at least one former taboo, being divorced, is no longer a relevant factor, at least for those who have been happily remarried for some time.

Finally, most recent presidential nominees have tended to be wealthy. Dwight Eisenhower, Gerald Ford, and, to a lesser extent, Richard Nixon were exceptions. While government subsidies have somewhat lessened the impact of personal wealth, they have not eliminated it entirely. Having a secure financial base contributes to one's ability to seek and win the nomination.

These informal characteristics for the presidential nomination apply to the vice presidential candidate as well. However, that choice has also been affected by the perceived need for geographic and ideological balance. Presidential aspirants have tended to select vice presidential candidates primarily as running mates and only secondarily as governing mates. Despite statements to the contrary, most attention is given to how the prospective nominee would help the ticket. Like the presidential nominee, parties have also insisted that the vice presidential aspirant possess all-American traits.

SUMMARY

Presidential nominating conventions have existed since the 1930s. Choosing the party's nominees, determining its platform, and unifying the party remain the principal tasks. There have been changes, however. Caused in part by the mass media and electoral reforms, these changes have resulted in greater emphasis on the public aspects of conventions and less on internal party matters.

Nominating conventions have become more visible and more open as a consequence of television. They have also become more theatrical. As news events of major proportions, they are replete with variety, drama, even suspense. Television emphasizes the activity and stresses conflict, often producing the impression of a divided convention. Party leaders have tried to counter this impression by streamlining and staging their convention to present the image of a unified group of delegates. To the extent that they have been successful, the convention has become more of an orchestrated political extravaganza and less of a participatory town meeting.

The big prize is the presidential nomination. It comes at the end of the convention, but early maneuvering can camouflage the continual quest for delegate votes. Disputes on rules or credentials are usually fought by candidate organizations and can forecast the presidential ballot. Platform issues, on the other hand, tend to reflect infighting within the party's electoral coalition. The increasing institutionalization of organized groups has increased their desire for recognition, publicity, and policy goals. This has affected not only the content of party platforms but the process of drafting them. The demands of these groups have also produced more platform challenges.

The tension between the needs of groups and the goals of the party indicates the changing nature of the political system and the increasingly difficult tasks that leaders face at the nominating conventions. In the past, state party officials made the principal demands. In most cases, their object was to extend their political influence rather than to achieve substantive policy goals. Today, the reforms have weakened state parties, strengthened candidate organizations, and led to the selection of fewer party professionals as delegates—a trend which the Democrats have attempted to reverse in 1984. These changes have made compromise more difficult, although they have also tended to make politicians of amateurs and purists. The hope of winning is still the most compelling reason for giving in—witness Ford's acquiescence on foreign policy planks in 1976 and Carter's on economic issues in 1980.

When the nomination is no longer in doubt, accommodation and conciliation are the order of the day. For the would-be standard-bearer the aim is to win in November and the immediate need is for a united party, as indicated by a supportive, nondivisive convention. Naturally, if the nomination is still in doubt, a more pressing goal is to amass or hold on to a majority of the delegates. A tight organization, geographically based, with a communications system that reaches into every state delegation, is an essential instrument. Promises made to different factions within the party may also be necessary. Creating a bandwagon or maintaining a lead requires that the candidate be poised and have a good organization in the background.

Since the object of the game is to win, having the image of a winner is crucial. Public prominence contributes to this. To party professionals especially, the best evidence of future success is past success. Factors which might detract from such success, whether political, ideological, or personal, lessen the odds of getting the nomination. This is the reason many presidential nominees possess very similar social and political attributes. In politics, the norm is often considered the ideal.

In the end, convention delegates seem to know what they are doing. The difference today is that most tend to be publicly committed. This has had two major consequences for national conventions. First, it has made them more predictable and less interesting (and, conversely, has made the preconvention process less predictable and more interesting), thereby placing an additional burden on convention organizers to make it a good show.

A second consequence is that the new delegate selection process seems to have enlarged the selection zone for potential nominees. It is unlikely that a Democratic convention prior to 1972 would have chosen a McGovern or even a Carter, or that a Reagan would have come as close as he did to defeating an incumbent President in 1976. Whether this represents a gain for democracy and/or a loss to the party system remains to be seen.

NOTES

1. The other attendants include media representatives, technicians, party leaders and rank-and-file supporters, government officials, and a host of other interested people. In 1980 the three major networks alone employed over 2,000 correspondents, technicians, and support personnel to cover the conventions. They spent an estimated $15 million each—far more than the parties themselves spent. Tom Shales, "Network vs. Network: TV at the Convention," *Washington Post,* July 13, 1980, p. G-1.

2. William Brock, quoted in Jonathan Moore (ed.), *The Campaign for President—1980 in Retrospect* (Cambridge, Mass.: Ballinger, 1981), p. 141.

3. Perhaps the most famous of all keynote addresses was William Jennings Bryan's. A relatively unknown political figure, Bryan at the age of thirty-six electrified the Democratic convention of 1896 with his famous "Cross of Gold" speech. His remarks generated so much enthusiasm that the delegates turned to him to lead them as standard-bearer. He did and lost.

4. In 1984, Democratic committees will be apportioned by the same formula used to determine the number of delegates for each state. Democratic rules also specify that state representation on the committees should be as evenly divided as possible between men and women. The composition of the Republican committees in 1984 will be similar to previous conventions—one man and one woman chosen by each state delegation.

5. In 1964, aides to presidential aspirant William Scranton, Republican from Pennsylvania, bused students from the University of California at Berkeley to the Republican convention to demonstrate on Scranton's behalf. Armed with signs supplied by the Scranton organization, they marched around the floor when Scranton's name was placed in nomination. Goldwater partisans were furious at this invasion of outsiders. After Goldwater received the nomination, some of his California supporters persuaded officials at the university's Berkeley campus to impose a rule preventing political solicitation on campus. Berkeley students protested this denial of their freedom of speech. Their protest, known as the Free Speech Movement, marked the first of the demonstrations on college campuses that rocked the 1960s.

6. Myra MacPherson, "Convention Outbursts: Artfully Rehearsed Spontaneity," *Washington Post,* August 19, 1976, p. A-13.

7. Malcom Moos and Stephen Hess, *Hats in the Ring* (New York: Random House, 1960), pp. 157–158.

8. Such protest votes have included ones for news commentators David Brinkley and Roger Mudd, Martha Mitchell (the late wife of Nixon's attorney general), Ralph Nader, Benjamin Spock, and even Eleanor McGovern, the 1972 nominee's wife. There is no law against nominating a husband and wife for President and Vice President. If

they live in the same state, however, the electors of that state could not vote for both of them.

9. Romney received 186 votes out of 1,333 cast and Bond 48½ out of 2,017¾.

10. In the course of his speech Carter made an embarrassing slip. In eulogizing the party's past heroes, he referred to the late Democratic senator and 1968 standard-bearer as "Hubert Horatio Hornblower . . . uh, Humphrey."

11. Tom Shales, "Tailored to TV," *Washington Post,* July 18, 1980, p. C-6.

12. Judith H. Parris, *The Convention Problem* (Washington, D.C.: Brookings Institution, 1972), p. 143.

13. Leonard Zeidenberg, "More Light, Less Heat in Wake of Miami Beach," *Broadcasting,* July 17, 1972, p. 16.

14. Thomas E. Patterson, *The Mass Media Election* (New York: Praeger Publishers, 1980), pp. 72–74.

15. David L. Paletz and Martha Elson, "Television Coverage of Presidential Conventions," *Political Science Quarterly,* 91 (1976), 124–127.

16. Ibid.

17. "Republicans Orchestrate a Three-Night TV Special," *Broadcasting,* August 28, 1972, p. 12.

18. Carter's renomination was assured because only a small percentage of the delegates were uncommitted and thus able to vote their consciences after the binding rule was accepted.

19. The new requirement means in essence that the convention will not force pledged delegates to exercise their pledges. However, presidential aspirants still have the right to approve delegates identified with their candidates. Once the delegates have been approved, they cannot be removed if they threaten to vote against "their" candidate.

20. Paul T. David, Ralph M. Goldman, and Richard C. Bain, *The Politics of National Party Conventions* (Washington, D.C.: Brookings Institution, 1960), p. 263.

21. This marvelously descriptive phrase comes from Jeff Fishel, "Agenda-Building in Presidential Campaigns: The Case of Jimmy Carter" (paper presented at the annual meeting of the American Political Science Association, Washington, D.C., September 1–4, 1977), p. 20.

22. Gerald M. Pomper, "Control and Influence in American Politics," *American Behavioral Scientist,* 13 (1969), 223–228; Gerald M. Pomper with Susan S. Lederman, *Elections in America* (New York: Longman, 1980), p. 161.

23. Naturally, the party controlling the White House has an advantage in accomplishing its goals. According to Pomper, between 1944 and 1968 the party in office achieved about four-fifths of its program, but even the losers gained some of their objectives. During the Nixon administration, the Democrats actually fulfilled more of their pledges than did the Republicans. Ibid.

24. Paul T. David, "Party Platforms as National Plans," *Public Administration Review,* 31 (1971), 303–315. In updating David's study, Jeff Fishel found that more than half of the 1976 Democratic platform contained future policy pledges and approximately half of them made detailed commitments. Fishel concludes, "If one compares the number of detailed pledges, the 1976 Democratic platform is considerably more specific than it was in 1960, slightly less so than in 1972." Jeff Fishel, "From Campaign Promise to Presidential Performance: The First Two (and half) Years of the Carter Presidency" (paper

presented at a colloquium of The Woodrow Wilson International Center, Smithsonian Institution, Washington, D.C., June 20, 1979), p. 27.

In examining promises and performances since 1960, Fishel also found variations among administrations. Ronald Reagan made fewer campaign promises than all his predecessors (except Johnson) and has redeemed fewer as well. For the first two years of his administration, Fishel found that Reagan had fulfilled 23 percent completely and 11 percent partially. Fishel, *Presidents and Promises: From Campaign Pledge to Presidential Performance* (Washington, D.C.: Congressional Quarterly, forthcoming).

25. Chester Bowles, *Promises to Keep: My Years in Public Life, 1941–1969* (New York: Harper & Row, 1971), p. 291.

26. Another civil rights dispute occurred in 1960—this one on the Republican side. The initial drafts of the Republican platform committee, approved by most of the party leadership, including President Eisenhower and Vice President Nixon, were criticized by Governor Nelson A. Rockefeller of New York as too weak. In an attempt to appease Rockefeller and win his active support in the forthcoming election, Nixon agreed to changes and then forced them on a reluctant platform committee. His success avoided a potentially divisive floor fight.

27. Under Democratic rules, the nominee must indicate in writing any reservations he has about the party platform. Carter glossed over his differences, emphasizing instead his agreement with the basic principals and goals of the party.

28. Fred G. Burke, "Senator Kennedy's Convention Organization," in Paul Tillett (ed.) *Inside Politics: The National Conventions, 1960* (Dobbs Ferry, N.Y.: Oceana Publications, 1962), pp. 25–39.

29. F. Christopher Arterton, "Strategies and Tactics of Candidate Organizations," *Political Science Quarterly*, 92 (1977–1978), 664–665.

30. Ibid., p. 664.

31. Donald S. Collat, Stanley Kelley, Jr., and Ronald Rogowski, "The End Game in Presidential Nominations," *American Political Science Review*, 75 (1981), 428.

32. By majority rule conventions is meant those in which the successful nominee needs only a majority of the delegates to win. Prior to 1940 the Democrats required a two-thirds vote. Ibid.

33. Ibid., p. 429.

34. William R. Keech and Donald R. Matthews, *The Party's Choice* (Washington, D.C.: Brookings Institution, 1976), pp. 160–167. The discussion of these three types of nominations is based on their description.

35. One testimony to the presence of such a consensus by the end of the nomination period is that the successful candidate has become the party's most popular leader. As Table 4–5 indicates, the candidate who was leading in the final public opinion poll won the nomination in twenty-two of the last twenty-three conventions. The lone exception was Estes Kefauver in 1952.

36. Survey data indicate that women and minority racial and religious candidates would have difficulty winning. According to a Gallup Poll conducted in the fall preceding the 1980 presidential campaign, a majority of people believed that blacks, Jews, and women would have slight, little, or no chance of being elected even if nominated by one of the major parties. Interestingly, the survey found that nonwhites were more pessimistic than whites about the chances of electing a nonwhite President, and women were more pessimistic than men about the odds against a woman winning that office. The degree

of pessimism also varied with age and education. Older and less well educated people rated the likelihood of electing such candidates lower than did those who were younger and more educated. Stephen J. Wayne, "Expectations of the President," in Doris Graber (ed.), *The President and the Public* (Philadelphia: Institute for the Study of Human Issues, 1982), pp. 32–33.

37. Historian Thomas A. Bailey reports that in his quest for the Presidency, Buchanan was greeted by a banner carried by a group of women reading, "Opposition to Old Bachelors." Thomas A. Bailey, *Presidential Greatness* (New York: Appleton-Century-Crofts, 1966), p. 74.

38. Ibid.

39. Kennedy was asked by his children not to run in 1984. They did not want their father, with whom they had lived since their parents had separated and divorced, subjected to the rigors of a full-time presidential campaign. The senator consented and announced his noncandidacy on December 1, 1982.

Selected Readings

Center, Judith A. "1972 Democratic Convention Reforms and Party Democracy," *Political Science Quarterly*, 89 (1974), 325–350.

Davis, James W. *National Conventions in an Age of Party Reform.* Westport, Conn.: Greenwood Press, 1983.

Keech, William R., and Donald R. Matthews. *The Party's Choice.* Washington, D.C.: Brookings Institution, 1976.

Malbin, Michael J. "The Conventions, Platforms, and Issue Activists," in Austin Ranney (ed.), *The American Elections of 1980.* Washington, D.C.: American Enterprise Institute, 1981.

Paletz, David L., and Martha Elson. "Television Coverage of Presidential Conventions," *Political Science Quarterly*, 91 (1976), 109–131.

Parris, Judith. *The Convention Problem.* Washington, D.C.: Brookings Institution, 1972.

Pomper, Gerald. *Nominating the President: The Politics of Convention Choice.* New York: Norton, 1966.

Reeves, Richard. *Convention.* New York: Harcourt Brace Jovanovich, 1977.

Roback, Thomas. "Amateurs and Professionals: Delegates to the 1972 Republican National Convention," *Journal of Politics*, 37 (1975), 436–468.

Sullivan, Denis, et al. "Candidates, Caucuses, and Issues: The Democratic Convention, 1976," in Louis Maisel and Joseph Cooper (eds.), *The Impact of the Electoral Process.* Beverly Hills, Calif.: Sage Publications, 1977.

Sullivan, Denis, Robert T. Nakamura, Martha Wagner Weinberg, F. Christopher Arterton, and Jeffrey L. Pressman. "Exploring the 1976 Republican Convention," *Political Science Quarterly*, 92 (1977–1978), 633–682.

Sullivan, Denis, Jeffrey Pressman, and F. Christopher Arterton, *Exploration in Convention Decision Making.* San Francisco: Freeman, 1976.

PART III

THE CAMPAIGN

Chapter 6

ORGANIZATION, STRATEGY, AND TACTICS

Introduction

Elections have been held since 1788, but campaigning by presidential candidates is a more recent phenomenon. For much of American history, major party nominees did not personally run for office. Personal solicitation was viewed as demeaning and unbecoming of the dignity and status of the Presidency.

It was not until 1860 that this tradition of nonparticipation by the nominees was broken. Senator Stephen A. Douglas, Democratic candidate for President, spoke out on the slavery issue in an attempt to heal the split that had developed within his party. However, he also denied his own ambitions while doing so. "I did not come here to solicit your votes," he told a Raleigh, North Carolina, audience. "I have nothing to say for myself or my claims personally. I am one of those who think it would not be a favor to me to be made President at this time."[1] Abraham Lincoln, Douglas's Republican opponent, refused to reply, even though he had debated him two years earlier in their contest for the Senate seat from Illinois, a contest Douglas won. Lincoln even felt that it was not proper to vote for himself. He cut his own name from the Republican ballot before he cast it for other officials in the 1860 election.[2]

Douglas did not set an immediate precedent. Presidential candidates remained on the sidelines, with party supporters making appeals on their behalf for the next eight elections. It was not until 1896 that another divisive national issue, this time free silver,[3] galvanized the country and elicited a public discussion by a presidential candidate. Again, it was the Democratic nominee who took to the stump. William Jennings Bryan, who had received the nomination following his famous "cross of gold" speech,[4] pleaded his case for free silver to groups around the country. By his own account, he traveled more than 18,000 miles, made more than 600 speeches, and, according to press estimates, spoke to almost 5 million people.[5]

Bryan's opponent that year, William McKinley, was the first Republican candidate to campaign, albeit from his own front porch. Anxious not to degrade the office to which he aspired, yet desirous of replying to Bryan's speeches, McKinley spoke to the throngs who came to his Canton, Ohio, home. Margaret Leech describes a typical McKinley performance:

> He bade them welcome to his home, and thanked them for the honor of their call. He said a few words on the campaign issues, adapting the discussion to suit the special interests of his audience. In conclusion, he expressed a desire to shake the hand of each and every one, and held an informal reception on the porch steps.[6]

In 1912, Theodore Roosevelt actively campaigned on the Progressive, or "Bull Moose," ticket. Republican candidates, however, did little more than front porch campaigning until the 1930s. Democrats, on the other hand, were more active. Woodrow Wilson and Al Smith took their campaigns to the public in 1912 and 1928, respectively. Wilson, a former university professor and president, spoke on a variety of subjects, while Smith, governor of New York and the first Roman Catholic to run for President, tried to defuse the religious issue by addressing it directly.

Radio was first used in a presidential campaign in 1928. Smith's heavy New York accent and rasping voice were faithfully captured on the air waves, probably to his detriment; the thunderous applause he received in a famous speech given in Oklahoma City on the subject of his religion was not nearly as clear. The applause and shouts sounded like a disturbance. Listeners could not tell whether Smith was being cheered or jeered.[7]

Franklin Roosevelt was the master of radio and employed it effectively in all his presidential campaigns. He also utilized the "whistle-stop" campaign train, which stopped at stations along the route to allow the candidate to address the crowds who came to see and hear him. In 1932, Roosevelt traveled to thirty-six states—some 13,000 miles. His extensive travels, undertaken in part to dispel a whispering campaign about his health, forced President Herbert Hoover onto the campaign trail.[8]

Instead of giving the small number of speeches he had originally planned, Hoover logged over 10,000 miles, traveling across much of the country. He was the first incumbent President to campaign actively for reelection. Thereafter, with the exception of Franklin Roosevelt during World War II, personal campaigning became standard for incumbents and nonincumbents alike.

Harry Truman took incumbent campaigning a step further. Perceived as the underdog in the 1948 election, Truman whistle-stopped the length and breadth of the United States, traveling 32,000 miles and averaging ten speeches a day. In eight weeks, he spoke to an estimated 6 million people.[9] While Truman was arousing the faithful by his down-home comments and hard-hitting criticisms of the Republican-controlled Congress, his opponent, Thomas Dewey, was promising new leadership but providing few particulars. His sonorous speeches contrasted sharply with Truman's straightforward attacks.

Unlike the Roosevelt years, when voter reactions to FDR were known long before the campaign began, Dewey's unexpected loss suggested that campaigns can affect election outcomes. The results of the election illustrated not only the need for incumbents to campaign but also the advantage of incumbency in campaigning, a lesson that was not lost on future Presidents.

The end of an era in presidential campaigning occurred in 1948. Within the next four years television came into its own as a communications medium. By 1952 the number of sets and viewers had grown sufficiently in the minds of campaign planners to justify a major television effort.[10] The Eisenhower organization budgeted almost $2 million for television, while the Democrats promised to use both radio and television "in an exciting, dramatic way."[11]

Television made a mass appeal easier, but it also created new obstacles for the nominees. Physical appearance became more important. Attention focused on the images candidates projected in addition to the positions they presented. The rules of the game changed accordingly.

The use of public relations techniques influenced how campaigns were planned and who planned them, what messages could be conveyed, and when and by what means. Large, complex organizations developed. Carefully calculated strategies and tactics based on fundamentals of market research were employed by candidates of both parties.

The players were also affected. Public relations experts were called on to apply the new techniques. Pollsters, media consultants, and fund raisers regularly supplemented savvy politicians in planning presidential campaigns. Even the candidates seemed a little different. With the possible exception of Johnson and Ford, who succeeded to the Presidency by the death or resignation of their predecessors, incumbents and challengers alike reflected in their appearances the grooming and schooling of the age of television.

This chapter and the one that follows discuss these aspects of modern presidential campaigns. Organization, strategy, and tactics serve as the principal focal points of this chapter, while image creation, projection, and impact are addressed in the next one.

The following section describes the structures of modern presidential campaigns and the functions they perform. It examines attempts to create hierarchical campaign organizations but also notes the decentralizing pressures. The tensions between candidate organizations and the regular party structure are discussed as well.

The basic objectives which every strategy must address are explored next. These include appealing to specific political constituencies, building an electoral coalition, and allocating financial resources. The effect of incumbency on campaign planning is also examined.

The last section of the chapter deals with tactics. It begins by describing some of the techniques used for gaining support, then turns to the targeting and timing of appeals during the campaign, and finally considers the turnout of voters on election day. Examples from past contests are used to illustrate some of these tactics of presidential campaigning.

ORGANIZATION

Running a campaign is a complex, time-consuming, nerve-racking venture. It involves coordinating a variety of functions and activities. These include advance work, scheduling, press arrangements, issue research, speech writing, polling, media advertising, finances, and party and interest group activities. To accomplish these varied tasks, a large, specialized campaign organization is necessary.

All recent presidential campaigns have had such organizations. The organizations have similar features. There is a director who orchestrates the effort and acts as a liaison between the candidate and the party, a manager charged with supervising the day-to-day activities, usually an administrative head of the national headquarters, division chiefs for special operations, and a geographic hierarchy that reaches to the state and local levels. Figure 6–1 outlines the major functional and geographic divisions of a presidential campaign organization.

Within this basic structure, organizations have varied somewhat in style and operation. Some have been very centralized, with a few individuals making most of the major strategic and tactical decisions; others have been more decentralized. Some have worked through or in conjunction with national and state party organizations; others seem to have disregarded these groups entirely and created their own field organization. Some have operated from a comprehensive game plan; others have adopted a more incremental approach.

The Goldwater organization in 1964 and the Nixon operation in 1972 exemplify the tight, hierarchical structure in which a few individuals control decision making and access to the candidate. In Goldwater's case, his chief advisers were suspicious of top party regulars, most of whom did not support the senator's candidacy. They opted for an organization of believers, one that would be run in an efficient military fashion.[12]

The initial purpose of the Goldwater organization was to take over and run the party, using its machinery to advantage. State chairmen were to coordinate and run the campaign within their states, but they were to be directed by a new national chairman, Dean Burch, and a new executive director, John Grenier, both strong supporters of the senator. Burch and Grenier appointed their own supporters to top positions within the party, including regional directors. These regional heads coordinated all campaign activities within their geographic areas. They had authority over state party chairmen. Only one of these regional directors had any national experience, however. As a consequence, when the campaign began, they turned to people they had worked within the preconvention period, not to state party leaders, for help. This produced tension between the regular Republican organization and the citizen groups which had helped Goldwater win the nomination.[13]

There are tensions in every campaign—between the candidate's organization and the party's, between the national headquarters and the field staff, between the research and operational units. Some of these tensions are the inevitable consequence of ambitious personnel frequently with large egos operating under severe time constraints and pressures. Some are the result of the need to coordinate a large, decentralized party system for a

Figure 6—1   PRESIDENTIAL CAMPAIGN ORGANIZATION

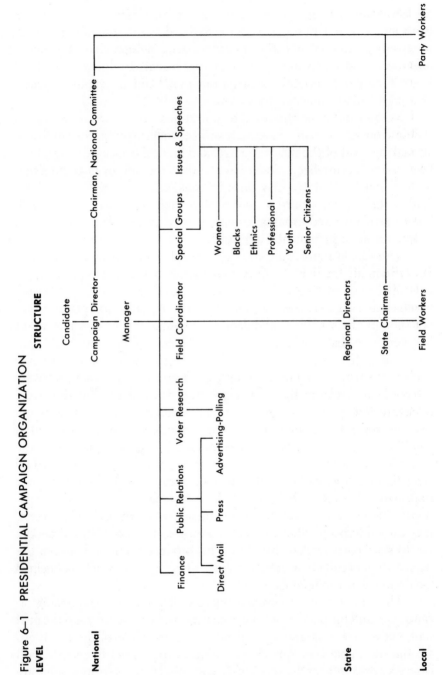

national campaign. Some result from limited resources and the struggle over who gets how much. In Goldwater's case, however, the tensions were aggravated by his circumvention of party regulars, by his concentration of decision making in the hands of a few, and by his attempt to operate with two separate campaign organizations in many states.

The same desire for control and for circumventing the party was evident in Richard Nixon's reelection campaign in 1972. Nixon's organization was larger than Goldwater's. He had a staff of 337 paid workers and thousands of volunteers.[14] Completely separated from the national party, his organization revealed no Republican connection, not even in title. The Nixon committee raised its own money, conducted its own public relations (including polling and campaign advertising), scheduled its own events, and even had its own security division, which planned and executed the dirty tricks and the Watergate burglary. The excesses of this division illustrate both the difficulty of overseeing all the aspects of a large campaign organization and the risk of placing nonprofessionals in key positions of responsibility. Had the more experienced Republican National Committee exercised more of an influence over the Nixon campaign, there might have been less deviation from the accepted standards of behavior.

Conflict can occur among individuals within a campaign organization itself. It normally results in a power struggle in which the losers are eased out of their positions and frequently forced to leave the campaign. Such a struggle occurred within the Reagan organization during the preconvention period. John Sears, the campaign director, desired to reduce the influence of several key advisers who were personally close to Reagan. Although he was initially successful, Sears eventually lost his job after Reagan's defeat in Iowa. A group of senior aides then took over and supervised the primary and later the general election campaign.

Democratic campaign organizations have tended to be looser in structure and more decentralized in operation than Republican organizations. Because Democrats for many years had stronger state parties and a weaker national financial base, their presidential candidates relied more heavily on state organizations. The Johnson organization in 1964 is a case in point.

With strong support throughout the party, President Johnson ostensibly chose the Democratic National Committee to run his campaign. John Bailey, the party chairman, was presumably in charge of coordinating state activities. However, since Bailey's task also included the election of other Democratic party hopefuls, Johnson's official campaign directors,

Lawrence O'Brien and Kenneth O'Donnell, really were the ones who co-ordinated the President's effort in the states. Theodore White reports:

> In a six-week period on the road O'Brien summoned 23 meetings of 43 state Democratic organizations, from state chairman to county level, and at night Johnson waited for O'Brien's report dictated over long-distance telephone to the White House. Meanwhile, O'Donnell directed Johnson's travel schedule.[15]

In addition to the field work done by party leaders, the Johnson campaign organization included a speech-writing team, which received input from a variety of government agencies, a public relations firm, which handled media advertising, and a group of young attorneys and government officials, who met regularly to respond to and anticipate Goldwater's statements and charges. Johnson had contact with all these groups and exercised influence over many aspects of the campaign. But so did others. Despite the President's penchant for directing the operation himself, there were many decision makers at many levels in the organizational structure.[16]

Carter's organizations in 1976 and 1980 were more centrally directed and more carefully planned than Johnson's. Since Carter did not owe his 1976 nomination to party regulars, a decision was made at the outset of his first campaign not to turn the running of it over to state parties. Out-of-state coordinators supervised state activities, creating some tension with party regulars in the process.[17] Moreover, there was little coordination with the Democratic National Commitee or with Democratic Congressional campaign committees.

At the top of Carter's organizational hierarchy were five principals: strategist and tactician Hamilton Jordan; pollster Patrick Caddell; media consultant Gerald Rafshoon; press aide Jody Powell; and policy analyst Stuart Eizenstat. Each operated with considerable autonomy within his own functional area. Major decisions were the result of group consultations in which the candidate usually participated.

The Reagan organization was less coordinated at the senior level but more efficient in the field. The staff was ostensibly headed by William Casey, a sixty-seven-year-old New York lawyer with limited political experience. Casey was asked to oversee the operation after John Sears was fired in February 1980. In actuality, a number of principal aides participated in most critical decisions. While the senior staff was loosely structured and somewhat factionalized, the regional operations were not.[18] Aided by Republican party funding and a large cadre of Reagan volunteers, state and local coordinators mobilized supporters more effectively than Republicans had in previous years.

STRATEGIC OBJECTIVES

All campaigns must have strategies. Most are articulated before the race begins; others develop during the election itself. In 1980, Carter and Reagan strategists designed elaborate plans well before their party's conventions. In contrast, Humphrey's 1968 strategy emerged after his nomination.

Certain decisions cannot be avoided when developing an electoral strategy. These decisions stem from the rules of the system, the costs of the campaign, and the character of the electorate. Each of them involves identifying objectives, allocating resources, and monitoring and adjusting that allocation over the course of the campaign. This is what a strategy is all about. It is a plan for targeting and tracking campaign resources.

Designing a Basic Appeal

In constructing a campaign strategy, it is important at the outset to identify the obstacles and opportunities that lie ahead. To do this, the strengths and weaknesses of the candidates must be carefully and continually assessed in the light of the current political environment. On the basis of this assessment, appeals can be generated and defenses prepared.

In recent times, pollsters have provided the initial assessments for the candidates. Their surveys can pinpoint changing perceptions and opinions of the public. In June 1980, Patrick Caddell gave Jimmy Carter a list of the negative perceptions of his candidacy. They included:

1. Doesn't seem to have a clear view of where he is going and why, doesn't seem to understand our problems or have solutions to them.
2. Does not think in terms of vision or quality of life and articulate these.
3. Administration decision process is often incapable of bold, rapid action; in seeking the "safe" course, often miss opportunities when timing is critical.
4. Not really on top of job.
5. Not decisive.
6. Not in control of government. Doesn't seem to want to use his power and authority.
7. Boring, not exciting.

8. He is politically expedient; seems inconsistent, swings one way and then another.
9. Is a poor communicator—often press considers speeches too poor to report seriously.[19]

To improve these perceptions, Caddell argued for a strong positive thrust in the campaign. "People must be given a positive reason to vote for Jimmy Carter," he wrote in a memo to the President.[20] Caddell's advice was difficult to translate into a popular appeal, however. By lauding the accomplishments of the administration, Carter's strategists were fearful they would convert the election into a referendum on his Presidency. Low public approval of his performance in office made this a risky undertaking. Instead, the campaign stressed personal themes: a man of the people, compassionate and concerned; a moderate, flexible decision maker; a hard-working and caring leader; a President who had learned on the job and would do better.[21] These traits, perceived as Carter's strengths, were also seen as Reagan's weaknesses.

The negative thrust of the Carter campaign was designed to accentuate personal and ideological concerns about Reagan: his lack of knowledge and energy, his insensitivity to the average person, his tendency to "shoot from the hip," his very conservative ideological and issue positions. Throughout the campaign the Carter effort was directed toward focusing attention on two candidates (Carter and Reagan) and two parties (Democratic and Republican) and not on an evaluation of the administration during the last four years. Within this thematic perspective John Anderson was considered a noncandidate. The strategy for dealing with him was to ignore him publicly and impede his ballot access privately.

In contrast, the Reagan appeal was designed to improve his image, criticize Carter's leadership, condemn the Democratic administration, and offer hope for the future. Polls conducted in the spring of 1980 by Richard Wirthlin indicated that Reagan had considerable name recognition but that little was known about him personally. Thus, the initial thrust of his presidential campaign was to provide the electorate with more personal information. Reagan's leadership abilities and his strength, competence, and decisiveness were all stressed. Only after this personal dimension was established did the campaign adopt an attack-Carter strategy.

The negative themes of the Reagan campaign strategy were directed almost exclusively against the Democratic candidate. Anderson was criticized but only enough to make him appear to be a viable contender, one who had to be taken seriously. Reagan pundits anticipated that Anderson would hurt Carter far more than their candidate, which turned out not to be the case.

The anti-Carter themes were designed to reinforce his weaknesses in the eyes of the voters. A Wirthlin memo to Reagan and other senior officials summarized these weaknesses as follows:

1. an ineffective and error-prone leader;
2. incapable of implementing policies;
3. mean-spirited and unpresidential;
4. too willing to use his presidential power politically;
5. vacillating in foreign policy, creating a climate of crisis.[22]

Building a Winning Coalition

The Electoral College strategies almost always require that both candidates concentrate much of their resources in the large industrial states with the most electoral votes. Failure to win a majority of these states makes it extremely difficult to put together a winning coalition. The question is, how much more of a candidate's resources should be allocated to these states?

A political scientist and a mathematician, Steven J. Brams and Morton D. Davis, have concluded that the larger states should receive even greater emphasis than their proportional share of the Electoral College would suggest. They have devised a mathematical formula for the most rational way to allocate campaign resources. According to the formula, resources should be allocated roughly in proportion to the 3/2's power of the electoral votes of each state. To calculate the 3/2's power, take the square root of the number of electoral votes and cube the result. Brams offers the following example: "If one state has 4 electoral votes and another state has 16 electoral votes, even though they differ in size only by a factor of four, the candidates should allocate eight times as much in resources to the larger state."[23] To illustrate:

	Electoral Votes	Square Root	Cube	Result
State A	16	4	64	=8
State B	4	2	8	

In examining the actual patterns of allocation between 1960 and 1972, Brams and Davis found that campaigns generally conformed to this rule.[24] This finding lends credence to the proposition that the large states exercise a disproportionate influence in the college, a conclusion which presidential candidates have apparently used as a guide for their own strategic planning.

In building their electoral majorities, candidates begin from positions of geographic strength, move to states in which they have some support, and compete in most of the large states regardless of the odds.

Since the establishment of their coalition in the 1930s, the Democrats have always focused on the northeastern and midwestern states. New York, Pennsylvania, Ohio, Michigan, Illinois, and Missouri form the core of the party's political base. With many of their support groups concentrated in these states, Democratic presidential candidates have an advantage. They need to win fewer states to gain an Electoral College majority. When other traditional Democratic states of the Northeast (Massachusetts, Rhode Island, and Connecticut), the Far West (Washington), the border states (Kentucky, Tennessee, and West Virginia), and the mid-Atlantic region (Maryland, the District of Columbia, and Delaware) are added to this list, the Democrats are close to victory.

For the Republicans, the task theoretically is more difficult. With none of the large states safely in their camp, the GOP must campaign and win in more states. Illinois, Michigan, Texas, and California usually figure high on any Republican list. In 1964, Goldwater was ready to concede the East and concentrate his efforts on the rest of the country. His basic strategy was to go for the states Nixon had won in 1960 plus several others in the South and Midwest. As one of Goldwater's aides put it:

> It was a regional strategy based on the notion that little campaigning would be needed to win votes in the South, no amount of campaigning could win electoral votes in New England and on the East Coast, but that votes could be won in the Midwest and on the West Coast. As the Senator said, "Go hunting where the ducks are."[25]

In 1968, Nixon strategists set their sights on ten battleground states—the big seven (see Table 6–1) plus New Jersey, Wisconsin, and Missouri—where Humphrey provided the main opposition and five peripheral southern states where Wallace was the principal foe. Together, these states had 298 electoral votes. Nixon needed to win at least 153 of them to combine with his almost certain 117 electoral votes from other states. He won 190.

Nixon's strategy of targeting the industrial states contrasted sharply with his previous presidential campaign. In 1960, he had promised to visit all fifty states, a promise he was to regret. On the day before the vote, he had to fly to Alaska to keep his campaign pledge, while Kennedy visited five East Coast states and ended with a torchlight parade in Boston.

In 1976, Ford found himself in a situation that required a broad-gauged national effort. Because of the nomination of a southerner by the Democrats, he could not count on the South or on as many other states as the Republicans had had in previous years. In fact, his strategists saw only 83 electoral votes from fifteen states as solidly Republican at the beginning of the campaign. Assuming these states to be theirs, and conceding ten states and the District of Columbia (87 electoral votes) to Carter, Ford's planners proposed a nationwide media effort to win the necessary 187 votes from the remaining twenty-five states. They were almost successful.

In contrast, Carter's strategy in 1976 was to retain the traditional Democratic states and regain the South. His goal was to win at least 71 votes from the large industrial states. He achieved each of these objectives, but only in the South was his performance really impressive. Not since 1960 had a majority of states from this region gone Democratic.

In 1980, Carter attempted to hold his 1976 coalition together. His Electoral College strategy, as designed by Patrick Caddell, had four key components:

1. Secure the South.
2. Focus on the larger industrial states (Ohio, Pennsylvania, Illinois, Texas, Michigan, New Jersey, Missouri, and Wisconsin).
3. Take New York or California.
4. Add small state targets of opportunity to the same base states.[26]

As the campaign progressed, Carter all but conceded the West to Reagan, mounting effective campaigns in only four Pacific coastal states: Washington, Oregon, California, and Hawaii.

The Reagan plan, a result of elaborate calculations,[27] was to build a western base that included California (where a Carter challenge was anticipated), target several states on the outer southern rim (Texas, Florida, and Virginia), and battle for the industrial heartland, specifically, Michigan, Illinois, and Ohio. Other states, including most of those in the South, were added during the campaign when polls showed them to be within the range of victory (see Table 6-1).

Table 6–1   EVOLUTION OF THE REAGAN GEOGRAPHIC COALITIONAL STRATEGY

Inventory of All States in Ronald Reagan's Geographic Coalition*	March Targets	June	Early September	Early October	Mid-October	Late October	Final Battleground
Large States							
California (45)	X	X	X	X	X	X	X
Illinois (26)	X	X	X	X	X	X	X
Texas (26)	X	X	X	X	X	X	X
Ohio (25)	X	X	X	X	X	X	X
Pennsylvania (27)	—	X	X	X	X	X	X
Michigan (21)	—	X	X	X	X	X	X
New York (41)	—	X	—	—	—	X	—
Medium States							
Indiana (13)	X	X	X	X	X	X	—
Virginia (12)	X	X	X	X	X	X	—
Tennessee (10)	—	—	—	X	X	X	X
Florida (17)	X	X	X	X	X	X	X
Maryland (10)	—	X	—	—	—	—	—
New Jersey (17)	X	X	X	X	X	X	X
Louisiana (10)	—	X	X	X	X	X	X
Wisconsin (11)	—	X	X	X	X	X	X
North Carolina (13)	—	—	—	—	X	X	X
Missouri (12)	X	X	—	—	—	X	X
Small States							
Idaho (4)	X	X	X	X	X	X	—
South Dakota (4)	X	X	X	X	X	X	—
Wyoming (3)	X	X	X	X	X	X	—

State (electoral votes)						
Vermont (3)	×	×	×	×	×	—
Utah (4)	×	×	×	×	×	—
Nebraska (5)	×	×	×	×	×	—
North Dakota (3)	×	×	×	×	×	—
New Hampshire (4)	×	×	×	×	×	—
Kansas (7)	×	×	×	×	×	—
Montana (4)	×	×	×	×	×	—
New Mexico (4)	×	×	×	×	×	—
Nevada (3)	×	×	×	×	×	—
Arizona (6)	—	×	×	×	×	×
Oregon (6)	×	×	×	×	×	—
Alaska (3)	×	×	×	×	×	—
Iowa (8)	×	×	×	×	×	—
Colorado (7)	×	×	×	×	×	—
Washington (9)	—	×	×	×	×	×
Maine (4)	×	×	×	×	×	×
Connecticut (8)	—	×	×	×	×	×
Oklahoma (8)	×	×	×	×	×	×
Kentucky (9)	—	—	×	×	×	×
Mississippi (7)	—	—	×	×	×	×
Alabama (9)	—	—	×	—	×	×
South Carolina (8)	—	—	×	—	×	×
Arkansas (6)	—	—	×	—	×	×

Source: Internal strategy memoranda and campaign strategy book. Reprinted in Richard B. Wirthlin, "The Republican Strategy and Its Electoral Consequences," in Seymour Martin Lipset (ed.), *Party Coalitions in the 1980s* (San Francisco: Institute for Contemporary Studies, 1981), pp. 254–255. © Copyright 1981 by the Institute for Contemporary Studies. Reprinted with permission from *Party Coalitions in the 1980s*. All rights reserved.

*Number of electoral votes is indicated in parentheses.

The geographic emphasis of independent John Anderson was dictated by his limited resources and small electoral base. Anderson had little choice but to spend much of his time and money in the big states, frequently in and around universities.

Targeting Voter Groups

Concentrating on certain states is only one aspect of a campaign design. Even within states, specific groups must be targeted and appeals directed toward them. The partisan disposition of the electorate is of primary importance in formulating and directing such appeals.

All things being equal, Democratic candidates enjoy an advantage. As the nominees of the majority party, they have a larger number of potential supporters within the electorate. By linking themselves to the party, these candidates try to maximize this numerical superiority. Every Democratic candidate since Roosevelt has adopted this tactic. In 1976 and again in 1980, Jimmy Carter mounted a strong partisan effort. By framing candidate differences in partisan terms, he hoped to induce Democrats to remain faithful to their political allegiances and support his candidacy.

Naturally, Republicans cannot depend on partisanship to win. With fewer Republicans in the electorate than Democrats, Republican nominees have tended to de-emphasize their party in their basic appeal. Ford's official campaign poster contained only his picture. His affiliation was not indicated. Nixon went so far as to separate his presidential campaign from congressional and gubernatorial races. In contrast, Ronald Reagan did not hide his partisan affiliation in 1980. He campaigned actively for other Republicans. His effort was aided by a $9 million advertising campaign which the Republican National Committee instituted on behalf of its candidates.

Normally the candidates of the minority party have tended to emphasize the issues of the day and their own leadership qualities. For the most part, they have not stressed ideology. Only Senator Barry Goldwater emphasized his conservatism. His defeat indicated that Republican presidential candidates have to do more than simply establish their conservative credentials in order to win—they must expand their coalition. In contrast, Democrats must maintain theirs.

Identifying or not identifying the party is only one way in which the partisan orientations of the electorate can be activated and reinforced. Recalling the popular images of the party is another. For the Democrats, common economic interests are still the most compelling link uniting the party's electoral coalition. Perceived as the party of common folks, the party that got the country out of the Great Depression, the party of labor and minority groups, Democrats tend to do better when economic issues are salient. This is why their candidates for President underscore the "bread and butter" issues: low unemployment, high minimum wage, maximum social security benefits, tax cuts for low- and middle-income families. Democratic candidates also emphasize the ties between the Republicans, their candidates, and big business.

For the GOP, the task seems to be to downplay economic issues. However, the increasing size of the upper middle class and its concern with high taxes and, particularly, inflation suggest that these two economic issues can be effectively used against an incumbent Democratic President, which is precisely what Ronald Reagan did in 1980. Blaming the country's economic ills on the party in power, he promised new and creative leadership to deal with these problems and improve the standard of living for millions of Americans. His appeal was directed toward those who were adversely affected by the policies of the Carter administration, particularly blue-collar workers, ethnic and religious minorities, and middle- to lower-income families in addition to the more well-to-do members of society, who are traditionally more sympathetic to the Republican appeal. In articulating his message, Reagan stressed traditional ethics, strong leadership, and a "Can Do, America" vision.[28] His themes met with increasing receptivity among the electorate as a whole, including Democratic partisans.

Table 6–2 indicates the movement of these target groups over the course of the campaign. Large gains were made among moderates, independents (particularly those who already leaned toward the Republican party), and young voters. The appeal was also successful in luring weak Democratic identifiers and blue-collar workers. An August poll by Wirthlin revealed only 34 percent of union households to be favorably disposed to Reagan's candidacy; in November he received approximately 43 percent of the vote of this group.[29]

Republican candidates usually do best when foreign and national security issues are dominant. Emphasis on their competence to deal with national security matters serves two purposes. It rekindles the more favorable perception which the electorate has of the Republican party's conduct of foreign and military policy, and somewhat conversely, it also serves to de-emphasize partisanship—which, in turn, works to the Republicans' advantage. An old adage says, "Politics stops at the water's edge." While

Table 6–2   CHANGES IN REAGAN VOTE SUPPORT BY KEY GROUPS* (IN PERCENTAGES)

	June	August	Early October	Late Oct./Nov. Tracking	Difference Oct./Nov. Minus June	Post-election
Political Groups						
Ideology						
Very conservative	54	65	57	61	+ 7	71
Somewhat conservative	50	50	49	53	+ 3	64
Moderate	26	36	31	38	+12	41
Somewhat liberal	20	24	24	27	+ 7	28
Very liberal	19	20	31	19	0	20
Partisan Strength						
Strong Republican	83	86	85	88	+ 5	91
Weak Republican	62	64	69	67	+ 5	83
Lean to Republicans	57	67	70	76	+19	83
Independent/no preference	33	36	38	41	+ 8	52
Lean to Democrats	19	15	18	14	− 5	22
Weak Democrat	24	30	24	30	+ 6	35
Strong Democrat	10	11	7	10	0	15
Demographic Groups						
Age						
17–20 years old	24	37	39	37	+13	46
20–24 years old	34			34	0	
25–29 years old	24	38	40	36	+12	48
30–34 years old	32			43	+11	
35–39 years old	42	46	40	46	+ 4	54

40–44 years old	44	43	42	48	+ 4	55
45–49 years old	51			48	– 3	
50–54 years old	40	41	38	45	+ 5	53
55–59 years old	29			45	+16	
60–64 years old	39			44	+ 5	
65 and over	36	41	38	45	+ 9	49
Education						
Some high school or less	34	34	28	37	+ 3	41
High school graduate	33	42	41	43	+10	51
Some college/vocational	41	43	39	45	+ 4	45
Postgraduate	30	37	44	42	+12	52
Income						
Under $5,000	31	24	23	NA	NA	39
$5,000–$9,000	28	39	37	NA	NA	40
$10,000–$14,000	32	41	38	NA	NA	46
$15,000–$19,999	36	42	42	NA	NA	49
$20,000–$29,999	39	40	38	NA	NA	52
$30,000–$39,999	45	46	46	NA	NA	54
$40,000 or more	48	55	55	NA	NA	67

Source: Unless otherwise noted, all surveys were conducted by Decision/Making/Information. June national survey (in person), N = 1,500; August national survey (telephone), N = 7,200; early October national survey (telephone), N = 1,300; tracking surveys (aggregate: telephone), N = 10,000; postelection survey, November 5–8 (telephone), N = 3,000. Reprinted in Richard B. Wirthlin. "The Republican Strategy and Its Electoral Consequences," in Seymour Martin Lipset (ed.), *Party Coalitions in the 1980s* (San Francisco: Institute for Contemporary Studies, 1981), pp. 246–247. © Copyright 1981 by the Institute for Contemporary Studies. Reprinted with permission from *Party Coalitions in the 1980s*. All rights reserved.

*Question: "If the full ticket for the presidential race in November were Ronald Reagan–George Bush, Republicans; Jimmy Carter–Walter Mondale, Democrats; and John Anderson–Patrick Lucey, Independents, for which ticket would you vote?"

this is not completely true, it has been the case that partisan divisions occur much more frequently over domestic matters. Thus, concentrating on foreign policy and national security affairs blurs partisanship in much the same manner as a domestic economic focus heightens it.

Dwight Eisenhower and Richard Nixon stressed their competence in foreign affairs. In 1952 Eisenhower campaigned on the theme "Communism, Corruption, and Korea," projecting himself as the most qualified candidate to end the war. Nixon did a similar thing in 1968, linking Humphrey to the Johnson administration and the war in Vietnam. Four years later, Nixon varied this tactic, painting McGovern as the "peace at any price" candidate and himself as the experienced leader who could achieve peace with honor. Gerald Ford was not nearly as successful in conveying his abilities in foreign affairs, in part because of the acknowledged expertise and statesmanship of his secretary of state and national security adviser, Henry Kissinger. Reagan pointed to the Russian invasion of Afghanistan and the Iranian hostage situation to criticize the foreign policy of the Carter administration and to urge greater expenditures for defense.

Candidates of both parties must show leadership potential regardless of their partisan affiliation, issue emphases, and policy positions. In many respects this task is more difficult and more important for the Republican candidate, given the partisan disposition of the electorate. Party identifiers tend to see their nominee in favorable terms. This puts the Republicans at a disadvantage because there are more Democrats. Thus, Republicans need to stress personal qualities. They need to have the more attractive candidate. Democrats can settle for equality.

The larger number of independents has increased Republican opportunities. It has also resulted in greater importance being placed on the personal evaluation by the public of those running for office. No longer can party affiliation alone carry a nominee to victory. Without demonstrating the potential for leadership, a candidate for the Presidency cannot hope to be successful.

Allocating Campaign Resources

The Campaign Finance Act of 1976 was supposed to equalize spending between the major party candidates in the general election. At the national level it has. If Republican and Democratic nominees accept public funds, their expenditures are limited by and to the amount they receive from the government. In 1980, this figure was $29.4 million each.

Although major party candidates who accept public funds cannot supplement their campaigns through private contributions, they can raise and spend money for the accounting and legal costs of complying with the law. In addition, the parties' national committees can spend a limited amount on behalf of their presidential and vice presidential nominees. In 1980 this amount could not exceed $4.6 million. The Republican National Committee spent most of this for the Reagan-Bush ticket; the Democratic National Committee raised only $4 million and spent about half on Carter and Mondale, with the rest going to support activities of other Democrats.

Major party candidates who do not accept public funds are not restricted to these expenditure limits. They can spend all they can raise. However, the law still prohibits them from accepting contributions of more than $1,000 per person. This makes fund raising harder and more expensive than it was when a few wealthy individuals could be counted on for very large donations.

The only way for a candidate's organization to raise sufficient sums from a large number of small contributors is by direct mail and/or television. Not only is this costly and time-consuming, but the results are unpredictable. Not knowing when and how much money will be available makes planning difficult.

Take television advertising, for example. Time must be purchased well in advance of the broadcast. The ads must be created, filmed, and edited. A shortage of money in the early stages of the campaign affects later purchases and can result in the loss of valuable prime-time slots. It can also cause a delay in producing and airing television spots. This hurt John Anderson in 1980.

Campaigning as an independent, Anderson was entitled to receive federal funds only if he received at least 5 percent of the popular vote. He ended up receiving $4.2 million, but *after* the election. As a consequence, he had to depend on private contributions to pay for most of his expenditures.

In 1976 and again in 1980 the Republican and Democratic candidates accepted government funds. The amount they had to spend was considerably less than what Nixon had in 1972. In order to maximize the impact of these limited funds and reach the largest number of voters, candidates spend relatively large proportions of their money on the media. In 1976, approximately half of the budget went to the media. In 1980 it was even more. Reagan spent an estimated $17 million on advertising, including $10.5 million for television, $1.4 million for radio, and $1.9 million for print media. Carter spent $20 million, with the bulk of it going to television. Anderson spent $2.3 million on media advertising, most of it in the final week of the campaign.[30]

Because of large media and polling expenditures, other aspects of the campaign such as field operations have received less support from the candidate organizations than in the past. State and regional coordinators have relatively less money available and less discretion over spending than they had before 1976. Not only must tight budget controls be exercised over all budget activities at the national level, but careful records of all expenditures must be kept and timely reports made.

Governmental and political activities have to be differentiated for Presidents and Vice Presidents seeking reelection. Thus, Presidents Ford and Carter had to reimburse the Treasury for the costs of using Air Force One during campaign trips. Aides budgeted to the White House can campaign for their President, but aides budgeted to other units in the Executive Office of the President cannot.

In summary, the allocation of resources is a critical element in any campaign strategy. Given the contribution limits, there seems to be little alternative to accepting public funds, yet the amount of public support is barely sufficient to mount an effective campaign for two months in all fifty states. As a consequence, most presidential candidates have devoted the bulk of their resources to the media. The situation for independent and third-party candidates has been even more desperate.

The financial plight of candidates for the Presidency has increased the importance of political action committees and state and local party committees. Their independent activities can have a significant impact on the results of the election. Labor's organizing efforts were instrumental in Carter's being elected in 1976; conservative PACs and state and local Republican party committees helped expand Reagan's margin of victory in 1980. These groups can be expected to play an even larger role in 1984.

Dealing with the Incumbency Factor

A final strategic consideration is incumbency. It insures visibility and respectability; it testifies to experience; it provides a record of accomplishments. The best testimony to the power of incumbency is the success of incumbent Presidents who have sought election or reelection. In the twentieth century, thirteen incumbent Presidents have run for election and nine of them have won. Franklin Roosevelt was reelected three times.

Three Republican Presidents, William Howard Taft, Herbert Hoover, and Gerald Ford, and one Democratic incumbent, Jimmy Carter, lost in the twentieth century. Extraordinary circumstances help explain the Republicans' defeats. The Bull Moose candidacy of Theodore Roosevelt in 1912 divided the larger Republican vote between Roosevelt (4.1 million) and Taft (3.5 million). Woodrow Wilson's 6.3 million was thus sufficient to win. The growing depression of the 1930s and the seeming incapacity of the Hoover administration to cope with it swung Republican and independent votes to Franklin Roosevelt. The worst political scandal in the nation's history and the worst economic recession in forty years adversely affected Ford's chances. Nonetheless, he almost won. Ford's narrow loss suggests how potent a factor incumbency can be.

Jimmy Carter's loss, however, portends another lesson, one that may increasingly beset modern Presidents. Incumbency is not necessarily an advantage in an age of high expectations, particularly if people believe that their standard of living has deteriorated over the course of an administration. Rightly or wrongly, the public places responsibility for economic conditions, social relations, and foreign affairs on the President. That he may actually exercise little control over some of these external factors seems less relevant to the electorate than their perception of the conditions, their desire that they be improved, and their expectation that the President do something about them.

The advantage of incumbency stems from the visibility of the office, the esteem it engenders, and the influence it provides. Being President guarantees recognition. The President is almost always known. A portion of the population usually has difficulty at the outset in identifying his opponent. Thus, a key element in most nonincumbents' strategies is to increase name recognition at the beginning of the campaign. Reagan was an exception because he was so well known as an actor, ex-governor, and presidential candidate.

Another advantage of incumbency is the credibility and respect which the office usually engenders. Naturally, this rubs off on the President. In the election, the incumbent's strategy is obvious: run as President. Create the impression that it is the President against some lesser-known and less qualified individual. In the words of Peter Dailey, Richard Nixon's chief media adviser in 1972:

Our basic effort was to stay with the President and not diffuse the issue. We thought that the issue was clearly defined, that there were two choices—the President (and I mean that distinction—not Richard Nixon, but the President) and the challenger, the candidate George McGovern. We wanted to keep the issue clearly defined that way.[31]

In 1980 that same media adviser was projecting Reagan's presidential qualities: his experience as California governor, his strong and decisive manner, his views on a variety of current issues.

The ability of a President to make news, to affect events, and to dispense the "spoils" of government can also magnify the disparity between an incumbent and a challenger. Presidents are in the limelight and can maneuver to remain there when it is to their advantage. The media focus is always on the White House. In the first phase of his 1980 campaign, President Carter adopted a "Rose Garden" strategy. He signed and vetoed legislation, made statements, held press conferences, received dignitaries, and, in general, visibly performed his duties as President. Television reported his activities at no cost to his campaign, while Governor Carter had to buy time to get himself and his views before the public.[32]

Presidents have another advantage. Presumably, their actions can influence events. Economic recoveries are geared to election years if possible. Foreign policy decisions can also be timed to maximize or minimize their electoral impact. In 1980 the Reagan campaign feared an "October surprise," an action by Carter late in the campaign that would build public support for the President. To minimize the impact of such an event (such as the return of American hostages from Iran), Reagan aides referred to the possibility of such an occurrence and even planned speeches and television advertisements to counter it.

Incumbents are generally perceived as more experienced and knowledgeable, as leaders who have stood the tests of the office in the office. From the public's perspective, this creates a climate of expectations that works to the incumbent's advantage most of the time. Since security is one of the major psychological needs which the Presidency serves, the certainty of four more years with a known quantity is likely to be more appealing than the uncertainty of the next four years with an unknown one, provided the initial four years were viewed as acceptable.

Translated into strategic terms, this requires that the incumbent play on public fears of the future. His campaign normally highlights his opponent's lack of experience and knowledge and contrasts it with his own experience and record in office. Johnson in 1964, Nixon in 1972, and Ford in 1976 all adopted this approach. Carter used a variation of it in 1980. He emphasized the arduousness of the job in order to contrast his energy, knowledge, and intelligence with Reagan's.

There is little a challenger can do in response other than act as presidential as possible to try to narrow the psychological gap in the voters' minds. The nonincumbent will also point to his own positions and criticize the President's lack of accomplishments. In 1980, Reagan's advertisements lauded his achievements as governor of California, a job which was described as "the biggest in the nation next to the Presidency."

Finally, being President provides an incumbent with the capacity to benefit certain individuals, groups, and areas of the country. The timing of grants, the making of appointments, the supporting of legislation, the stating of positions—all have political impact. White House staff and cabinet officials, acting as surrogates of the President, can be used effectively to promote the President's programs and policies around the country. While these activities occur throughout an administration, they are more newsworthy and potentially more influential during a campaign. A President can damage his reputation, however, if his actions appear to be solely or primarily for political purposes, such as Ford's pardon of Nixon in 1974 and Carter's announcement of grants during his reelection campaign.

Having a record in office helps to generate an image of leadership. Clearly, this tends to benefit incumbents. But a record, or especially a lack of achievement, can be harmful as well. Carter's inability to obtain the release of the Iranian hostages illustrates how inaction can adversely affect a President's image.

Incumbency is a two-edged sword. It can strengthen or weaken a claim to leadership. That is why incumbents point to their accomplishments, note the work that remains, and sound a "let us continue," "stay the course" theme. Challengers, in contrast, will argue that it is time for a change and that they can do better, while at the same time alluding to their own presidential qualities. In the end the advantage may not always be with the incumbent if the times are bad or a sufficient number of grievances have accumulated.

THE REAGAN STRATEGY IN 1980*

(1) Without alienating the Reagan base, we can beat Jimmy Carter twenty-five days from now if we continue to expand it to include more
  • Independents
  • Anderson voters
  • Disaffected Democrats—union members, Catholics
  • Urban ethnics and Hispanics
  to offset Carter's larger Democratic base and the incumbency advantage.

We should *not* break any major new issue ground except in the foreign policy and highly targeted "social" issue areas. The thrust of our speeches to accomplish this condition must be directed toward:
- Inflation
- Jobs
- Economic growth and
- A more responsible and more efficient federal government

(2) Allocate all campaign resources carefully against the target list of battleground states.

We must remember that the successful outcome of many months of effort hinges on just the few percentage points we garner marginally in less than ten states.

Sufficient media funds should be available to purchase heavy spot market exposure in a few key states during the final two weeks.

The time commitments of Ronald Reagan and George Bush must be assessed and assigned against state target priorities.

Event schedules should be kept free of low-milage meetings or events and provide sufficient personal time to *recharge* during the closing days of the campaign.

(3) Focus campaign resources to reinforce the Governor's image strengths that embody the presidential values a majority of Americans think are important:
- Leadership
- Competence
- Strength and
- Decisiveness

At the same time, we must minimize the perception that he is dangerous and uncaring.

Ultimately the voters will choose the man they believe best suited to *lead* this country in the decade of the 80s. In addition to the above general "leader perceptions" we need to reinforce, we must give the voter the opportunity to get a glimpse of the quality, skill, and experience of the men and women that a Reagan Administration would attract.

(4) Reinforce through our media and spokespersons Carter's major weaknesses—that he is:
- An ineffective and error-prone leader
- Incapable of implementing policies
- Mean-spirited and unpresidential
- Too willing to use his presidential power politically, and
- Vacillating in foreign policy, creating a climate of crisis

A sharp contrast must be drawn between Carter's political promises and his performance.

Given Carter's proclivity to mount personal and vindictive attacks, we have the opportunity to play it very cool and come out of those exchanges more "presidential" than "President" Carter. In sum, the voters do not want Carter, but are not yet quite sure of us. His outbursts help. They may be muted, but they will continue.

(5) Neutralize Carter's "October Surprise," and avoid fatal, self-inflicted blunders.

(6) Position the campaign to pick up as much of the Anderson vote as possible as Anderson fades in the stretch.

It appears Anderson has not achieved the national momentum necessary to sustain a viable candidacy. Anderson's national base may be no larger than 6–8 percent and significant only in New York, Massachusetts, and the Northeast generally.

Furthermore, on November 4th, many loyal Anderson voters will be confronted with the reality of "throwing away" their votes if they stay with Anderson. In all probability many of these voters will opt not to vote for Anderson, and will cast a vote for either Reagan or Carter because they are vehemently against one of the candidates.

Now, Carter carries more negative baggage than Reagan. Every effort should be made to appeal to these voters, giving them every reason to vote for Reagan. The target Anderson states—Illinois, Connecticut, Pennsylvania, Ohio, Michigan and New England generally.

(7) Maintain control of the thrust of our campaign by refusing to let it become event-driven especially in the last two weeks. Be prepared to end the campaign either on a hard note or a high note depending on the momentum and level of support we achieve next week.

*Richard B. Wirthlin, "Memorandum to Ronald Reagan, October 9, 1980," in Richard Wirthlin, Vincent Breglio, and Richard Beal, "Campaign Chronicle," *Public Opinion*, IV (1981), p. 44. © 1981, American Enterprise Institute for Public Policy Research, Washington, D.C. 20036.

THE CARTER STRATEGY IN 1980*

FIRST, and foremost, *the campaign had to be a question of the future, not the past. It had to be a choice for president, not a referendum on the Carter administration.* To this end, we wanted to focus on the presidency itself, to stress the importance and extreme sensitivity of the office, and to emphasize the question of which individual might better be trusted with the responsibility.

SECOND, it was imperative that the perception of Carter's job performance be improved, and that the incumbency be used to the best advantage. "Hard" news—governmental, noncampaign actions and results—was more valuable than softer, campaign news.

THIRD, Carter had to be portrayed as a president who had learned and who would be a better president in a second term. Polls indicated that most voters accepted this argument, and we believed that if Reagan faltered, many would need to utilize this rationale in voting for the president.

FOURTH, the campaign wanted to portray the president as being in the mainstream of American political beliefs, in contrast to Ronald Reagan.

FIFTH, the issue had to be Ronald Reagan. Nineteen eighty was a negative political year when every contender was burdened with high negative ratings. It was imperative that Reagan, his positions, and his weaknesses be the focus of public attention. This was particularly true on the issue of "war and peace"—the most "presidential" of issues.

SIXTH, the Democrats must be united. Carter was the nominee of the majority party. His chief electoral problems, many stemming from the primaries, lay among Democratic constituencies: liberal, blue-collar, union, Catholic, Jewish, and weak-preference Democrats.

SEVENTH, the South and Northern industrial states were of necessity the core of the electoral college strategy. Those two regions elected Carter in 1976, and would have to do so again in 1980. Carter's regional appeal had to be capitalized upon. Initial efforts had to be directed to the North, and particularly to the suburbs, where Carter had run poorly in 1976 but where Reagan was highly suspect.

EIGHTH, John Anderson had to be weakened. Anderson's independent candidacy initially hurt Carter among key constituencies in most major Northern states.

TACTICAL CONSIDERATIONS

Whereas the basic objectives set the contours of the campaign strategy, tactical considerations influence day-to-day decisions. Tactics are the specific ways in which the ends are achieved. They involve techniques, targets, and timing: how appeals will be made, to whom, and when. Unlike strategy, which can be planned well in advance, tactics change with the environment and events, ideology and issues, party and participants. The circumstances, in short, dictate different tactical responses.

Techniques

There are a variety of ways to convey a political message. They include door-to-door canvassing, direct mail, and media advertisements. At the local level especially, door-to-door campaigning may be a viable option. Obviously, presidential candidates and their national staffs cannot directly engage in this kind of activity in the general election even though they may have in the early primaries. However, presidential staffs can help generate such a canvass by prodding or coordinating the efforts of state parties, citizen volunteers, and interest groups.

The Kennedy organization in 1960 was one of the first to mount such a campaign on the local level. Using the canvass as a device to identify supporters and solicit workers, Kennedy's aides built precinct organizations out of the newly recruited volunteers. The volunteers, in turn, distributed literature, turned out the voters, and monitored the polls on election day. They were instrumental in Kennedy's narrow victory in several states.

The procedures for coordinating a door-to-door campaign are fairly straightforward, but they do involve a lot of work. A national field coordinator, designated by the national headquarters, normally oversees the operation. He is assisted by regional coordinators who, in turn, supervise the activity of the state organizers.

The object is to identify potential supporters, provide them with information, and get them to vote. Canvassers usually follow a set routine that carefully avoids alienation and argumentation. Here's an example of a typical approach—the one, incidentally, that Nixon campaigners used in 1972.

"Hello, my name is ————. I am a volunteer working for the reelection of President Nixon. We believe President Nixon is an outstanding President. May we count on your support and vote for President Nixon on November 7?"

IF NO: "Thank you for your time. Goodbye."

IF UNDECIDED: "We think President Nixon is the best man for the job, and we hope you decide to join us in voting for him."
"We certainly thank you for your time. Goodbye."

IF YES: 1. "Do you usually vote Republican?"
    2. "Are all Nixon supporters in your home registered to vote at this address?"

IF NOT REGISTERED: "Could you give me (your/their) name(s)? Here is information on how to register to vote. Please register soon."

IF REGISTERED: "Good."
    3. "Would you volunteer to help us in President Nixon's campaign?"

IF YES: "That's great. I'll be happy to have our volunteer chairman call you."

IF NO: "I understand."
    4. "Is there a chance that you may be away on November 7th and will need to vote absentee for President Nixon?"

IF YES: "Here is complete information on how to vote absentee."

IF NO: Go on to closing statement.
    5. "Thanks so much for your time. May we have your name and phone number for our records? Thanks again. Goodbye."[33]

The Nixon organization was not trying for a hard sell. Its object was simply to identify voters and get them to the polls. Nixon campaign officials were so confident that they felt no persuasion was necessary.

Personal contact is generally considered to have a greater impact on voters than any other kind of campaign activity. It is most effective in stimulating voting. To a lesser extent, it may also influence the decision on how to vote. Other appeals, such as direct mail and media advertising, are less effective. However, they are also easier to make and are less of a drain on the campaign organization. In fact, outside experts are usually "brought in" or hired to do them.

Direct mailings, frequently utilized in fund raising, have also been employed to distribute information about the candidate and the party. Letters can be made to look personal. They are designed for the specific people to whom they will be sent. Modern computers can even include the addressee's name in different parts of the letter. For conveying a substantive message to a specific audience, direct mail is efficient and effective. It has been used extensively in congressional elections and will be used increasingly by presidential candidates in their quest for the nomination.

Another option is television, but it is more costly and less personal. Its benefits are many, however. Television can reach large numbers of people. It is less taxing on the candidate than extensive personal campaigning. It facilitates control over the political environment. While messages cannot be tailored as precisely as they can in individualized letters, they can be designed to create and project favorable images and can be aimed at specific groups of voters.

But no matter how extensive a candidate's use of television may be, a certain amount of personal campaigning will always be necessary. Appearances by presidential hopefuls create news, often becoming media events. These appearances can also promote a sense of unity in the party that benefits all of its nominees, not just the presidential and vice presidential candidates. Appearances make the candidate seem real to the voters and testify to his concern for them. No area or group likes to be taken for granted.

The problem with personal appearances is that they are personally wearing, have limited impact, cost a lot of money, and can be dangerous. Making arrangements is itself a complex, time-consuming venture. It requires the work of experts to make certain that everything goes smoothly, from scheduling to physical arrangements to the rally itself. Jerry Bruno, who advanced Democratic presidential campaigns in the 1960s, described his task in the following manner:

> It's my job in a campaign to decide where a rally should be held, how a candidate can best use his time getting from an airport to that rally, who should sit next to him and chat with him quietly in his hotel room before or after a political speech, and who should be kept as far away from him as possible.
>
> It's also my job to make sure that a public appearance goes well—a big crowd, an enthusiastic crowd, with bands and signs, a motorcade that is mobbed by enthusiastic supporters, a day in which a candidate sees and is seen by as many people as possible—and at the same time have it all properly recorded by the press and their cameras.[34]

Bruno did not work alone. Numerous people are employed on advance staffs. In 1968, when Humphrey desperately needed to create an impression of public support at his speeches and rallies, his national organization had more than 125 people doing this kind of work.[35]

Even with all the advance preparations, the public appearance may have a limited impact—or, even worse, a negative one. If the crowds are thin, if the candidate is heckled, if a prominent public figure refuses to be on the platform with the candidate or if a controversial one does appear, or if the candidate makes a verbal slip, the appearance may do more harm than good.

In 1964, for example, a number of prominent Republicans declined to appear with Senator Goldwater. Their unwillingness to be on the same platform with the party's nominee testified to the continued split in the Republican party. Similarly, in 1972, prominent Democrats, particularly from the South, shied away from endorsing Senator McGovern's candidacy or even appearing to support him in public. A great effort was made by Jimmy Carter in 1980 to get Senator Kennedy to appear on the same platform with him at the Democratic convention. Kennedy did, but only briefly, and then failed to raise his hands with Carter in the traditional victory pose.

The arduous and exhausting schedules of modern campaigns have also contributed to displays of emotion by candidates that have embarrassed them and damaged their public image. One of the most highly publicized of these incidents occurred during the 1972 New Hampshire primary. Senator Edmund Muskie, the Democratic front-runner, broke into tears when defending his wife from the attacks of William Loeb, publisher of the *Manchester* (New Hampshire) *Union Leader*. In the minds of some, the crying incident made Muskie look weaker and less presidential. It raised the question, could he withstand the pressures of the Presidency? George McGovern, who benefited from the Muskie episode, expressed his own frustration toward the end of his presidential campaign. When passing a vociferous heckler at an airport reception, McGovern told his critic, "Kiss my ass!" The press dutifully reported the senator's comment.[36]

In 1976 and again in 1980 each of the major party candidates made questionable statements that were highlighted by the media. In the midst of the Democratic primaries in 1976, Carter stated that he saw nothing wrong with people trying to maintain the "ethnic purity" of their neighborhoods. After some people interpreted his remarks as racist, Carter indicated that he had made an error in his choice of words, promptly retracted them, and apologized. During the general election of 1980 he indirectly accused Reagan of being warlike and a racist by suggesting to his audience that the choice was not only between two men but two futures: "whether this nation will make progress or go backward . . . whether we have war or peace . . . whether Americans might be separated, black from white, Jew from Christian, North from South, rural from urban."[37] Although Carter denied he was making specific references to Reagan, his comments were viewed as mean and nasty, and his presidential image suffered accordingly.[38]

Republican nominees have also made verbal slips, factual errors, and offhand comments which adversely affected their candidacies. During his second debate with Jimmy Carter, President Ford asserted that the Soviet Union did not dominate Eastern Europe. His comment, picked up and repeated by the media, led critics to wonder whether he really understood the complexities of international politics, much less appreciated the Soviet Union's influence in Eastern Europe. Ronald Reagan's much-quoted reference to trees as being a primary source of pollution brought him considerable ridicule during the campaign, although the remark was made prior to it. Reagan's statements doubting the theory of evolution, favoring the reestablishment of government relations with Taiwan, and contrasting his Labor Day appearance in Michigan with Carter's in Tuscumbia, Alabama, "the city that gave birth to and is the parent body of the Ku Klux Klan,"[39] also raised concerns about his intelligence, knowledge, and competence to be President.

Targeting Issues

Candidates are normally very careful about their public utterances. Knowing that the press focuses on inconsistencies and highlights controversies, presidential candidates tend to stick to their articulated public positions. In fact, they often give the same basic speech many times during the campaign.

When speeches are tailored to specific groups, the general practice is to tell the audience what they want to hear. Naturally, this creates a favorable response which, in turn, helps to project a positive image when covered by the media.

Occasionally, however, candidates will use the opposite tactic. In order to exhibit their courage and candor, they will announce a policy to an unsympathetic audience. Carter did this in 1976 when he told an American Legion convention of his intention, if elected, to issue a blanket pardon to Vietnam draft dodgers. Barry Goldwater took a similar approach. In order to emphasize the purity of his conservative convictions,

Goldwater made a speech in Appalachia in 1964 criticizing the war on poverty as phony, and in Tennessee he suggested the possibility of private ownership of the Tennessee Valley Authority.[40] While the senator did not win many converts, he did succeed in maintaining his image as a no-nonsense conservative.

A third approach when discussing issues is simply to be vague. This allows potential supporters to see what they want to see in a candidate's position. Dwight Eisenhower succeeded with this approach in 1956, but Thomas Dewey did not eight years earlier. Many candidates use this tactic effectively by conveying a plan of action without encumbering it in a myriad of details. Reagan was able to pull this off in 1980 by virtue of his impressive communicative skills and strong ideological stands. Carter was less successful when he was a challenger in 1976. His emphasis on his own personal attributes, combined with his centrist position, left the impression that he waffled on the issues, an impression that the Ford campaign was quick to reinforce. In general, taking positions tends to be more important in the primaries, when party is not a factor, than during the general election, when it is.

Timing

In addition to the problem of whom to appeal to and what to say, it is also important to decide when to make the appeal. Candidates naturally desire to build momentum as their campaigns progress. This usually dictates a phased effort, especially for the underdog. Phasing frequently includes a combination of unifying negative and positive thrusts.

Goldwater's campaign of 1964 illustrates the plight of the challenger. Having won the Republican nomination after heated primary contests with Nelson Rockefeller, the senator initially had to reunite the party. The first month of his campaign was directed toward this goal. Endorsements were obtained; the party was reorganized; traditional Republican positions were articulated. Phase two was designed to broaden Goldwater's electoral support. Appeals to conservative Democratic and independent voters were made on the basis of ideology. The third phase was the attack. Goldwater severely criticized President Johnson, his Great Society program, and his liberal Democratic policies. In phase four, the Republican candidate enunciated his own hopes, goals, and programs for America's future. Finally, at the end of the campaign, perceiving that he had lost, Goldwater became increasingly uncompromising in presenting his conservative beliefs.[41]

In 1976, Gerald Ford also faced the problem of unifying the Republican party after a divisive selection process. The first stage of his campaign was directed to this goal as well as to broadening his popular appeal. Cutting Carter down to size was the focus of stage two. Like Goldwater, Ford also trailed his Democratic rival in the polls. Unlike Goldwater, he was able to close the gap by pointing to Carter's personal and political vulnerabilities. In the third part of his campaign, Ford sought to accentuate the positive. His speeches and advertisements stressed the achievements of his administration and his goals for the future. The theme of his ads, feeling good about America, was designed to generate a positive feeling toward the President and build momentum in the final days of the campaign.

In 1980 the Reagan organization also divided its campaign into three phases. The first, from the end of the primaries until Labor Day, was aimed at solidifying the Republican base of support. The second, from early September to mid-October, was designed to expand that base by appealing to blue-collar workers, ethnic and religious minorities, and political moderates. The final phase was directed at turning out a large Reagan vote.[42]

In staging any campaign it is necessary to build some flexibility into the strategic design. The allocation of resources, the use of techniques, even the projection of appeals may have to be tempered by changing political conditions. However, an effective strategy should not be controlled by events. That was the Reagan campaign's rationale for anticipating an October surprise. In the words of Richard Wirthlin, "a campaign strategy survives the rigors of a crisis-driven presidential election to the degree that it . . . evolves without surrendering its basic propositions every time pressures mount demanding a new direction."[43]

Turnout

When all is said and done, it is the electorate who makes the final judgment. Who votes can be the critical factor in determining the winner in a close election. Turnout is influenced by a number of variables: the demographic characteristics and political attitudes of the population, registration laws and procedures, the kind of election and its competitiveness, and even the weather. Turnout can also be affected by the campaign itself.

On balance, lower turnout tends to hurt the Democrats more than the Republicans because a larger proportion of their party identifiers are in the lower educational and socioeconomic levels, where people are less likely to vote. Thus, a key element in the strategy of most Democratic candidates since Franklin Roosevelt has been to maximize the number of voters by having a large registration drive.

Traditionally it is the party, not the candidate's central headquarters, that mounts the drive. The party, through its state affiliates, is usually in a better position than a fledgling candidate organization to conduct a large-scale effort. Besides, increased registration benefits the entire party, not just its presidential candidate.

Since the party plays a major role in the registration of voters, a party divided at the time of its convention can seriously damage its chances in the fall. This is especially true for the Democrats. A case in point was the Humphrey campaign of 1968. Humphrey received the nomination of a party which took until late October to coalesce behind his candidacy. This was too late to register a large number of voters. Were it not for organized labor's efforts in registering approximately 4.6 million voters, Humphrey probably would not have come as close as he did.

Whereas Humphrey's loss in 1968 can be partially attributed to a weak voter registration drive, Carter's victory in 1976 resulted in part from a successful one. The Democratic National Committee coordinated and financed the drive. With the support of organized labor, Democrats out-registered Republicans. Labor's efforts in Ohio and Texas contributed to Carter's narrow victory in both states. A successful program to attract black voters also helped increase Carter's margin of victory.

In 1980, Carter's lukewarm support from labor and his party's weak financial position adversely affected Democratic registration efforts. In contrast, the Republican party in conjunction with the Reagan campaign, stepped up its registration activities. The party's superior financial base enabled it to use telephone banks to identify potential supporters, and state and local Republican committees thereby mounted highly successful get-out-the-vote drives.

SUMMARY

Campaigning by presidential nominees is a relatively recent phenomenon. Throughout most of the nineteenth century, presidential campaigns were fairly simple in organization and operation and rather limited in scope. With the exception of William Jennings Bryan, there was little active involvement by the candidates themselves.

Changes began to occur in the twentieth century. They were largely the consequence of developments in transportation and communications that permitted more extensive travel and broader public appeals. First the railroad and then the airplane encouraged campaigning across the country; first radio and then television enabled the candidates to reach millions of voters directly. These developments made campaigning more complex, more expensive, and more sophisticated. They also required more personal activity by the candidates. Organizations expanded, and strategy and tactics became more highly geared to the mass media.

Campaign organizations have increased in size and expertise. Supplementing the traditional cadre of party professionals are the professionals of the new technology: pollsters, media consultants, direct mailers, lawyers, accountants, and a host of other specialists. Their inclusion in the candidate's organization has had two major effects: it has increased the tendency toward decentralized decision making and has accelerated the division between the party and its nominee. Two separate organizations, one very loosely coordinated by the national committee and the other more tightly controlled by the candidate and his senior aides, function in presidential elections, sometimes working in tandem and sometimes not.

The job of campaign organizations is to produce a unified and coordinated campaign effort. Most follow a general strategy prepared in advance to accomplish this primary objective. In designing such a strategy, planners must consider the attitudes and perceptions of the electorate, the geography of the Electoral College, the allocation of campaign resources, and, frequently, the performance of the incumbent.

In designing a basic appeal and targeting it to specific groups within the population, partisan factors must be considered, since the voting behavior of a sizable portion of the electorate is affected by their political attitudes. Democratic candidates emphasize their link to the party and stress those bread-and-butter economic issues that have held their majority coalition together in most presidential elections since the 1930s. Republican candidates, on the other hand, often de-emphasize party, stressing instead personality and leadership qualities. The issues they are likely to accentuate are in the foreign policy and national security spheres.

Most strategies have a geographic emphasis. For Democrats, this normally includes the large industrial states of the East and Midwest plus Texas and California. For the Republicans, the Midwest, Rocky Mountain, and Far West states offer the most promise, with the southern states not far behind. Certain highly competitive states that appear on both "must" lists enjoy more activity and greater media focus.

Financial planning is an important strategic consideration. As a consequence of legislation passed during the 1970s, fund raising is no longer a principal concern for major party candidates who accept federal funds in the general election. It still is, however, for independent and third-party candidates. Public support for the campaigns of the Democratic and Republican nominees has not eased their expenditure problems. In fact, it has made them more difficult because the amount of money is barely sufficient and it cannot be directly supplemented.

As a consequence, presidential campaigns in 1976 and 1980 have maintained their heavy media emphasis by allocating a large proportion of their funds for television. Organizational support and nonmedia activities suffered in 1976. In 1980, state and local party committees helped to fund some of these activities with the Republicans the principal beneficiary.

In 1976 and again in 1980, incumbency was a factor and issue that weighed heavily in the strategies of the principal candidates. The incumbents campaigned as President and tried to take advantage of the prestige, power, and publicity of their position. The challengers criticized the President, not the Presidency, and promised to provide new, stronger, and more decisive leadership for the next four years. The results of both elections indicate that the voters chose to rely on this promise for the future not on the performance of the past.

While strategy is more long-term in conception and even in execution, tactics have a greater effect on day-to-day events. Key tactical decisions include what techniques will be utilized, when, and by whom. They also include what appeals will be made, how they will be made, and when they should be made. Other than being flexible, it is difficult to generalize about tactics. Much depends on the basic strategic plan, the momentum of the campaign, and the development of events. In the end, the methods that mobilize the electorate by getting people excited about a candidate are likely to be of the greatest benefit in turning out and influencing the vote. Image creation, production, and projection lie at the heart of this process. The next chapter explores this aspect of campaigning.

NOTES

1. Stephen A. Douglas, quoted in Marvin R. Weisbord, *Campaigning for President* (New York: Washington Square Press, 1966), p. 45.

2. Ibid., p. 5.

3. In 1893 the country suffered a financial panic and slid into a depression. Particularly hard hit were the farmers and silver miners of the West. Angered at the repeal of the Sherman Silver Purchase Act, which had required the government to buy a certain

amount of silver and convert it into paper money, farmers, miners, and other western interests wanted new legislation to force the government to buy and coin an unlimited amount of silver at the ratio to gold of 16 to 1. Eastern financial interests opposed the free coinage of silver, as did President Cleveland. Their opposition split the Democratic party at its convention of 1896 and in the general election of that year.

4. The speech was made during the platform debate. Bryan, arguing in favor of the free and unlimited coinage of silver, accused eastern bankers and financiers of trying to protect their own narrow interests by imposing a gold standard. "You shall not press down upon the brow of labor this crown of thorns, you shall not crucify mankind upon a cross of gold," he shouted at the end of his remarks. Bryan's speech moved the convention. Not only did the free silver interests win the platform fight but Bryan himself won the presidential nomination on the fifth ballot.

5. William Jennings Bryan, *The First Battle* (Port Washington, N.Y.: Kennikat Press, 1971), p. 618.

6. Margaret Leech, *In the Days of McKinley* (New York: Harper & Brothers, 1959), p. 88.

7. Weisbord, *Campaigning for President,* p. 116.

8. Roosevelt had been crippled by polio in 1921. He wore heavy leg braces and could stand only with difficulty. Nonetheless, he made a remarkable physical and political recovery. In his campaign, he went to great lengths to hide the fact that he could not walk and could barely stand.

9. Cabell Phillips, *The Truman Presidency* (New York: Macmillan, 1966), p. 237.

10. Stanley Kelley reports, "By mid-October of 1952, advertising men calculated, there would be some 19,000,000 sets in use and some 58,000,000 viewers; television stations would cover the most populous areas of some of the states most critical politically." Stanley Kelley, *Professional Public Relations and Political Power* (Baltimore: Johns Hopkins Press, 1956), p. 161.

11. Ibid., pp. 161–162.

12. Raymond Moley, an early Goldwater supporter, sent the senator a comprehensive plan for running his campaign in October 1963, more than nine months before he received the nomination. The Moley plan called for the coexistence of two distinct Goldwater groups: the thinkers and the doers. In the first category were the researchers, analysts, and speech writers. Their job was to articulate Goldwater's conservative philosophy. Most of the members in the second category were politicians and technicians: party professionals, advance people, schedulers, media consultants, fund raisers, and others. Their job was to run the campaign. Both groups reported directly to Goldwater. In theory, neither was to interfere with the other's business. In practice, a strict division was difficult to maintain, resulting in some intrusion and some uncoordinated efforts. Karl A. Lamb and Paul A. Smith, *Campaign Decision-Making: The Presidential Election of 1964* (Belmont, Calif.: Wadsworth, 1968), pp. 59–63.

13. This description is based primarily on the discussion that appears in ibid., pp. 114–116, 129–130.

14. Robert Agranoff, *The Management of Election Campaigns* (Boston: Holbrook Press, 1976), p. 182.

15. Theodore H. White, *The Making of the President 1964* (New York: Atheneum, 1965), p. 349.

16. Lamb and Smith, *Campaign Decision-Making*, p. 206.

17. Carter chose to keep his campaign headquarters in Atlanta, Georgia, rather than move it to Washington, D.C., for symbolic as well as practical reasons. An Atlanta address underscored the outsider image Carter desired to project and made it more difficult for Washington-based Democrats to interfere with the conduct of his campaign.

18. Albert R. Hunt, "The Campaign and the Issues," in Austin Ranney (ed.), *The American Elections of 1980* (Washington, D.C.: American Enterprise Institute, 1981), p. 162.

19. Patrick H. Caddell, "Memorandum on General Election Strategy," June 25, 1980, as reprinted in Elizabeth Drew, *Portrait of an Election* (New York: Simon & Schuster, 1981), p. 391.

20. Ibid., p. 400.

21. Patrick H. Caddell, "Memorandum on Debate Strategy," October 21, 1980, in Drew, *Portrait of an Election*, pp. 421–423.

22. Richard Wirthlin, Vincent Breglio, and Richard Beal, "Campaign Chronicle," *Public Opinion*, 4 (1981), 44.

23. Steven J. Brams, *The Presidential Election Game* (New Haven: Yale University Press, 1978), pp. 106–107. See also Steven J. Brams and Morton D. Davis, "The 3/2's Rule in Presidential Campaigning," *American Political Science Review*, 68 (1974), 113.

24. Brams notes that the rule held up reasonably well for Ford and Carter in 1976. Brams, *The Presidential Election Game*, p. 114.

25. Lamb and Smith, *Campaign Decision-Making*, p. 95.

26. Patrick H. Caddell, "Memorandum on General Election Strategy," in Drew, *Portrait of an Election*, pp. 394–395.

27. In devising an Electoral College strategy, Reagan's strategists first calculated the odds of winning each state. To do this they utilized historical and current survey data. Information from polls was added as the campaign progressed. Those states in which the probability of winning was less than 70 percent but more than 30 percent were then ranked in order of population size and geographic area. Priority targets were then identified among the large, middle, and small states. The initial calculations were made in March 1980. The targets were revised in June and over the course of the campaign. Wirthlin, Breglio, and Beal, "Campaign Chronicle," p. 46.

28. Richard B. Wirthlin, "The Republican Strategy and Its Electoral Consequences," in Seymour Martin Lipset (ed.), *Party Coalitions in the 1980s* (San Francisco: Institute for Contemporary Studies, 1981), pp. 242–243.

29. Ibid., p. 249.

30. Herbert E. Alexander, "Making Sense About Dollars in the 1980 Presidential Campaigns," in Michael J. Malbin (ed.), *Financing Politics in the 1980s* (Washington D.C.: American Enterprise Institute/Chatham House, forthcoming).

31. Peter Dailey quoted in Ernest R. May and Janet Fraser (eds.), *Campaign '72* (Cambridge, Mass.: Harvard University Press, 1973), p. 244.

32. In an interesting study on the uses of incumbency, William Lammers has found that Presidents do not concentrate their public activities in the year in which they stand for reelection. Rather he found a general increase in these activities in the three years prior to reelection. Foreign travel, in particular, has consumed greater presidential time. These findings led Lammers to conclude, "the incumbent does indeed have a tremendous advantage in his opportunities for public exposure, but the major shift has come in the period between elections rather than during elections." William W. Lammers, "Presiden-

tial Uses of Incumbency: Attention-Focusing Strategies in the Re-Election Year" (paper presented at the annual meeting of the American Political Science Association, Washington, D.C., August 28–31, 1980), p. 28.

33. Committee to Re-Elect the President, "60 Days to Victory," Washington, D.C. (September 1972), quoted in Agranoff, *The Management of Election Campaigns*, pp. 433–434.

34. Jerry Bruno and Jeff Greenfield, *The Advance Man* (New York: Morrow, 1971), p. 299.

35. Agranoff, *The Management of Election Campaigns*, p. 302.

36. Another well-reported incident, this one involving Vice President Nelson A. Rockefeller, occurred in 1976. It too was precipitated by heckling. The Republican vice presidential candidate, Robert Dole, accompanied by Rockefeller, was trying to address a rally in Binghamton, New York. Constantly interrupted by the hecklers, Dole and then Rockefeller tried to restore order by addressing their critics directly. When this failed, Rockefeller grinned and made an obscene gesture, extending the middle fingers of his hands to the group. The Vice President's response was captured in a picture that appeared in newspapers and national magazines across the country, much to the embarrassment of the Republican ticket.

37. Jimmy Carter, "Remarks at the California State AFL-CIO Convention," Los Angeles, California, September 22, 1980, in *Weekly Compilation of Presidential Documents*, Vol. 16, No. 39, p. 1,884; "Remarks at a Democratic National Committee Fund-Raiser," Chicago, October 6, 1980, ibid., p. 2,092.

38. In 1976 Carter damaged his image by comments he made during an interview with *Playboy* magazine. In articulating his religious views, Carter quoted Christ as saying, "anyone who looks on a woman with lust has in his heart already committed adultery." He went on to add, "I've looked on a lot of women with lust. I've committed adultery in my heart many times." Jimmy Carter, interview, *Playboy*, November 1976, p. 86.

39. Ronald Reagan was incorrect. Tuscumbia was not the birthplace of the Klan or its main headquarters. The Klan, however, was active in the city.

40. The Tennessee Valley Authority is a government corporation that produces and sells fairly cheap electric power to residents of the Tennessee River Valley.

41. This discussion of the five steps of the Goldwater campaign is based on the description in John Kessel, *The Goldwater Coalition* (Indianapolis: Bobbs-Merrill, 1968), pp. 193–217.

42. Wirthlin, Breglio, and Beal, "Campaign Chronicle," pp. 44–45.

43. Ibid., pp. 43–44.

Selected Readings

Agranoff, Robert. *The Management of Election Campaigns*. Boston: Holbrook Press, 1976.

Caddell, Patrick H. "The Democratic Strategy and Its Electoral Consequences," in Seymour Martin Lipset (ed.), *Party Coalitions in the 1980s*. San Francisco: Institute for Contemporary Studies, 1981.

Drew, Elizabeth. *Portrait of an Election*. New York: Simon & Schuster, 1981.

Kessel, John. *The Goldwater Coalition*. Indianapolis: Bobbs-Merrill, 1968.

Lamb, Karl A., and Paul A. Smith. *Campaign Decision-Making: The Presidential Election of 1964.* Belmont, Calif.: Wadsworth, 1968.

May, Ernest R., and Janet Fraser. *Campaign '72: The Managers Speak.* Cambridge, Mass.: Harvard University Press, 1973.

Moore, Jonathan, ed. *The Campaign for President: 1980 in Retrospect.* Cambridge, Mass.: Ballinger, 1981.

Schram, Martin. *Running for President 1976: The Carter Campaign.* New York: Stein & Day, 1977.

Weisbord, Marvin R. *Campaigning for President.* New York: Washington Square Press, 1966.

White, Theodore H. *The Making of the President 1960.* New York: Pocket Books, 1962.

————. *The Making of the President 1964.* New York: Atheneum, 1965.

————. *The Making of the President 1968.* New York: Atheneum, 1969.

————. *The Making of the President 1972.* New York: Atheneum, 1973.

————. *America in Search of Itself: The Making of the President, 1956–1980.* New York: Harper and Row, 1982.

Wirthlin, Richard B., "The Republican Strategy and Its Electoral Consequences," in Lipset (ed.), *Party Coalitions in the 1980s.*

Wirthlin, Richard, Vincent Breglio, and Richard Beal, "Campaign Chronicle," *Public Opinion,* 4 (1981), 43–49.

Chapter 7

IMAGE BUILDING
AND THE MEDIA

Introduction

Images are mental pictures that people rely on to make the world around them understandable. These pictures are stimulated and shaped by the environment as well as by personal attitudes and feelings. What is projected affects what is seen. However, people also see the same thing differently. This suggests that their attitudes color their perceptions. To some extent, beauty is in the eye of the beholder; to some extent, it is in the object seen.

The electorate forms different images of the parties, candidates, and issues. These perceptions help make and reinforce judgments on election day. The images of the party affect how the candidates and the issues are perceived. Strong party identifiers tend to see "their" candidate in a more favorable light than the opposition and perceive his position on the issues as closer to their own. Independents also use their beliefs and feelings to shape their perceptions of the candidate and the issues, although they are less likely to be encumbered by preconceived partisan perspectives in making their evaluations.

This is not to imply, however, that what candidates say and do or how they appear is irrelevant. On the contrary, even strong party supporters can be influenced by what they see, read, and hear. George McGovern's poor showing among Democrats in 1972 dramatically illustrates how a candidate's image can adversely affect his partisan support. He was perceived as incompetent by much of the electorate.[1]

Candidate images are short-term factors that are more variable than party images. In addition to being affected by partisan attitudes, they are also conditioned by the situation and the environment. It is difficult to separate a candidate's image from the events of the real world. Incumbents, especially, tend to be evaluated on the basis of their performance in office. Richard Nixon's image improved from the election of 1968 to 1972, while Jimmy Carter's declined from 1976 to 1980. The changes were a consequence of their Presidencies. Nixon's reputation was subsequently tarnished by the Watergate burglary and his participation in its coverup.

Personal qualities are also important. Inner strength, moral integrity, seriousness of purpose, candor, empathy, and style all contribute to the impression people have of public figures. In fact, these personal characteristics are frequently cited as the reason for voting for or against a particular person.

In view of the weakening of party loyalties and the media's emphasis on personality politics, this is not surprising. For many, the images of the candidates provide a cognitive handle for interpreting the campaign and making a qualitative judgment. Candidates who enjoy a higher assessment have an advantage. A Republican can use it to offset his minority status; a Democrat can use it to insure victory.

The task for presidential candidates is to create as beneficial an image as possible. Normally, just being a presidential candidate helps. The public's inclination to look up to the President usually extends to his opponent. The year 1980 was an exception. Both Carter and Reagan were perceived negatively by a majority of the electorate.

A favorable image, of course, cannot be taken for granted. It has to be built or at least polished. To do this, it is necessary to know what qualities the electorate looks for in its presidential candidates and how to project those qualities. It is the job of pollsters to identify these traits; it is the job of media experts to help project them to the voters.

The first section of this chapter discusses those traits which the public considers most desirable for the Presidency. Illustrations from recent campaigns are used as examples. In the following sections, the creation and projection of presidential images in the media are explored. The second section looks at political advertisements and how they have been used to generate positive and negative images. The third section examines campaign coverage that is subject to less control by the candidates. The debates and other news events are assessed in the light of the conflictual relationship between media and candidates. The final section of the chapter evaluates the impact of the media. Do they affect turnout? Can they change attitudes? Do they influence the vote?

PRESIDENTIAL TRAITS

The American electorate has traditionally valued certain traits in its presidential candidates.[2] These reflect the public's psychological needs and its expectations of those in office.[3] These traits also provide a model of an ideal President, one that is used to evaluate an incumbent and to rate a challenger.

Surveys of public opinion indicate that certain qualities are absolutely essential.[4] The contemporary President is expected to be strong, assertive, dominant—a father figure to millions of Americans. He is expected to be skillful, knowledgeable, and competent—a product of the technological age. He is also expected to be a person who can understand and solve a range of highly intricate problems—a savior in time of trouble. Finally, the President should be able to empathize with the people as well as to embody their most redeeming qualities. He must be understanding and inspiring, honest and honorable, reasonable and rational. In presenting himself to the voters, a candidate must naturally try to project these traits and create the image of an ideal President.

Strength, boldness, and decisiveness are intrinsic to the public's image of the office. During times of crisis or periods of social anxiety these leadership characteristics are considered absolutely essential. The strength that Franklin Roosevelt was able to convey by virtue of his successful bout with polio and Eisenhower by his military command in World War II contrasted sharply with the perceptions of Stevenson in 1956, McGovern in 1972, and Carter in 1980 as weak, indecisive, and vacillating.

The Presidency usually implies strength. When Gerald Ford and Jimmy Carter were criticized for their failure to provide strong leadership, their organizations countered by focusing on their presidential activities. For nonincumbents the task of seeming to be assertive, confident, and independent (one's own person) can best be imparted by a no-nonsense approach, a show of optimism, and a sense of conviction and direction. Kennedy's rhetorical emphasis on activity in 1960 and Nixon's tough talk in 1968 about the turmoil and divisiveness of the late 1960s helped to generate a take-charge impression. Kennedy and Nixon were perceived as leaders who knew what had to be done and would do it. Reagan's references to his economic and defense policies combined with his "Can Do, America" appeal were designed to convey a similar impression.

In addition to seeming tough enough to be President, it is also important to appear competent, to exhibit sufficient knowledge and skills for the job. In the public's mind, personal experience testifies to the ability to perform. However, all experience is not equal. Having held an executive or legislative office at the national level is usually considered necessary, since the public does not think of the Presidency as a position that any political novice could easily or adequately handle.

The advantage of incumbency is obvious when attempting to create and project an image of competence. Presidents are presumed to be knowledgeable because they have been President. They have met with world leaders, dealt with national and international crises, and coped with everyday problems of running the country. Nonincumbents have to prove they can do the same.

A trip abroad is a first step that many take even before declaring their candidacy. The trip, which pictures the candidate conversing with officials of other countries, is designed to convey a well-traveled, diplomatic impression. Similarly, if a candidate's background does not indicate a wide range of presidential-like experiences, then assembling a group of experts and receiving their support may help to demonstrate the potential for these capabilities.

Most candidates can refer to some direct and relevant personal experience. In 1960, Kennedy pointed to his service in the Senate, particularly on the Foreign Relations Committee, as evidence of his competence in foreign affairs; in 1972, McGovern spoke of his years as an Air Force bomber pilot to lend credence to his views on the war in Vietnam and to his patriotism; in 1976, Carter noted his involvement with the Trilateral Commission, a group of prominent individuals interested in the United States' relations with Western Europe and Japan, as an indication of his interest and proficiency in foreign relations; in 1980, Reagan talked about his governorship of California as qualifying him to handle the executive duties of the Presidency as well as the policy problems of the country.

Citing figures and facts in a seemingly spontaneous manner is a tactic frequently employed by candidates to exhibit their knowledge and intelligence. Kennedy in 1960, Carter in 1976, and Reagan in 1980 used the forum of the debates to recite, without notes, a series of statistics on the economy, foreign policy, and national security matters. Their objective was to equalize the information advantage that their opponents were perceived to have had by virtue of their positions as Vice President and

President. So concerned were Ford's supporters about the public's perception of his intellectual abilities that they released information about his record in college and law school. Reagan was frequently pictured in a library-like setting during his 1980 campaign to suggest learning ability and knowledge about current issues.

In addition to strength, decisiveness, and knowledge, empathy is an important attribute for presidential candidates. The public wants a person who can understand feelings and respond to emotional needs. As the government has become larger, more powerful, and more distant, empathy has become more important. Roosevelt and Eisenhower radiated warmth. By comparison, McGovern and Nixon appeared cold, distant, and impersonal. Carter was particularly effective in 1976 in generating the impression that he cared, creating a vivid contrast with the conception of the imperial Presidency and the stereotypical image of his Republican opponents. In 1980, however, his vicious personal criticism of Ronald Reagan undercut his own attractive qualities of compassion and fair play. His rhetoric made him look mean, nasty, and petty—all very undesirable traits.

Candor and integrity emerge periodically as important attributes in presidential image building. Most of the time these traits are taken for granted. Occasionally, however, a crisis of confidence, such as Watergate, dictates that political skills be downplayed and these qualities stressed. This occurred in 1952 and 1976, but in 1980 being politically savvy once again was considered important.

In summary, candidates try to project images consistent with public expectations of the office and its occupant. Traits such as inner strength, decisiveness, competence, and experience are considered essential for the office, and others, such as empathy, sincerity, credibility, and integrity, are viewed as necessary for the individual. Which traits are considered most important varies to some extent with the assessment of the strengths and weaknesses of the incumbent. That is why candidates must constantly monitor public opinion to discern which qualities are most salient during a particular election. Candidates who seem to be lacking one of them may have an image problem but one that can be rectified; candidates who appear to lack more than one of them, however, are in more serious trouble.

The next section discusses some of the ways positive traits can be projected and negative ones overcome.

CONTROLLED MEDIA

Candidates are marketed. Their advertisers use "Madison Avenue" techniques to persuade people to vote for them on election day. Gaining attention, making a pitch, and leaving an impression are all part of the basic objective.

Political ads on television take many forms. They include short spots interspersed with other commercials in regular programming, longer advertisements that preempt part of the standard fare, and full-length productions, such as interviews, documentaries, speeches, and telethons, that utilize a news-entertainment format.

Developed for the candidate, each of these forms of advertising allows a message to be communicated directly on the screen. There are no intermediaries, nor is there any interference from the media. Candidates can say and do what they want. The problem, however, is to make it look real. Candidate-sponsored programs are not unbiased, and the public knows it. Generating interest and convincing viewers are more difficult for advertisers than newscasters.

Short spots of thirty and sixty seconds were used exclusively in the 1968 presidential campaign. The Nixon campaign tried to shape a more favorable image of its candidate by associating him with peace, order, and unity and Humphrey with domestic turmoil and war. The messages were short, the images were repeated, and the audience was captive.[5] There was little issue content. Adverse reaction to the slickness of some of these commercials convinced political advertisers in 1972 that they should produce longer ones in which an issue-oriented message could be conveyed. These ads, which lasted over four minutes, were repeated in 1976 and 1980 along with the shorter ones.

For advertising to be effective, the material must be presented in an interesting and believable way. Having a candidate interact with people is one way of doing this. The use of ordinary citizens rather than professional actors increases the sense of authenticity. Joseph Napolitan, Humphrey's media consultant in 1968, recalled an advertisement that was not shown for precisely this reason. It looked stilted.

One of the storyboard presentations DDB [Doyle Dane Bernbach] made at the convention in Chicago showed a little old lady talking about why she was going to vote for Humphrey, why she couldn't possibly vote Republican. In the drawing, she looked like everybody's grandmother; we thought it would be a good medicare/senior citizen kind of spot, so we told DDB to go ahead and produce it.

Most *political* film producers would have gone out and found a real person and filmed her. But DDB, and I suppose this is common procedure in their sphere, hired a model. Instead of the sweet little old lady, we were shown an elegantly coifed, beautifully gowned woman wearing a string of pearls that looked as though it had just come out of Harry Winston's window, filmed against a brocaded chair in a lavishly appointed setting, acting for all the world as though she had to get through the spot quickly because she was keeping her chauffeur waiting. And I swear to God she spoke with at least a hint of an English accent.[6]

Political documentaries also provide a sense of realism. They have the added advantage of combining a story with a message in pictorial form. Film biographies are particularly good at image building for lesser-known candidates or for explaining the accomplishments of those who have been in office but whose records have not jelled in the minds of the voters. Even President Ford ran a short biography in 1976 to draw attention to parts of his career that were not well known to the general public.

In addition to the format of the ad, timing and targeting have an impact as well. For the candidate who appears ahead, the advertising should be scheduled at a steady rate over the entire campaign in order to maintain the lead. Nixon in 1968 and 1972 and Carter in 1976 followed this course.

When a candidate needs to catch up, however, a concentrated series of ads that builds toward the end of the campaign is more desirable. Humphrey in 1968 and Ford in 1976 adopted this approach. Humphrey had no choice. With no postnomination campaign plan in place, no usable television commercials on file, and no money to purchase time on television, his organization had to create, purchase, and package the advertising and then buy slots when money became available. John Anderson in 1980 was in a similar financial bind and was forced to run all of his ads in the final ten days. Ford's election blitz, on the other hand, was carefully calculated to take advantage of the free coverage he received as President. By adopting a "Rose Garden" strategy at the beginning of the campaign, Ford was able to save his advertising until the end without jeopardizing his media exposure to the voters. In 1980 Ronald Reagan also ran much of his advertising in the last two weeks of the campaign. With a large number of voters undecided, Reagan's strategists desired to maximize their flexibility, maintain their momentum, and offset the gain which an incumbent usually makes in the final week.

Whether ads are spaced or consolidated, they are usually targeted to different sections of the country and to different groups within the electorate. The objective of targeting is to bring the campaign home, to influence specific groups of voters who share many of the same concerns. This requires that issues and positions be relevant to the audience. The candidate's appearance, message, and language must mesh. One good example of targeted advertising was Carter's Hispanic commercials. In a series of television and radio ads, he discussed the issues in Spanish.

Targeting takes great skill and considerable knowledge. Timing is critical. When and where commercials are aired affects who will see them. Media buyers will normally code stations by their viewers and their program format so that the messages fit the audience both demographically and regionally.

Underlining all television advertising is the need to maintain viewer interest. Frequently, this means action. The ad must move. The Carter campaign in 1976 was particularly skilled in creating this effect. Carter was seen walking on his farm, talking with local citizens, speaking to business and professional groups, and addressing the Democratic convention. His movement gave the impression of agility, of a person who was capable of meeting the heavy and multiple responsibilities of the Presidency. His 1980 ads pictured him as an active President—meeting with foreign leaders, working in the White House, talking with members of Congress. In contrast, Reagan's advertising was more static. Fearful that a slick presentation would bring attention to his career as an actor, the commercials presented the candidate as a talking head with as few gimmicks and diversions as possible.

Candidates usually supplement their television appeals with advertising on radio and in newspapers and magazines. Cheaper in cost, print ads and radio commercials normally reach a smaller but more clearly defined audience. As a consequence, these advertisements can be more effectively targeted to readers or listeners than television commercials usually can be to viewers.

The Nixon campaign sought to take advantage of this type of advertising in 1968 and especially in 1972. In a series of radio addresses, heard by as many as 10 million people per broadcast,[7] Nixon delved more deeply into the issues than he did or presumably could have on television. Moreover, his speeches were made available immediately to the press, which generated additional coverage.

In 1968 and 1972, newspaper ads, paid for by the Nixon organization, listed the names of professional and community leaders who endorsed his candidacy and the reasons for their support. The ads created the impression of widespread backing for the Nixon-Agnew ticket. In 1976 and in 1980, both major party campaigns attempted to create a similar effect through radio and print advertising.

Projecting a Positive Image

To mount a successful advertising campaign, a team of experts must be assembled and a plan put into effect. The size of the effort and the time constraints normally dictate that an advertising firm be hired to supplement the regular campaign staff. Even when an in-house group directs campaign advertising, they are normally recruited from an outside firm. In 1976, Bailey, Deardourff and Associates of Washington, D.C., created, produced, and marketed Ford's media campaign, and Gerald Rafshoon's advertising agency in Atlanta did the same for Carter. Rafshoon continued as Carter's media adviser in 1980, while Peter Dailey, who designed Nixon's 1972 advertising, handled Reagan's 1980 effort.

The media plan is a strategic blueprint, setting out the assumptions and objectives of the campaign. These include the personality traits that need to be emphasized, the issues that should be raised, and the basic images that have to be created. The plan, designed with the mood of the country in mind, outlines the form that the advertising should take and the way it should be marketed, targeted, and phased.

The assumptions of the plan relate to the environment and the candidate's position at the beginning of the campaign. The objectives indicate where the candidate would like to be at the end. The goal, of course, is to get him there. Take the situation in which Carter found himself in the summer of 1980. He was perceived as a weak, indecisive, inconsistent leader, a President who seemed unable to devise solutions that would revive the nation's economy and reverse setbacks in foreign affairs. The task, as his advisers saw it, was to change significant portions of that image. They developed an advertising plan designed to emphasize Carter's activities as President and to highlight the incumbent-challenger contrast.[8] (See box.) Presidents Nixon and Ford also used their office to enhance their personal images. Nixon's advertisements in 1972 pictured him meeting with the heads of other governments, presiding over a cabinet meeting, awarding medals of honor, and so on. Similarly, Ford's commercials in 1976 showed him negotiating with foreign leaders, working in the White House, and talking seriously with members of Congress.

To counter this approach, challengers presented themselves in their commercials in as presidential a posture as possible. Carter's 1976 ads stressed his versatility, decisiveness, sincerity, and responsiveness. Untainted by a Washington affiliation, Carter was portrayed as a fresh, independent, people-oriented candidate who would provide new leadership. His slogan, "A leader, for a change," his less formal appearance, even the deep green color of his literature,[9] conveyed how different he was from the old-style Washington politican and the two recent Rebublican Pre-

CARTER'S ADVERTISING PLAN IN 1980

There should be a positive and negative media campaign plan for the Fall. The positive campaign should begin Sept. 4th. The negative campaign should begin in October. *1. The Positive Campaign. Jimmy Carter should run for re-election on his record.* It is a sign of how bad things have become that this suggestion would be ridiculed if made publicly. The public is now convinced that Jimmy Carter is an inept man. He has tried hard but he has failed. He is weak and indecisive—in over his head. *We have to change peoples' minds.*

This is a formidable task. If we adopt this approach we will not be doing "responsive chord" type spots—quick and easy re-inforcements of existing perceptions. We will be trying to turn perceptions around; to educate. Not an easy thing to do with television spots.

The first step must be to properly analyze the public psychology concerning Carter. People are confused about him—they always have been. People used to *like* Carter but they have been bombarded with evidence (through the media) that he's inept. Many people voted for him in 1976 and many more in 1980. They want to think that they voted intelligently. But the media insists daily (and nightly) that they didn't.

If properly exploited, this can work for us. People would feel more comfortable if they could get their thoughts and perceptions about Jimmy Carter straight. Either: "yes, he is a good man *and* a good President"; or "He's a lousy President and he's not a particularly nice man either. He tricked us."

If we're going to elicit the first response ("a good man *and* a good President") we're going to have to make it easy for people to change their minds about the competence issue. We have to give them a reason—a rationale—that explains why they've been so wrong. . .

The message should be this: "We know you think Carter has not done much as President. But give us your attention—and an open mind—for a few minutes and we think you may be surprised by what you learn. . .

Obviously, the effectiveness of this approach will depend upon the believeability of the case we make. The spots will have to be long (probably five minutes) and packed with hard and surprising facts. The presentation can't be dull. We may want to use an actor to present our case. We'll need pictures, shots of the President, some use of the Cabinet, endorsement from world leaders (out of introduction, if that's acceptable), Governors, Mayors, business leaders, labor leaders, other groups and common people. The over-all should present a *lot* of information presented in an interesting and credible way.

The advantages to this are many. We contrast Carter's record with Reagan's. We take Carter's biggest negative head-on. We get credit—with the public, if not the press—for running "on the issues and the record." We raise questions in people's minds about *why* they think Carter is inept . . . We may even make it respectable to be "for" Carter.

The other positive message that we have to offer is this: CARTER IS SMARTER THAN REAGAN. The President is a man who grasps what is going on. We must show Carter as a man who comprehends the facts. A cornerstone of our positive media campaign will be the town meetings held during the general election. We will film these, then produce 30 minute programs, run them in the key states within a week of the President's visit.

2. The Negative Campaign

CARTER	*REAGAN*
SAFE/SOUND	UNTESTED
YOUNG	OLD
VIGOROUS	OLD
SMART	DUMB
COMPREHENSIVE MIND	SIMPLISTIC
ENGINEER	ACTOR
EXPERIENCED PRESIDENT	NAIVE/INEXPERIENCED
COMPASSIONATE	REPUBLICAN
MODERATE	RIGHT/WING

The negative campaign will be similar to the primary media campaign against Kennedy.

In his strategy memo, Pat Caddell wisely suggests the Election Definition as "The Presidency—A Serious Business." This is an excellent definition. We plan to make this the tone of our media campaign. Wrapping Carter—the only President running—in the mantle of the Presidency should give pause to those misguided souls who perceive Reagan as the lesser of two evils.

We are already producing a 15–16 minutes convention film which touches on this—talking about Carter's real accomplishments in the context of the qualities that we expect of our Presidents and setting Jimmy Carter in a historic perspective while pointing out WHAT IT TAKES TO BE PRESIDENT.

What Does it Take to be President?

A DEEP UNDERSTANDING of the difficult and complex problems that face our country and our world. Never before in history has one man had to grasp so much about such a wide range of issues. And never before has so much depended upon his ability to grasp it.

EXPERIENCE with a staggering number of procedures and institutions—Congress, the federal bureaucracy, our nation's defense system, state and local governments, foreign policy. There's no adequate preparation outside the Office itself.

A SENSE OF MODERATION to avoid the dangers of ideological excess. The ability and the temperament to deal with all the complexities of the big problems that reach the Oval Office. The willingness to search for the proper balance among the many competing needs and demands of our society.

COMPASSION for those who need government most—the poorest and the weakest in society as well as for the working person trying to bring the American Dream within his grasp.

THE COURAGE to do what is best even when it's not popular and to tell the truth to the American people even when it hurts.

Rafshoon Communications, "1980 General Election Media Plan," July 3, 1980.

sidents.[10] In 1980, Reagan's media efforts showed him talking confidently about the economy and the military. They projected a personal dimension of the man and were designed to utilize his acting skills without making him look like an actor.

The focus on personal qualities has been dominant in recent presidential campaigns. Typically, the Republican candidate has not emphasized his partisanship. Reagan's ads were directed at undecided voters, not Republicans. In contrast, Democratic commercials have connected the candidate to the party and made the link explicit: "McGovern, Democrat, for the people," "Carter, Democrat, a leader, for a change."

Within the electorate, appeals must be made to specific groups. Campaign advertising typically pictures the candidates with senior citizens talking about the problems of the elderly, with farmers asserting their commitment to agriculture, with labor reiterating their concern for the working man, with veterans discussing the difficulties of readjustment. For Democrats, the object of this targeted advertising is to hold their fragile electoral coalition together. For Republicans, the minimum goal is to destroy their stereotype as the party of business and the rich; a longer-range objective is to enlarge their base of support. The failure to appeal to black voters in 1976 hurt Ford's chances and effectively surrendered the South to Carter.

Criticizing an Opponent

Frequently a campaign works as hard to destroy the opponent's favorable image as it does to build a positive image for its own candidate. Most media plans also include negative or confrontation advertising. Instead of playing to a candidate's strength, negative advertising exploits the opposition's weaknesses. Perhaps the most famous (or infamous) negative political commercial was created by advertising executive Tony Schwartz in 1964 for use against Barry Goldwater. It was designed to reinforce the impression that Goldwater was a trigger-happy zealot who would not hesitate to use nuclear weapons against a communist foe.

Pictured first was a little girl in a meadow plucking petals from a daisy. She counted to herself softly. When she reached eleven, her voice faded and a stern-sounding male voice counted down from nine. When he got to zero there was an explosion, the little girl disappeared, and a mushroom-shaped cloud covered the screen. The announcer stated soberly, "These are the stakes, to make a world in which all of God's children can live or go into the dark. . . . The stakes are too high for you to stay at home." The ad ended with a plea to vote for President Johnson.

The commercial was run only once. Goldwater supporters were outraged and protested vigorously. Their protest kept the issue alive. In fact, the ad itself became a news item, and parts of it were shown on television newscasts. Schwartz had made the point stick.

In 1972 and 1976 the Republican candidates ran a series of very effective negative commercials. The anti-McGovern ads were sponsored by Democrats for Nixon and introduced by John Connally, former Democratic governor of Texas, but paid for by Nixon's Committee to Re-Elect the President. One showed a profile of McGovern, with an announcer stating a position that McGovern had taken and later changed. When the change in position was explained, another profile of McGovern, but one looking in the opposite direction, was flashed on the screen. This tactic of position change and profile rotation was repeated several times. Finally, when the announcer asked, "What about next year?" McGovern's face spun rapidly before viewers. A similar negative ad was directed against Carter in 1980.

In 1976, Bailey, Deardourff created a very effective negative ad referred to as the "Man in the Street" commercial. It began with interviews with a number of people in different areas of the country who indicated their preference for Ford. The focus then gradually changed. Some people were uncertain; others voiced reservations about Carter. Most convincing were the Georgia critics. "He didn't do anything," stated one man from Atlanta. "I've tried, and all my friends have tried, to remember exactly what Carter did as governor, and nobody really knows." The commercial concluded with an attractive woman, also from Georgia, saying in a thick southern accent, "It would be nice to have a President from Georgia—but not Carter." She smiled. The ad ended.

The "Man in the Street" commercials showed a contrast. They not only suggested that President Ford enjoyed broad support but also served to reinforce doubts about Carter, even among Georgians. Moreover, the fact that the people interviewed were not actors gave the ads more credibility. They seemed like news stories, and that was not coincidental. They were so effective, in fact, that Carter used similar commercials in his 1980 primary and general election campaigns. The anti-Reagan ads presented Californians talking critically about their former governor:

I think it's a big risk to have Reagan as President.

Reagan scares me.

As a governor it really didn't make that much difference, because the state of California doesn't have a foreign policy and . . . isn't going to be going to war with a foreign nation. It was just amusing. But as president—you know, it's scary.

These spots were supplemented by others that forced people to picture Reagan as President. In one, an empty Oval Office was seen with an announcer saying:

When you come right down to it, what kind of person should occupy the Oval Office? Should it be a person who, like Ronald Reagan, has opposed Medicare, and is a strong opponent of national health insurance, and has summed up his position by saying, "There is no health crisis in America"? Or should a man sit here who has already put together a workable national health program?

In the final days of the campaign, "Man in the Street" ads that showed people explaining why they intended to vote for Carter were also aired.

One object of negative advertising is to goad the opposition into a mistake. In 1964, the uproar generated by the daisy commercial worked to keep the issue of Goldwater's military posture foremost in the voters' minds. In 1976, Carter did not reply to Ford's ads; in 1980, Reagan did not respond directly to Carter's. Instead, Reagan hammered away at economic issues and Carter's inept leadership. "Everywhere I travel in America," he said in his ads, "I hear this phrase over and over again. Everything is going up. Where is it going to end? Record inflation has robbed the purchasing power of your dollar. And for three and one-half years the administration has been unable to control it. I'm prepared to do something about it."

Financial problems forced Anderson to rely on news coverage for much of his campaign. In the final days advertisements were shown that combined the "Man in the Street" approach with the candidate talking very specifically about the issues. The specificity was intended to demonstrate Anderson's knowledge and his directness. He did not want to appear as just another politician.

Negative advertising has not been used only against presidential candidates. In recent campaigns, Democrats have directed their barbs to the vice presidential candidate as well. One of the most clever of these ads appeared in 1968. It was a twenty-second spot that began with the words "Agnew for Vice President" on the screen. The audio consisted almost entirely of a man laughing. As the laughter began to fade away, a solemn-sounding announcer stated, "This would be funny if it weren't so serious."

In 1976 the Democrats sought to take advantage of the impression left by the debate between vice presidential candidates Mondale and Dole with an ad dubbed "Mondole." Shown everywhere except in the South, it pictured the two vice presidential candidates as the announcer asked, "What kind of men are they? When you know that four out of the last six vice presidents have wound up as presidents, who would you like to see a heartbeat away from the Presidency?"[11]

UNCONTROLLED MEDIA

From the perspective of image building, political advertising gives the campaign the most control over what the voters see. The environment can be predetermined, the words and pictures can be created and coordinated, and the candidate can be rehearsed to produce the desired effect. Moreover, the message can be targeted.

News events are more difficult to influence. A candidate's media advisers neither determine the environment nor produce the product. In some cases, the message is partially mediated by the structure of the event. Interviews and debates provide a format which shapes but does not always control the discussion. In other cases, the message and the image are directly affected by the media's orientation. Remarks are edited for the sake of the story. A candidate can be interrupted, his comments interpreted, and his policies evaluated. Major statements can even be ignored—if, for example, hecklers are present or if the candidate makes some goof, such as slipping and bumping his head. Under these circumstances, aspirants for the Presidency exercise much less leverage. They are not powerless, however.

The Debates

Candidates have viewed presidential debates as vehicles for improving their images and/or damaging their opponents'. In 1960, Kennedy wanted to counter the image of him as being too young and inexperienced. Nixon, on the other hand, sought to maintain his stature as Eisenhower's knowledgeable and competent Vice President and the obvious person to succeed his "boss" in office. In 1976, Ford saw the debates as an opportunity to appear presidential and to chip away at his Democratic rival's "soft" backing. The Carter camp, however, saw them as a means of shoring up their own support. In the words of pollster Patrick Caddell, "Debates would give him [Carter] exposure in depth, would demonstrate his competence in the same arena with an incumbent president, would retain his solid vote—and keep reinforcing it."[12] In 1980 the rationale was similar. From Reagan's perspective, it was an opportunity to reassure voters about himself and his qualifications for office. For Carter, it was another chance to exaggerate the differences between himself and Reagan, between their parties, and between their issue and ideological positions. With the possible exception of Nixon, candidates have achieved their principal objective but they have not benefited equally from their participation in debates.

More than any other campaign event, debates have attracted public attention. Kennedy and Nixon held four debates of sixty minutes each. Three of them were face to face; one was conducted on a split screen, with the candidates in different cities. Ford and Carter held three ninety-minute debates, and their vice presidential candidates held one. Reagan and Carter had only one but held it one week before the election.

There was also a debate between Reagan and independent candidate John Anderson. Carter did not participate in that debate, although he was invited to do so. He was not anxious to incur the criticism of two challengers.

It is estimated that more than half the adult population in the United States watched all of the Kennedy-Nixon debates and almost 90 percent saw one of them.[13] The first Ford-Carter debate in 1976 attracted an estimated viewing audience of 90 million to 100 million and was seen in 35 million to 40 million homes. The Carter-Reagan debate had an audience of approximately 120 million.

With so many people watching, the candidates went to great lengths to project themselves in a favorable light. The debates presented a unique opportunity to do so. As news events, they were more believable than political advertisements. Yet, they also gave the candidates considerable flexibility in how they appeared, what they said, and the extent to which they chose to respond to the questions. Even the format was negotiated.[14]

Careful planning went into each debate. Representatives of the candidates studied the locations, tried to anticipate the questions, and briefed and rehearsed the candidates. Mock studios were built and the debate environment simulated. Here's how Jules Witcover described Ford's training for his debates with Carter:

> The family theater at the White House was converted into a rough mockup of the actual set to be used in Philadelphia. The podium was identical, down to the same television camera angles, so that Bill Carruthers, Ford's television adviser, could recommend the most attractive position for the President to assume. As Ford stood at his lectern, cardboard cards were held up by hand indicating "one minute," "thirty seconds," "cut"—similar to the electric timing devices that would be used in the actual studio to monitor the time of his answers.

> Various aides . . . took turns at the reporters' panel and threw questions at him by the hour. Then a complete videotape was played back so they could all study what he said, and how he looked and sounded as he said it. At one session, a television set was even brought in and set up on Carter's lectern. On a closed-circuit arrangement, old tapes of Carter answering reporters' questions on panel shows like "Meet the Press" were run off in Ford's presence, to familiarize him with Carter's style. Ford would be asked and would answer a question, and then Carter, on tape, would have his "turn."[15]

In 1980 this elaborate preparation took a bizarre twist. The Reagan campaign obtained one of Carter's three briefing books. Knowing the questions Carter anticipated and the answers he was advised to give helped Reagan's strategists prepare responses for him. In general, all debate participants with the exception of Nixon, in his first debate with Kennedy, were well prepared.

Throughout the debates the candidates repeated basic themes. Despite the appearance of spontaneity, what was said was hardly new. Analyses of the debates reveal that the candidates gave their standard campaign speeches in response to or in spite of the questions they were asked. The debates, in short, were an extension of the media campaign. The candidates sounded like their ads.

There were, however, stylistic differences. Kennedy and Carter talked faster than their opponents. They accentuated action-oriented issues. Both tried to display their knowledge of the intricacies of the governmental process. Ford and Reagan spoke in more general terms, expressing particular concern about the size and structure of government. Both tried to convey their capacity for leadership.

Public reaction to the debates focused on the performance of the candidates and not on their issue stands. The media contributed to this reaction by their emphasis on controversy and on personal style. In at least one instance, the media directly affected the image a candidate was attempting to project. By highlighting Ford's statement during his second debate with Carter that the Soviet Union did not dominate Eastern Europe, network commentators damaged the President's claim to be more capable and knowledgeable in foreign affairs.

The media have tended to assess debates in terms of winners and losers. Their evaluation conditions how the public judges the results. Since most people do not follow the content very closely and do not put much faith in their own evaluation, media commentary can have a considerable impact on public opinion. It can modify the immediate impressions people have, moving it in the direction of the acknowledged winner. This happened in 1976 and again in 1980.

The impact is not immediate. It takes time for a general assessment to take hold and affect the public's judgment. Ford's second debate with Carter is an excellent illustration. Surveys taken within the first twelve hours following the debate indicated that viewers, by almost two to one, believed Ford had won. Few mentioned his remarks on Eastern Europe. Polls taken two to three days following the debate, however, presented a very different picture. By more than two to one, Carter was perceived the winner.[16]

A time lag was also apparent in the reaction to the 1980 debate. Table 7–1 reports the results of two polls taken by CBS News. The first, conducted the day after the debate, indicated that 8 percent more people believed Reagan to be the winner than believed Carter to be. The second, taken two to four days later, showed a difference of 15 percent in Reagan's favor. What seemed to happen was that those perceiving Carter the winner became less certain of their judgment in light of the postmortems which concluded that Reagan had won. Memories fade quickly. The percentage believing the debate was a tie almost doubled in the few days following the event.

Do debates have a long-term impact? Do they affect voting behavior? Do they affect the outcome of the election? Most analysts believe they do, although measuring their influence is very difficult.

Debates have two principal effects. For partisans, they solidify support. Those who are more involved are more likely to watch them; those who are more knowledgeable are more likely to learn from them; those who are most partisan are more apt to be convinced by them.[17] The debate confirms their perceptions.

For weaker partisans and independents the debates can increase their interest and clarify, color, or even change their perceptions. Before debating, Kennedy was thought by many to be less knowledgeable and less experienced than Nixon; Carter was seen as an enigma, as fuzzier than Ford; Reagan was perceived to be more doctrinaire and less informed than his Democratic opponent. The debates enabled each of these candidates to overcome these negative perceptions. In the end this proved to be critical to the success of their candidacies.

Kennedy and Carter might not have won without the debates. Reagan probably would not have won by as much. According to a private poll by Patrick Caddell, voters evaluated Reagan more negatively than posi-

Table 7–1   PERCEPTIONS OF THE WINNER OF THE CARTER-REAGAN
DEBATE* (IN PERCENTAGES)

Perceived Winner	CBS News Poll October 28, 1980	CBS News/New York Times Poll October 30–November 1, 1980
Carter	36	26
Reagan	44	41
Tie	14	27
No Opinion	6	6

Source: *Public Opinion*, III (1981), 34. © 1981, American Enterprise Institute for Public Policy Research, Washington, D.C. 20036.
*Question: "Which candidate do you think did the best job—or won the debate—Carter or Reagan?"

tively two days before his debate with Carter. Three days after the debate another Caddell poll found that Reagan's favorable rating had increased and his unfavorable rating had decreased. During the debate, Reagan simply did not look or talk like the ogre he had been represented as. In fact, he appeared more personable, sounded as reasonable, and talked more confidently than Carter.

The Kennedy, Carter, and Reagan experiences suggest why debates tend to help challengers more than incumbents. Being less well known, challengers tend to have more questions raised about them, their competence, and their capacity to be President. The debates provide them with an opportunity to satisfy some of these doubts in a believable setting and on a comparative basis. By appearing to be at least the equal of their incumbent opponents, the presidential images of the challengers are enhanced. There are fewer reasons for voting against them.

News Coverage

News coverage is not as likely to benefit a candidate in the same manner as debates or interviews do. The *modus operandi* of news reporting is to inform and interest the public. Rather than improve an image, news coverage can distort or destroy it.

Knowing how the media cover the campaign is critical to understanding how campaign organizations can affect the media. Most people follow presidential campaigns on television. It is the prime source of news for approximately 60 percent of the population.[18] Newspapers are a distant second, with only about 20 percent listing them as their principal source. Radio and magazines trail far behind.

News on television seems more believable. People can see what is happening. Being an action-oriented, visual medium, television reports the drama and excitement of the campaign. It does so by emphasizing the contest. Who is ahead? How are the candidates doing? Is the leader slipping? It is this horse-race aspect of the campaign that provides the principal focus for television as well as for the print media.

Issues, on the other hand, get little in-depth coverage. According to Thomas Patterson, "about 60 percent of television election coverage and 55 percent of newspaper election coverage in 1976 were devoted to 'game' topics, such as winning and losing, strategy, tactics, and logistics. Only 30 percent of television coverage and 35 percent of newspaper coverage were devoted to the campaign issues and leadership subjects."[19] Robinson and Sheehan found a similar emphasis in 1980. Their analysis of the CBS "Evening News" during the campaign revealed an average of ninety seconds per program devoted to policy issues, approximately 20 to 25 percent of the total coverage.[20] Five out of six stories emphasized the competition.[21]

Not only does the horse race pervade the coverage, but the race is between the major party candidates. The principal aspirants for the nomination receive coverage roughly in proportion to their standing, with the front-runners receiving the most. After the conventions are over, it becomes a two-person contest. Minority-party and independent candidates receive little, if any, attention. The exception was John Anderson. In 1980, he received one-fourth of the coverage given to Reagan and Carter.[22]

The race is for the Presidency. Even the vice presidential candidates of the major parties get practically no coverage. Robinson and Sheehan's analysis of UPI revealed one story featuring Walter Mondale, two featuring George Bush, and none featuring Patrick Lucey, Anderson's running mate. Similarly, on CBS, there was only one story featuring Bush, one on Lucey, and none on Mondale.[23] In fact, the only time vice presidential candidates seem to be in the news is when they are nominated. Once they receive the nomination, they seem to disappear from the scene.

The contest shapes the coverage. Candidates understand this. They know that what is new and unexpected is newsworthy. A fresh face winning or an old face losing receives attention. That is why doing well in the early primaries brings mixed blessings. It gains media coverage but it also increases the likelihood of more negative news.

The media emphasize change. Inconsistent policy positions get more attention than do consistent ones. Verbal slips make news, while stump speeches and canned answers do not. As a consequence, candidates try to speak in careful, calculated language, fearing the worst possible interpretation of their remarks. Ad lib comments are discouraged. Reagan's advisers in 1980 were particularly fearful that his penchant for making off-the-cuff remarks would get him into trouble. After several faux pas at the beginning of his campaign, he was advised to stick to his prepared text and avoid informal contacts with the press.

The media need to simplify complex statements, issues, and events, to infuse politics with drama, to tap the human dimension. To do this, a framework of interpretation is necessary. As with the debates, the winner-loser orientation provides such a framework. It is an easy way to evaluate the campaign. Issues are difficult to assess, but the relative positions of the candidates are not.

Candidates take this orientation into account when trying to affect the quantity and quality of the coverage they receive. Naturally, they desire more and better coverage. Their need is most acute at the beginning of the primary process, especially for those who lack public recognition. Without such coverage, it is difficult to be taken seriously by the electorate or to mount a successful fund-raising drive. Jimmy Carter attacked this problem in 1976 by directing his attention to the local press at the beginning of his drive for the nomination. In 1980 most of the lesser-known candidates adopted a similar strategy.

How the media interpret the early primaries is particularly important, since voters have less information and are more manipulatable at the outset of the nomination process. With the popular and delegate vote often divided among several candidates, the media pay attention to expectations and performance. When expectations are exceeded, a candidate can be judged a winner, regardless of the vote. Similarly, when expectations are not met, the results are usually interpreted as a disappointment at best and a loss at worst, regardless of popular or delegate vote. This basis for judgment affects campaign strategy. The reason why candidates tend to underestimate their vote in public is in order to be able to claim victory when the results come in, whatever they may be.

Not only is the outcome of the primaries subject to interpretation, but so is the importance attached to particular elections. Generally speaking, the media tend to provide more coverage of early contests than later ones; they give primaries more attention than caucuses (with the exception of Iowa), close elections more emphasis than one-sided ones, and statewide contests better coverage than district elections. Candidate organizations can also influence the evaluation by the importance they place on individual primaries, especially when a number of them occur on the same day. For example, in 1976 and again in 1980, there were three major Democratic primaries in early June. In both elections, the Carter organization successfully diverted attention from New Jersey and California, which it thought Carter would lose, to Ohio, which it believed he would win. This diversion contributed significantly to the media's perception that Carter had the nomination sewed up by his victory in Ohio.

While the media's influence tends to be magnified during the preconvention period, when voters have less information at their disposal, candidate strategists believe the media to be important throughout the campaign. They see their ability to mobilize resources, to get endorsements, to raise money, and to create an organization as all related to the coverage they receive. Hence, they plan campaigns with the media in mind.

The tactics used to influence the media are many and varied. They include the timing and staging of events, the access given to reporters, and the release of information by the candidate and his aides. Major announcements are made early enough to get on the evening news. Speeches are timed to maximize the viewing audience. Quiet periods, such as Saturday, are considered a good time to hold a press conference or schedule interviews. In addition to receiving same-day coverage by television, a Saturday event usually gets prominent treatment in the Sunday papers.

Access is a valuable commodity. At the beginning of the nomination process, access is cheap, especially for lesser-known candidates, who need attention. As the campaign progresses, access becomes more important and, at the same time, more difficult to obtain. There is more competition among journalists, the candidates have a more demanding schedule, and a larger public relations staff stands between the correspondents and the nominees. Granting interviews under these circumstances can do much to affect the quantity and quality of coverage received.

So can the careful release of information, not only the position papers, but items on the personal life of the candidate and his family. To a large extent, those who report the news are dependent on this material. An analysis of news stories in twenty papers in 1968 found that candidates were the principal source of more than half of them.[24] Similar findings were reported by Robinson and Sheehan:

> On UPI, just over 40 percent of the Carter news came directly from Carter, his press office, his staff, or his administration. Fewer than 10 percent came via the investigative route. On CBS, it was the same story, so to speak, only more so. A full two-thirds of the "official" news about Carter came via a Carter-controlled news source. Investigative journalism again accounted for less than 10 percent of the reporting.[25]

In short, the candidates can exercise a major influence on their own images in the news. They cannot control the news, however. They cannot define their coverage completely, counter uncomplimentary evaluations, or divert the media from controversial statements or actions. As Jody Powell said of Jimmy Carter's 1976 candidacy:

> There was no way on God's earth we could shake the fuzziness question in the general election, no matter what Carter did or said. He could have spent the whole campaign doing nothing but reading substantive speeches from morning to night and still have had that image in the national press.[26]

In summary, there is both tension and cooperation between the media and the candidate. The tension is compounded by the media's need to highlight controversy and accentuate the negative and the candidate's desire to suppress unfavorable news. The cooperation is generated by the media's need for information and access and the candidate's desire to accentuate the positive. The key questions are: What impact does all this have on the voters? How does media coverage affect image creation during the campaign? The final section proposes some answers to these questions.

THE IMPACT OF THE MEDIA

The time, money, and energy spent on image building suggest that it has a major impact on voting behavior. Why else would so many resources be devoted to the media effort? Yet, it is difficult to document the precise effect. There is little tangible evidence to support the propositions that television changes people's minds on the candidates and the issues, or that news programs raise their level of knowledge, or that mass appeals affect many voting decisions.

Studies of campaigning in the 1940s indicated that the principal impact of the media was to activate predispositions and reinforce attitudes rather than to convert voters. Newspapers and magazines provided information but primarily to those who were most committed. The most committed, in turn, used the information to support their beliefs. Weeding out opposing views, they insulated themselves from unfavorable news and opinions that conflicted with their own.[27]

With the bulk of campaign information coming from printed matter, voters, particularly partisan voters, tended to minimize cross-pressures and to strengthen their own preexisting judgments. In contrast, the less committed also had less incentive to become informed. They maintained their ignorance by avoiding information about the campaign. The format of newspapers and magazines facilitated this kind of selective perception and retention.

Television might have been expected to change this. It exposes the less committed to more information and the more committed to other points of view. Avoidance is more difficult, since viewers become more captive of the picture than of the printed page.

While the same events get reported, the reports often differ. Robinson and Sheehan found the news on television to be "more mediating, more political, more personal, more critical, [and] more thematic than old-style print."[28] Newspapers describe events. They indicate what candidates say and do. Television presents drama. It provides a visual slice of reality, *not* a compendium of people, places, and things. In this way it mediates between candidates and the public more than newspapers do. It is also more analytic and more negative. Robinson and Sheehan report, "In the end, every major candidate in Campaign '80 got a more critical press on CBS than on UPI, explicitly or implicitly."[29]

The amount of coverage also differs. Television compartmentalizes. The evening news fits a large number of stories into a thirty-minute broadcast. Of necessity, this restricts the time that can be devoted to each item. Campaign stories average ninety seconds on the evening news, the equivalent of only a few paragraphs of a printed account. This helps explain why viewers do not retain much information from it.

Two political scientists, Thomas E. Patterson and Robert D. McClure, who studied how television reported the news during the 1972 campaign, found:

1. Most election issues are mentioned so infrequently that viewers could not possibly learn about them.
2. Most issue references are so fleeting that they could not be expected to leave an impression on viewers.
3. The candidates' issue positions generally were reported in ways guaranteed to make them elusive.[30]

"Television news adds little to the average voter's understanding of election issues," they wrote. "Network news may be fascinating. It may be highly entertaining. But it is simply not informative."[31]

The need to emphasize the contest affects which issues are covered when issues are covered. The media focus on those which provide clear-cut differences between the candidates, those which provoke controversy, and those which can be presented in a simple, straightforward manner. These are not necessarily the issues which the candidates have stressed during their campaigns. In his research, Patterson has found that "candidates talk mostly about 'diffuse' issues, ones in which the differences between the candidates are either indirect or mostly those of style and emphasis. . . . Such issues in 1976 accounted for about 65 percent of the issue appeals in the candidates' speeches. These issues, however, accounted for only 35 percent of the issue messages in election news."[32]

In addition to its de-emphasis of diffuse issues, news coverage also fails to present background information needed to assess issue stands. While policy positions of the candidates may be reported, these positions are rarely analyzed.[33] Nor are personal histories or public records of the principal candidates explored in any depth. It is no wonder that people learn so little about their voting choices from the news.

Where, then, do people receive information? One of the most interesting findings of the Patterson and McClure study is that people actually get more information from the advertisements they see on television than from the news.[34] The reason seems to be that ads are more repetitive and more compact. When placed with other commercials in popular shows, they are difficult to avoid.[35] In fact, studies have shown that television watchers pay about twice as much attention to political advertisements as they do to other kinds of commercials.[36] Special election programs also add to the public's information. Together with advertising, these programs broaden the electorate's understanding and contribute to their images of the candidates.

Does political advertising pay? Most media consultants and campaign managers believe that it does. It is apt to be more influential during the preconvention period, when less is known about the candidates and partisan affiliation is not a factor. During the general election campaign, advertising tends to reinforce the loyalties of strong partisans. The campaign is simply too short and the defenses of these partisans too resilient for large-scale changes of attitude.

For those without strong partisan identities, those who are marginally interested in the election but have limited knowledge about the candidates and issues, television may have a different effect. It can alter their perceptions, although it usually does not change their beliefs or necessarily even improve their knowledge of the issues. What happens is that some people begin to see the candidates in a different light. They are persuaded to vote for or against a particular individual.

With the decline of strong partisans in the electorate and the increase of independents, the audience who may be affected in this manner has become larger. That is why campaigns spend so much time and energy on television advertising and why they try to affect news coverage of their candidates.

SUMMARY

The creation and projection of images are important to a presidential campaign. They are important because the electorate's assessment of the candidates, issues, and parties affects its voting behavior. Influencing that assessment is the goal of the image makers. They work on the assumption that what candidates say affects their image, and their image, in turn, affects their chances for winning the election.

The increasing dependence on television as a communications medium has forced greater emphasis to be placed on candidate images and less on the party and issues. Candidates try to project images that embody traits people desire in their Presidents. These include the institutional need for strong, decisive, and intelligent leadership and the personal qualities of empathy, sincerity, candor, and integrity. In 1976 personal qualities received special emphasis because of the abuses of Vietnam, Watergate, and the so-called imperial Presidency; in 1980, institutional needs once again predominated.

Images must be conveyed primarily through the media. Relatively few people come into direct contact with the candidate. The objective of the campaign organizations in communicating information is, of course, very different from that of the media in covering the campaign. Thus, the task from the candidate's perspective is to get the message across as clearly, as frequently, and as cogently as possible.

The easiest way to do this (and also the most costly) is to create, project, and air an advertisement that sells the candidate much as any product is marketed. Political advertising can be targeted and timed to maximize its impact. It can also be made to look like news. The more credible the ad, the more likely it is to have an effect.

Advertising can tap positive or negative personality dimensions. All candidates have to project their presidential characteristics. Incumbents have an advantage, since they can be pictured on the job and in the White House. Nonincumbents have to show their experience, knowledge, and versatility in other ways. Kennedy referred to his Senate days, McGovern to his Democratic affiliation, and Carter to his experience as a farmer, engineer, naval officer, and governor but not as a born-again Christian. Reagan pointed to his California governorship as qualifying him for the job.

The other personal characteristics that are emphasized depend on the candidate and his perception of the times. Presidents Kennedy and Carter stressed activity and decisiveness in the aftermath of conservative Republican years; Johnson and Nixon promised mainstream politics, in contrast to their more reactionary or radical opponents; Ford pointed to his decency and honesty in a not-so-subtle contrast to his predecessor. Reagan articulated traditional values and conservative policies as the best way of attacking the country's political and economic malaise. Each of these traits was reinforced by slogans repeated throughout the campaign—"A choice, not an echo"; "A leader, for a change"; "Now is the time for Reagan."

Confrontation advertising has also been effective, particularly against candidates with image problems. Goldwater's inflexibility, McGovern's inconsistency, Carter's fuzziness, and Reagan's intellectual deficiencies were highlighted by their opponents to accentuate the differences between the candidates. Most campaigns utilize both types of commercials to bolster their candidate's image while trying to weaken their opponent's.

There are other ways of influencing perceptions through the media. Candidates exercise considerable discretion in the words they use and the demeanor they present in interviews, in debates, and even on the news. Despite the appearance of spontaneity, their comments are carefully prepared and well rehearsed. In fact, throughout the entire campaign, public utterances and actions are almost always made with the press in mind.

How the media cover campaigns affects how candidates attempt to influence that coverage. The media emphasize the contest. They highlight drama and give controversial statements and events the most attention. There is little a campaign organization can do to affect that focus or divert attention from major blunders and conflicts. There is much, however, it can do to affect the regular reporting of everyday events of the campaign. Its release of information, its timing and staging of activities, and even the access provided the candidate and his senior aides can influence the quantity and quality of coverage and thereby affect the image that is projected to the public.

The overall impact of the media varies with the type of communication. The print media tend to attract a smaller but better-educated, higher-income, more professional audience than do radio and television. Newspapers and magazines require more active involvement of their readers than television does of its viewers, but they also facilitate selective perception to a larger extent. Television, on the other hand, has a more captive and passive audience.

None of the media emphasizes issues. Television news deemphasizes them the most. Instead it focuses on the principal candidates in action, capsuling the major events of their day. Paid media compensate for this focus by providing more substantive information in addition to the favorable or unfavorable profiles they present.

What effect does all this have on the voters? The literature suggests that newspapers and magazines work primarily to activate and reinforce existing attitudes. For strong party identifiers, television does the same.

For weaker partisans and independents, however, television can alter perceptions of the candidates, although it is unlikely to change political attitudes or affect issue positions. How many people are actually influenced is difficult to measure. In a close election, however, even a small number can affect the results. Few campaign managers would be willing to discount the impact of the media. This is why candidates are very careful what they say and how they appear whenever cameras and reporters are around.

NOTES

1. Samuel Popkin, John W. Gorman, Charles Phillips, and Jeffrey A. Smith, "Comment: What Have You Done for Me Lately? Toward an Investment Theory of Voting," *American Political Science Review*, 70 (1976), 779–805.

2. An excellent examination of presidential traits appears in Benjamin I. Page, *Choices and Echoes in Presidential Elections* (Chicago: University of Chicago Press, 1978), pp. 232–265. This discussion draws liberally from Page's description and analysis.

3. Fred I. Greenstein, "Popular Images of the President," *American Journal of Psychiatry*, 122 (1965), 523–529; Greenstein, "What the President Means to Americans: Presidential 'Choice' Between Elections," in James D. Barber (ed.), *Choosing the President* (Englewood Cliffs, N.J.: Prentice-Hall, 1974), pp. 121–147; Dan Nimmo and Robert L. Savage, *Candidates and Their Images* (Pacific Palisades, Calif.: Goodyear Publishing, 1976), pp. 45–80; Roberta S. Sigel, "Image of the American Presidency—Part II of an Exploration into Popular Views of Presidential Power," *Midwest Journal of Political Science*, 10 (1966), 123–137.

4. One of the most comprehensive of these surveys was conducted by the Gallup organization in 1979 for WHYY-TV (Philadelphia-Wilmington) for its public television series "Every Four Years." The poll included forty-five open- and closed-ended questions on the President. The results are reported in Stephen J. Wayne, "Expectations of the President," in Doris Graber (ed.), *The President and the Public* (Philadelphia: Institute for the Study of Human Issues, 1982), pp. 17–38.

5. Short commercials are difficult to turn off or tune out, especially if they come in the midst of an entertainment program. They are over before most people could or would change them. Their brevity, however, is also a problem, since only a limited message can be conveyed. Typically, advertisers repeat short spots to hammer home a point. In this way they produce an effect over time.

6. Joseph Napolitan, *The Election Game and How to Win It* (Garden City, N.Y.: Doubleday, 1972), p. 41.

7. Robert Agranoff, *The Management of Election Campaigns* (Boston: Holbrook Press, 1976), p. 394.

8. Rafshoon Communications, "1980 General Election Themes-The Media Campaign," *Memorandum to the President* (July 3, 1980).

9. Carter was the first candidate in some time not to use the traditional red, white, and blue colors. His deep green conveyed the freshness and purity of a new day.

10. Carter literally got dressed in his ads. A first shot pictured him in a short-sleeve shirt and dungarees on the farm. It would be difficult to imagine Eisenhower, Nixon, or Ford in similar garb. Another scene showed him in casual slacks and a long-sleeve shirt open at the collar, talking informally with several people. Finally, he was seen in a coat and tie addressing a group of business people. These ads were so effective in conveying a human dimension and in suggesting Carter's ability to move from the informality of the farm to the formality of the White House that Ford had to get undressed. He rolled up his sleeves, loosened his tie, and puffed his pipe in the Oval Office to demonstrate how hard he was working as President. Ford's advertisers also used his dress to create the image of a person who could adjust to different situations, who was a regular guy. He wore a University of Michigan jacket when speaking on that campus and was seen in other informal attire when pictured with his family or with small groups.

11. The "Mondole" ad was similar in theme to a heartbeat commercial the Democrats ran in 1968. This ad pictured an oscillograph that was recording a person's heartbeat. The message followed: "Muskie. Agnew. Who is your choice to be a heartbeat away from the Presidency?"

12. Patrick Caddell, quoted in Stephen Lesher with Patrick Caddell and Gerald Rafshoon, "Did the Debates Help Jimmy Carter?" in Austin Ranney (ed.), The Past and Future of Presidential Debates (Washington, D.C.: American Enterprise Institute, 1979), p. 141.

13. Elihu Katz and Jacob J. Feldman, "The Debates in the Light of Research: A Survey of Surveys," in Sidney Kraus (ed.), The Great Debates (Bloomington: Indiana University Press, 1962), p. 190.

14. The debates had to be sponsored by an outside group in order to get around a law which forces television to provide equal time for all candidates, not simply those of the major parties. Congress had suspended this provision of the law in 1960 but did not do so in 1976 and 1980. The League of Women Voters agreed to sponsor the debates, and television carried them as a news event.

15. Jules Witcover, Marathon (New York: New American Library, 1977), pp. 611–612.

16. Thomas E. Patterson, "Television and Election Strategy," in Gerald Benjamin (ed.), The Communications Revolution in Politics (New York: Academy of Political Science, 1982), p. 31.

17. George F. Bishop, Robert W. Oldendick, and Alfred J. Tuchfarber, "Debate Watching and the Acquisition of Political Knowledge," Journal of Communication, 27 (1978), 109.

18. Agranoff, The Management of Election Campaigns, p. 311.

19. Patterson, "Television and Election Strategy," p. 30.

20. Michael J. Robinson and Margaret A. Sheehan, Over the Wire and on TV: CBS and UPI in Campaign '80 (New York: Russell Sage Foundation, 1983), p. 146.

21. Ibid., p. 148.

22. Ibid., p. 74.

23. Ibid., p. 168.

24. Doris A. Graber, "Presidential Images in the 1968 Campaign" (paper delivered at the annual meeting of the Midwest Political Science Association, Chicago, April 30–May 2, 1970), p. 3.

25. Robinson and Sheehan, Over the Wire and on TV, p. 184.

26. Jody Powell, quoted in F. Christopher Arterton, "The Media Politics of Presidential Campaigns," in James David Barber (ed.), *Race for the Presidency* (Englewood Cliffs, N.J.: Prentice-Hall, 1978), p. 36.

27. Paul Lazarsfeld, Bernard Berelson, and Hazel Goudet, *The People's Choice* (New York: Columbia University Press, 1948); Bernard Berelson, Paul Lazarsfeld, and William McPhee, *Voting: A Study of Opinion Formation in a Presidential Campaign* (Chicago: University of Chicago Press, 1954).

28. Robinson and Sheehan, p. 9.

29. Ibid., p. 271.

30. Thomas E. Patterson and Robert D. McClure, *The Unseeing Eye* (New York: Putnam, 1976), p. 58.

31. Ibid., p. 54.

32. Thomas Patterson, "The Miscast Institution: The Press in Presidential Politics," *Public Opinion*, 3 (1980), 47.

33. In his study, Patterson found that knowledge of the candidates' issue stands improved over the course of the campaign. However, he also noted, "As the November election day approached, there were, on average, more voters who did not know where Ford and Carter stood on an issue than those who did." Ibid., p. 50.

34. This is a conclusion that people are not quick to admit. See Walter DeVries, "Taking the Voter's Pulse," in Ray E. Hiebert et al., *The Political Image Merchants* (Washington, D.C.: Acropolis Books, 1971).

35. Patterson and McClure, *The Unseeing Eye*, pp. 109, 122.

36. Patterson, "Television and Election Strategy," p. 32.

Selected Readings

Adams, William C. *Television Coverage of the 1980 Presidential Campaign.* Norwood, N.J.: Ablex, 1983.

Barber, James D., ed. *Race for the Presidency.* Englewood Cliffs, N.J.: Prentice-Hall, 1978.

Crouse, Timothy. *The Boys on the Bus: Riding with the Campaign Press Corps.* New York: Random House, 1973.

Graber, Doris. "Personal Qualities in Presidential Images: The Contribution of the Press," *Midwest Journal of Political Science,* 16 (1972), 46–76.

Greenstein, Fred I. "What the President Means to Americans: Presidential 'Choice' between Elections," in James D. Barber (ed.), *Choosing the President.* Englewood Cliffs, N.J.: Prentice-Hall, 1974.

Kraus, Sidney, ed. *The Great Debates.* Bloomington: Indiana University Press, 1962.

McGinnis, Joe. *The Selling of the President, 1968.* New York: Trident Press, 1969.

Napolitan, Joseph. *The Election Game and How to Win It.* Garden City, N.Y.: Doubleday, 1972.

Nimmo, Dan. *The Political Persuaders.* Englewood Cliffs, N.J.: Prentice-Hall, 1970.

Nimmo, Dan, and Robert L. Savage. *Candidates and Their Images.* Pacific Palisades, Calif.: Goodyear Publishing, 1976.

Page, Benjamin I. *Choices and Echoes in Presidential Elections.* Chicago: University of Chicago Press, 1978.

Patterson, Thomas E. *The Mass Media Election: How Americans Choose Their President.* New York, Praeger, 1980.

Patterson, Thomas E., and Robert D. McClure. *The Unseeing Eye.* New York: Putnam, 1976.

Ranney, Austin, ed. *The Past and Future of Presidential Debates.* Washington, D.C.: American Enterprise Institute, 1979.

Robinson, Michael J., and Margaret A. Sheehan. *Over the Wire and on TV: CBS and UPI in Campaign '80.* New York: Russell Sage Foundation, 1983.

PART IV

THE ELECTION

Chapter 8

THE VOTE AND
ITS MEANING

Introduction

Predicting the results of an election is a favorite American practice. Politicians do it; the media do it; even the public anticipates the outcome far in advance of the event. It is a form of entertainment—somewhat akin to forecasting the winner of a sporting event.

Presidential elections are particularly prone to such predictions. Public opinion polls report on the choices of the American public at frequent intervals during the campaign. Television projects a winner long before most of the votes are counted. Election-day surveys of voters exiting from the polls assess the mood of the electorate and present the first systematic analysis of the results. Subsequently, more in-depth studies reveal shifts in opinions and attitudes.

Predictions and analyses of the election are not conducted solely for their entertainment/news value. They provide important information to candidates running for office and to those who have been elected. For the nominees, they indicate the issues that can be effectively raised and those that should be avoided. They also suggest which audience would be most receptive to what policy positions. For the successful candidates, they provide an interpretation of the vote, the range of acceptable policy options, and the extent of presidential discretion—all matters which newly elected Presidents need to know.

This chapter will examine the presidential vote from three perspectives. The first section deals with predictions. It discusses national polls, describes their methodology, and evaluates their effect on the conduct of the campaign. The election-eve predictions of the media will also briefly be described.

The next section turns to an examination of the vote. After alluding to the election-day surveys, it reports on the findings of studies conducted since 1952 by researchers at the University of Michigan. The major components of the Michigan model are reviewed and the principal conclusions of its evaluation of recent presidential elections are summarized. In this summary, the interplay of partisan, issue, and candidate orientations is emphasized.

The final section of the chapter discusses the relationship between campaigning and governing, between issue debates and public policymaking, between candidate evaluations and presidential style. Do the campaign issues determine the form of agenda building? Does the projected or perceived image of the candidate affect the tone of his Presidency or his actions as President? Can an electoral coalition be converted into a governing party? Does the selection process help or hinder the President in meeting the expectations it creates? These questions will be explored in an effort to determine the impact of the election on the operation of the office, the behavior of the President, and the functioning of the political system.

PREDICTING PRESIDENTIAL ELECTIONS

Public Opinion Polls

The most popular question during a campaign is, who is going to win? The public is naturally interested in the answer and the media and candidates are obsessed with it, although for different reasons. In focusing on the horse-race aspect of the election, the media feel compelled to report who is ahead and, to a much lesser extent, what the dominant issues are. In forging a winning coalition, candidates and their organizations need to know how the electorate is reacting to their appeals. Both require this information at frequent intervals during the campaign. Waiting until it is all over is obviously too late.

Much of these data can be obtained from surveys of the population. Since 1916 there have been nationwide assessments of public opinion during elections. The largest and most comprehensive of these early surveys were the straw polls conducted by The *Literary Digest,* a popular monthly magazine. The *Digest* mailed millions of ballots and questionnaires to people who appeared on lists of automobile owners and in telephone directories. In 1924, 1928, and 1932, the poll correctly predicted the winner of the presidential election; in 1936, it did not. A huge Landon victory was forecast and a huge Roosevelt victory occurred.

What went wrong? The *Digest* mailed 10 million questionnaires over the course of the campaign and received 2 million back. As the ballots were returned, they were counted and the results totaled. This procedure tended to cloud, not highlight, trends in the responses.[1] But this was not the major problem. The problem was the sample of people who responded; it was not representative of the total voting population. Automobile owners and telephone subscribers were simply not typical voters in 1936, since most people did not own cars or have telephones. This mattered more in 1936 than it had in previous years because of the depression. There was a socioeconomic cleavage within the electorate. The *Literary Digest* sample did not reflect this cleavage; thus, its results were inaccurate.[2]

While the *Digest* was tabulating its 2 million responses and predicting that Landon would be the next President, a number of other pollsters were conducting more scientific surveys and correctly forecasting Roosevelt's reelection.[3] The polls of George Gallup, Elmo Roper, and Archibald Crossley differed from the *Digest*'s in two principal respects: They were considerably smaller, and they tried to approximate the characteristics of the population in their sample.

The *Digest* went out of business, but Gallup, Roper, and Crossley continued to poll and perfect their sampling techniques. In 1940, Gallup predicted Roosevelt would receive 52 percent of the vote; he actually received 55 percent. In 1944, Gallup forecast a 51.5 percent Roosevelt vote, very close to his actual 53.2 percent. Other pollsters also correctly predicted the results. As a consequence, public confidence in election polling began to grow.

The confidence was short-lived, however. In 1948, all major pollsters forecast a Dewey victory. Their errors resulted from poor sampling techniques, from the premature termination of polling in the middle of the campaign, and from incorrect assumptions about how the undecided would vote. In attempting to approximate the population in their samples, the pollsters had resorted to filling quotas. They interviewed a certain number of people with different sexual, religious, ethnic, economic, and social characteristics until the percentage of these groups in the sample resembled those in the population as a whole. However, simply because the percentages were approximately equal did not mean that the sample was representative of the population. For example, interviewers avoided certain sections in cities, which biased the results.

Moreover, the interviewing stopped several weeks before the election. In mid-October, the polls showed that Dewey was ahead by a substantial margin. Burns Roper, polling for *Fortune* magazine, saw the lead as sufficiently large to predict a Dewey victory without the need for further surveys.

A relatively large number of people, however, were undecided. Three weeks before the election, Gallup concluded that 8 percent of the electorate had still not made up their minds. In estimating the final vote, he and other pollsters assumed the undecided would divide their votes in much the same manner as the electorate as a whole. This turned out to be an incorrect assumption. Most of those who were wavering in the closing days of the campaign were Democrats. In the end, most voted for Truman or did not vote at all.

The results of the 1948 election once again cast doubt on the accuracy of public opinion polls. Truman's victory also reemphasized the fact that surveys reflect opinion at the time they are taken, not necessarily two weeks later. Opinion and voter preferences may change.

To monitor shifts within the electorate better, pollsters began extending their surveying to the weekend before the election. They changed their method of selecting people to be interviewed. They also developed more effective means of anticipating who would actually vote. These changes, plus the continued refinement of the questions, have produced more accurate forecasts.

Between 1936 and 1950, the average error of the final Gallup Poll was 3.6 percent; between 1952 and 1970, it was 1.65 percent; and between 1972 and 1980, it was 1.5 percent. In 1980, the average error was 3.8 percent.[4] Very close elections in 1960, 1968, and 1976, however, resulted in several wrong predictions, and in 1980, the polls underestimated the magnitude of Reagan's victory. (See Table 8–1).

Some of the problems in 1980 were similar to those in 1948. Polling stopped too early. With partisan ties weakening, voting behavior has become more volatile in recent years. The electorate tends to make up its mind later in the campaign and seems more susceptible to influence by candidates, issues, and events. In 1980 there were a large number of undecided voters. The CBS News/*New York Times* poll estimated that approximately 20 percent of the electorate made up their minds in the final

Table 8–1   FINAL PREELECTION POLLS AND RESULTS, 1948–1980

Year	Gallup Poll	Roper Poll	Harris Poll	Actual Results*
1948				
Truman	44.5	37.1		49.6
Dewey	49.5	52.2		45.1
Others	6.0	4.3		5.3
1952				
Eisenhower	51.0			55.1
Stevenson	49.0			44.4
1956				
Eisenhower	59.5	60.0		57.4
Stevenson	40.5	38.0		42.0
1960				
Kennedy	51.0	49.0		49.7
Nixon	49.0	51.0		49.5
1964				
Johnson	64.0		64.0	61.1
Goldwater	36.0		36.0	38.5
1968				
Nixon	43.0		41.0	43.4
Humphrey	42.0		45.0	42.7
Wallace	15.0		14.0	13.5
1972				
Nixon	62.0		61.0	60.7
McGovern	38.0		39.0	37.5
1976				
Carter	48.0	51.0	46.0	50.1
Ford	49.0	47.0	45.0	48.0
Others	3.0	2.0	3.0	1.9
Undecided			6.0	
1980				
Reagan	47.0		46.0	50.7
Carter	44.0		41.0	41.0
Anderson	8.0		10.0	6.6
Others				1.7
Undecided	1.0		3.0	

Source: Final Gallup Poll, "Record of Gallup Poll Accuracy," *Gallup Opinion Index,* December 1980, p. 12. Reprinted with permission.
*Except in 1948, 1976, and 1980 the percentage of votes for minor candidates is not noted in the table.

week of the campaign; many did so on the final day. Since most of the public polls were completed by November 1, four days before the election, they did not detect the late surge for Reagan. The candidates' polls, which continued until the eve of the election, did. (See Table 8–2).

Moreover, predicting levels of turnout continued to prove difficult. Since more people indicate that they will vote than actually do vote, pollsters must try to identify the most likely voters. In 1980 the decline in turnout did not affect the candidates equally. Carter suffered more than Reagan. A larger percentage of his supporters failed to cast ballots.[5]

The tendency to give socially acceptable responses also seemed to affect the poll results in 1980. Reagan appeared to gain from a "closet vote"—that is, the votes of people who did not wish to admit publicly that they were supporting him. The closet Reagan voter was most likely to be a Democrat, a liberal, and, in some cases, a member of a minority group.[6]

Finally, the attention given the polls accentuated the differences between their findings and the actual returns. With the print and visual media emphasizing the closeness of the contest and documenting this emphasis with the latest surveys, it is no wonder that the results came as something of a surprise. Nonetheless, they remained within the relatively small range of sampling error.

Methods and Uses of Surveys

The main reason that polls have become increasingly accurate is the improvement in sampling procedures. Since the objective of surveying is to generalize from a small number to the population as a whole, it is essential that the people interviewed be representative of the electorate. The odds of the sample's being representative can be estimated when it is randomly selected.

Random selection does not mean haphazard choice. Rather, it means that every element in the population (in this case, the eligible elec-

Table 8–2 FINAL PREELECTION MEDIA AND CANDIDATE POLLS, 1980*

	Media Polls		Candidate Polls		Actual Results†
	CBS/New York Times‡	NBC-AP‡	Caddell (Carter)‡	Wirthlin (Reagan)‡	
Reagan	41	42	46	45	50.7
Carter	40	36	36	34	41.0
Anderson	7	9	9.5	9	6.6
Undecided	11	10	8	12	
N	2,264	1,574	1,200	2,000	

*The percentage may not equal 100 due to rounding and the existence of preferences for minor party candidates (not indicated in table).

†Other candidates received approximately 1.7 percent of the total vote.

‡The CBS/New York Times poll was conducted October 30–November 1; the NBC-AP poll, October 22–24; and the Caddell and Wirthlin polls, November 3.

torate) has an equal chance of being included in the sample, and the choice of any one element would not preclude the choice of any other. The *Literary Digest* sample of 1936 and the quota sample of 1948 were not random.[7] There was no way to determine whether the people interviewed were typical. As it turned out, they were not—at least, not of those who voted on election day.

Random selection is thus the key to sampling. There are many ways of doing it. Most pollsters employ what is known as a cluster random sample. In such a sample, the population is divided into geographic units and stratified on the basis of the size of communities. This procedure is used to make sure that the sample conforms to Census Bureau estimates. Within each stratum, smaller and smaller units are then randomly selected until a block in a city or part of a township is isolated. Then, a number of interviews are conducted according to a carefully prescribed procedure at each of these sampling points. Interviewers have no choice whom they interview or where they conduct the interviews. In 1980, the Gallup organization randomly selected 350 sampling points and held about five interviews at each.[8]

Since sampling is based on probability theory, the likelihood of being right or wrong can be calculated. In a random sample the odds of being right are determined primarily by the size of the sample. The closer the sample approximates the size of the population, the more likely it will be accurate and the more confidence that can be placed in the results. For national surveys, a sample of approximately 1,100 will yield an error of ± 3 percent.[9] This means that the results of the sample may deviate 3 percent in either direction from the population as a whole. Thus, if a poll with a sampling error of ± 3 percent indicated candidate A had 49.5 percent and candidate B had 50.5 percent, its findings could be generalized as follows: A will receive between 46.5 and 52.5 percent of the total and B will receive between 47.5 and 53.5 percent. The results of such a contest would be hazardous to predict.

The way to improve the accuracy of a sample is to enlarge it. However, enlarging it adds to its cost. At $25–$35 per interview, the expense can be substantial.[10] At some point a law of diminishing returns sets in. For example, to increase the accuracy of a nationwide sample to ± 2 percent, a total of approximately 2,400 randomly selected respondents would be needed as opposed to about 9,600 for ± 1 percent and 600 for ± 4 percent.[11] Surprising as it may seem, so long as the sample size is less than 5 percent of the entire population, the size of the population does not directly affect the error in the sample.

The accuracy of a poll in measuring public opinion is also affected by the interview and the interviewer.[12] A survey is only as good as its questions: how they are worded and what order they are in. The focus of the questions is normally dictated by the objectives of the study. Public polls, such as those conducted by independent research organizations like Gallup and Harris and syndicated to newspapers and magazines, usually focus on who is ahead and how different groups of people feel about the candidate. "If the election were held today, for whom would you vote?" is the key question.[13]

Finally, pollsters and candidates alike are interested in the currency of their polls. A survey of public opinion measures that opinion only during the time in which interviews were conducted. To monitor changes as rapidly as possible, a new technique known as tracking polls was used by the Republicans during the 1982 congressional elections. Instead of simply interviewing the entire sample in one or two days and then analyzing the results, interviews were conducted continuously. As new respondents were added, old ones were dropped. This produced a rolling sample. Continuous analyses of this sample discerned trends within the population. Pollsters of all persuasions can be expected to use this technique over the course of the 1984 campaign.

Television Forecasts

Predictions continue right to the end, until all the votes are tabulated. The national pollsters normally conduct their final surveys on the Friday and Saturday before the Tuesday vote.[14] The results, which appear in the Sunday and Monday newspapers, constitute their final preelection poll but not the final prediction. That comes on election night as the returns are counted.

In presenting the results the media have three objectives: to report the vote, to forecast the winners, and to analyze the returns. To accomplish the first of these objectives, the major networks and news services have pooled their resources. In 1964 they established a consortium known as the News Election Service (NES). Operating on election night to report the results, the NES assigns thousands of reporters to precincts and county election boards around the country. Their job is to telephone the presidential, congressional, and gubernatorial vote to a center which feeds the returns into a giant computer. Each of the networks (ABC, CBS, and NBC) and news services (Associated Press and United Press International) that participate in the consortium have terminals that indicate how the vote is progressing until it is completed.[15]

If all the media wished to do was report the results of the vote as rapidly as possible, the NES system would suffice. However, the winners and losers might not be obvious for some time. Moreover, the initial reports of who is ahead and likely to win might be misleading. The NES results do not reveal which precincts have reported, whether they tend to be Democratic or Republican, or how their returns compare with those of past elections.

Since the name of the game is accuracy and speed, the networks have developed projection systems to anticipate the results and exit polls to analyze them. The projections are based on identifying sample precincts. They may be randomly or purposely selected. In either case, they should be roughly proportional to the number of urban, suburban, and rural precincts within the state. If they are purposely chosen, they should have a history of mirroring the state vote (barometer precincts) or should be reflective of a particular ethnic, racial, or religious group within the state (bellweather precincts). Finally, they must report early.[16]

The object of the analysis is to discern trends. As the votes are received, they are compared with the results from the same precincts in previous years. Computers are used to calculate the various combinations of voting patterns. On the basis of these calculations, analysts call elections. Normally, the vote is not called until a number of different checks, usually made by different people, confirm the same results. Occasionally, however, the race to beat the other networks is so compelling that analysts will go out on a limb, sometimes with embarrassing results.

The classic faux pas in election predictions happened in 1960, when CBS News forecast a Nixon victory at 7:15 P.M. Eastern Standard Time. The CBS error occurred because its computer had been programmed to evaluate the vote in the order in which it had been received in the last election and not on the basis of geographic areas. Thus, when midwestern votes were received more quickly than they had been four years earlier, the computer predicted Nixon would win. Once the returns from the East Coast began to be recorded, the computer revised its prediction.

The CBS error in 1960, combined with some hasty predictions by the other networks, has led to greater caution in election-eve forecasts. In 1976, all three networks waited until the early hours of the morning before projecting a Carter victory. In 1980, however, they did not. Prior to 7:30 P.M., before the other networks even began their election coverage, NBC had forecast the results of the presidential elections in six states. It called Ohio for Reagan forty seconds after the polls closed in that state! By 8:15 P.M. NBC had reported that Reagan had won the election.[17]

How were such quick projections made? Obviously, the results could not have been predicted on the basis of precinct votes, since they could not have been counted and reported so quickly. What NBC did in 1980, and what the other networks can be expected to do in 1984, was to project the results on the basis of exit polls, which survey voters after they have cast their ballots.

Exit polls work in the following manner: A large number of precincts across the country are randomly selected. Representatives of the networks, often college students, interview voters as they leave the polls. In the course of the interview, each voter is asked to complete a printed ballot and deposit it into a sealed box. Throughout the day, these ballots are collected and tabulated. Results are telephoned to a central computer bank. After the election in a state has been completed, the findings of the poll are broadcast.

The survey is usually very accurate. The large number of people who are interviewed, anywhere from 12,000 to 15,000, reduces the sampling error to much less than that of the national surveys conducted by Gallup, Harris, and the Center for Political Studies at the University of Michigan. As a consequence, the attitudes, opinions, and choices of the electorate can be discerned in a fairly precise manner.

All three networks have depended on exit polls in recent years to analyze the vote. NBC, however, was the first to rely on them to forecast the winner of a presidential election. While its 1980 projections were the most rapid in television, they were not the first to be made before the voting had been completed in the nation as a whole. In 1964, Johnson's victory over Goldwater was announced by all the networks prior to the close of voting on the West Coast. Similarly, Nixon's win in 1972 was forecast by the media two hours before the Pacific states had completed voting.

Considerable criticism of these early projections has been made on the grounds that they discourage turnout and affect voting in states in which the polls are still open. A number of researchers have examined the question, but their results are inconclusive. In a 1964 survey of approximately 1,700 registered voters in California, Harold Mendelsohn uncovered little evidence of vote switching as a consequence of television. Relatively few people watched the broadcasts and then voted. Most voted first.[18] A similar study in 1968 conducted by other researchers reached a similar conclusion.[19] However, in the 1972 election, political scientists Raymond Wolfinger and Peter Linquiti concluded that there was a small decline in the West Coast vote after the Nixon victory had been predicted.[20]

The issue was raised again in 1980 but with a slightly different twist. When the early returns and private polls all indicated a Reagan landslide, President Carter appeared before his supporters at 8:30 P.M. Eastern Standard Time, while polls were still open in most parts of the country, and acknowledged defeat. His concession speech was carried live on each of the major networks. Almost immediately Carter's early announcement incurred extensive criticism, particularly from defeated West Coast Democrats. They alleged that the President's remarks discouraged many Democrats from voting, thereby contributing to their defeat as well. However, it is difficult to substantiate this claim. In general, turnout declined more in the East and Midwest than it did in the Far West. Even if there was a decline after Carter's concession, there is little evidence to suggest that Democrats behaved any differently from Republicans and independents. Hawaii, the last state to close its polls, voted for Carter.

In short, it is difficult to prove or disprove the impact of election-eve broadcasts on the vote. In all likelihood they affect turnout or the rationale for not turning out more than they affect the actual decision of how to vote.

INTERPRETING THE ELECTION

In addition to predicting the results, the television networks also provide an instant analysis of them on election night. This analysis, based primarily on exit polls, relates voting decisions to issue positions, ideological perspectives, and partisan preferences. Patterns between demographic characteristics, issue stances, and electoral choices are noted and used to explain why people voted for particular candidates.

Exit polls present a detailed picture of the electorate on election day. They do not, however, provide a longitudinal perspective. To understand changes in public attitudes and opinions, it is necessary to survey people over the course of the election, asking the same questions and, if possible, interviewing the same people. The nationwide polls conducted by Gallup and Harris often repeat questions but not respondents. Surveys conducted by the University of Michigan repeat both. Utilizing the interview-reinterview technique, these surveys have provided social scientists with a wealth of data on the behavior of the American voter.

The Normal Vote

According to the Michigan studies, the identification of people with political parties is the most stable and resilient factor affecting the voting decision. It is considered to be the single most important long-term influence on voting. Party identification has both direct and indirect effects. Partisan attitudes provide voting cues to party identifiers. They also influence their perceptions of the candidates and the issues, which, in turn, affects their vote. Orientations toward the candidate and issues are short-term factors which change from election to election. If strong enough, they can, of course, cause people to vote against their partisan inclinations. Usually, however, they do not. In most cases, they serve as an inducement and a rationalization for supporting the party and its candidates.

The stability of partisan attitudes explains why much of the electorate votes as it does in election after election. To be influenced by partisanship is normal for people who identify with a party and even for many who technically consider themselves independent. Since a large majority of the electorate does identify with a political party or leans in a partisan direction, the candidate of the major party should win—*all other things being equal.*

That partisan attitudes are enduring and constant for much of the electorate permits analysts to calculate the vote in any given election. By examining the rate of turnout among strong and weak partisan identifiers, researchers can project an expected or normal vote.[21] Actual votes can then be compared with the expected vote and the difference explained on the basis of short-term factors.

Some deviation from the expected partisan division of the electorate occurs in every election. Since 1952, the deviation seems to be increasing at the presidential level. The weakening of partisan ties, growth of media campaigning, and increasing ideological/issue awareness on the part of some of the electorate have contributed to the influence of short-term factors on the outcome of the election. What are these factors, and which have been the most important?

In its evaluation of presidential elections since 1952, the Center for Political Studies of the University of Michigan has attempted to identify the major components of the electorate's decisions. Focusing on the interplay of candidate evaluation, issue awareness, and ideological attitudes, the center's analysts have sought to provide an explanation of the elections, an interpretation of the votes. What follows is a summary of their conclusions.

1952–1960: The Impact of Personality

In 1952, the short-term effect of the issues and the candidates contributed to the Republican victory. "Communism, corruption, and

Korea" were the three principal issues.[22] The Republicans were seen as the party better able to deal with the problems of fighting communism, promoting efficiency and better government, and ending the war in Korea. General Eisenhower was also perceived in a more favorable light than his opponent, Adlai Stevenson. While the public still regarded Democrats as more capable of handling domestic problems, the appeal of Eisenhower, combined with the more favorable attitude toward the Republican party in foreign policy and government management, resulted in an election that deviated from what would have been expected if only partisanship had affected the vote.

The presidential election of 1956 also deviated from partisan voting patterns. However, Eisenhower's reelection was far more of a personal triumph for the President than it was a political victory for the Republicans. The Republican party did not win control of Congress, as it had in 1952.

One major factor seems to explain the presidential voting in 1956—the very positive evaluation of Eisenhower and the slightly negative evaluation of Stevenson in contrast to 1952, when Stevenson was favorably perceived by most of the electorate.[23] At other levels of government, however, the Democrats continued to benefit from their partisan majority. Their reputation within the domestic sphere more than compensated for the Republicans' image as the party best able to make and conduct foreign policy.[24] In electoral politics, it is the impact at home that counts the most.

Because he was the candidate of the majority party in 1960, Kennedy's victory was not surprising. What is surprising is the closeness of the election. Despite the Democrats' large partisan advantage, Kennedy received only 115,000 more votes than Nixon, 0.03 percent more of the total vote. Why was the presidential contest so close?

Most analysts agree that Kennedy's Catholicism cost him votes. The Michigan researchers estimate that he lost about 2.2 percent of the popular vote, or approximately 1.5 million votes, because of the religious issue.[25] The decline in Democratic voting was particularly evident in the heavily Protestant South, where 16.5 percent of the expected Democratic vote went to Nixon. Analysis of the Protestant defection reveals that it varied directly with church attendance. The more regular the attendance, the less likely the individual would vote for Kennedy.[26]

Outside the South, however, Kennedy registered a small net gain over the expected Democratic vote. The main reason for this gain was the heavy vote he received from Catholics. In 1960, it rose to almost 80 percent, 17 percent more than normal. The concentration of Catholics in the large industrial states may, in fact, have contributed to the size of his Electoral College majority.[27]

Religion, in short, was the main issue even though the candidates focused on other concerns and generally downplayed the religious question.[28] Nonetheless, Kennedy's religion dominated the attention of the voters and affected their assessments of the candidates. Nixon had a better image than Kennedy. His Vice Presidency during the popular Eisenhower years contributed to the public perception that he was the more experienced candidate, the more capable in foreign affairs, and surprisingly, in the aftermath of his own Presidency, the more personable of the two candidates. In contrast, Kennedy was viewed as young, immature, and lacking in experience. His performance during the debates, however, helped to counter Nixon's image advantage, especially among Democratic partisans.

The Michigan analysis of the election suggests that the vote turned on partisanship as modified by religion.[29] The Democratic candidate won, but barely. Kennedy's vote fell 4 percent below the expected Democratic vote.[30]

1964–1972: The Rise of Issue Voting

Lyndon Johnson's victory in 1964 can also be attributed to his being the candidate of the majority party. The size of his victory, however, exceeded the Democrats' partisan advantage. Moreover, there were significant deviations from the voting patterns of the past. The traditionally Democratic South voted for Goldwater and the Republican Northeast went Democratic.

Short-term factors explain the magnitude of the Johnson victory.[31] Goldwater was perceived as a minority candidate of a minority party, ideologically to the right of most Republicans. Moreover, he did not enjoy a favorable public image. In the Michigan survey, negative comments about Goldwater outnumbered positive ones two to one.[32] For Johnson, the pattern was reversed. He received twice as many complimentary remarks as uncomplimentatry ones. Policy attitudes also favored the Democrats even in foreign affairs. Goldwater's militant anticommunism scared many voters. They saw Johnson as the peace candidate.

Some analysts have concluded that voters in 1964 were more aware of and influenced by issues than in previous elections.[33] Goldwater's strong ideological convictions, coupled with his attempt to differentiate his position from Johnson's, undoubtedly contributed to greater issue awareness. When voting, however, most of the policy-conscious electorate had their views on the issues reinforced by their partisan attitudes.

One group that did not were southern Democrats. Fearful of the party's civil rights initiatives, they cast a majority of their votes for Goldwater. There was also a sizable defection of northern Republicans, who voted for Johnson.

In retrospect, Nie, Verba, and Petrocik conclude that 1964 was a critical transitional year for presidential elections. They write:

> 1964 . . . is the year when the public becomes more issue oriented and when its issue positions develop a coherence they did not previously have. At the same time citizens begin to vote consistently with their issue positions. It is the year when partisan commitment begins to erode. Pure party voting—that is, a vote for the candidate of the party with whom one identifies even if that vote is not in accord with one's issue inclination—declines.[34]

By 1968, the Vietnam war, urban riots, campus unrest, and the continuation of the civil rights struggle divided the electorate, particularly the Democratic party. A significant portion of that party deserted its presidential candidate.

The Wallace candidacy demonstrated the importance of issues in the presidential vote in 1968.[35] The Alabama governor did not have as much personal appeal for those who voted for him as his positions had. Unhappy with the Democratic party's handling of a wide range of social issues, white Democratic partisans, particularly in the South, and to a limited degree in the urban North, turned from their party's presidential candidate to vote for Wallace. He received 13.5 percent of the total vote cast.[36]

For those who stayed with their party, partisanship reinforced issue positions and candidate preferences. Republican defectors of 1964 returned to their party in 1968 and the Republican portion of the vote rose accordingly, from 39 percent in 1964 to 43 percent in 1968. The Democrats, on the other hand, suffered a 19 percent decline during the same period. It is estimated that a majority of Wallace's supporters were Democrats.[37] Had Wallace not run, the Republican presidential vote undoubtedly would have been larger. Nixon was the second choice of most Wallace voters.[38]

The results of the 1968 presidential election thus deviated from the partisan alignment of the electorate primarily because a significant number of Democrats had grievances against their party and expressed them by voting for Wallace and, to a much lesser extent, for Nixon. A decline in the intensity of partisanship and growth in the number of independents contributed to the issue voting that occurred in 1968. Were it not for the Democrats' large partisan advantage and the almost unanimous black vote that Humphrey received,[39] the presidential election would not have been nearly as close.

The trend away from partisan presidential voting for the Democratic candidate continued in 1972. With a nominee who was ideologically and personally unpopular, the Democrats suffered their worst presidential defeat since 1920. On the other hand, the party retained control of Congress, a majority of the state legislatures, and most of the governorships.

What factors contributed to Nixon's win? According to the Michigan researchers, the withdrawal of Senator Eagleton, McGovern's choice as vice presidential candidate, after Eagleton's history of mental depression became known was not a factor, nor was McGovern's identification with the new left.[40] These issues affected the Democratic standard-bearer's image, but they were not directly associated with the vote he received. Neither did distrust in government or Nixon's defense of traditional values make a crucial difference, although these factors also were related to the assessments of the candidates.[41] The fact was that Nixon enjoyed a better image than McGovern. He was perceived as the stronger presidential candidate. The electorate reacted to him positively, although less so than in 1960.[42] McGovern, on the other hand, was viewed negatively by non-Democrats and neutrally by Democrats. These perceptions contributed to Nixon's victory, but they were not its principal cause.

According to the Michigan analysts, Nixon's positions on the issues when contrasted with McGovern's account for the magnitude of his win.[43] Most of the electorate saw Nixon as closer to their own positions than McGovern. The latter was perceived as liberal on all issues and ideologically to the left of his own party. The Michigan researchers concluded, "The outcome of the election was the result of the ideological polarization within the Democratic ranks that pitted the left wing Democrats against those of the right."[44]

This conclusion, however, has been criticized by a number of political scientists. Samuel Popkin and his colleagues have argued that it was McGovern's perceived incompetence, not his issue positions, that was the primary cause of the sizable partisan defection to Nixon.[45] David RePass arrived at a similar conclusion. He wrote, "The 1972 election was, above all else, an election decided by the candidate factor."[46] The Michigan survey revealed that 42 percent of the self-identified Democrats and 66 percent of the independents cast ballots for Nixon.

Whereas the Democrats defected in considerable numbers in 1972, the Republicans did not: 94 percent of them voted for Nixon. For Republicans, partisanship remained the critical influence on their vote, reinforcing their issue and candidate images. For Democrats who stayed with McGovern, party identity, not issue preferences or candidate evaluation, seemed to be the principal reason for doing so.

The large defection of Democrats in 1972 and 1968 and of Republicans in 1964 led election analysts to reevaluate the impact of partisanship and issues in voting. Some studies of electoral behavior during this period indicated that more people than before were holding consistent issue positions and were being influenced by them when voting.[47] Not only was the proportion of party voters declining, but the partisan influence on issue voters also appeared to be declining. Nie, Verba, and Petrocik conclude that by 1972,

> the majority of the voters with coherent issue attitudes in 1964 were voters whose issue positions reinforced their party identification. By 1972 the majority of those with coherent issue positions were either Independents or partisans whose issue position was not congruent with their party identification.[48]

How much more important issues and ideology had become, however, remained the subject of considerable controversy. The instruments that survey researchers used to measure issue awareness and relate it to candidate choice were challenged; the number of issue voters in the survey was said to be too small for generalization; the contention that the decline in partisan identities contributed to issue voting was questioned; even the existence of consistent views on a range of issues that would allow voters to make an ideological judgment was disputed.[49]

1976–1980: The Evaluation of Potential and Performance

Neither Ford nor Carter emphasized the social and cultural concerns that played so large a role in the McGovern-Nixon contest. Rather, they both focused their attention on trust in government and domestic economic matters. Carter benefited from this dual emphasis. In the wake of Watergate, it is not surprising that the issues of trust and integrity worked to the Democrats' advantage. Similarly, with a recession occurring during the Ford Presidency, the public could be expected to blame the Republicans and look to the Democrats for its solution. By stressing these matters, Carter united his party and divided the electorate along partisan lines.

Despite the decreased attention given to sociocultural issues, which had split the electorate along liberal and conservative lines in 1972, some ideological thinking was still evident in 1976.[50] The difference was that in 1976 it translated more easily into Republican or Democratic votes, whereas in 1972 ideology had split the Democrats.

Approximately 60 percent of the electorate can place themselves on an ideological scale. Of those, the Michigan survey found that 79 percent who considered themselves liberal voted for Carter and 80 percent who thought of themselves as conservatives voted for Ford.[51] Whether ideology was a cause of the voting or simply a consequence of partisanship is unclear. What is clear, however, is that ideology and issues were reinforced by partisanship in 1976. They contributed to the influence of party on voting behavior. Four years earlier, they accounted for much of the Democratic defection.

Carter received 50.1 percent of the vote in 1976. If party alone were an influence, he would have been expected to receive 51.8 percent. Democratic defections declined by more than 50 percent. Twenty percent of the Democrats voted for Ford, compared with 42 percent four years earlier. Republican defections, on the other hand, increased to 14 percent.[52]

Most of the defections appeared to be generated by unfavorable assessments of the candidates. Ford was judged on the basis of his performance in office, whereas Carter was judged on the basis of his potential for leadership.[53] Normally, an incumbent would enjoy an advantage in such a comparison. Ford did not. His association with the Nixon administration, highlighted in the public mind by his pardon of the former President, his difficult struggle to win his own party's nomination, and his seeming inability to find a solution to the country's economic problems and to articulate discernible policy objectives appear to be the principal reasons for the low public appraisal of his performance in office. Ford's ratings improved as the campaign progressed, demonstrating that he was having some success in convincing the voters of his presidential ability. By the end of the campaign, his personal evaluation almost equaled Carter's.[54] In contrast, Carter's personal evaluation declined as the campaign progressed. Whereas he was initially viewed as an acceptable Democrat and evaluated on the basis of long-term partisan expectations, by the end of the campaign the public's judgment became more closely tied to his performance as a campaigner and less to his being an acceptable Democrat. The campaign concluded with Carter having only a slightly more favorable image.

With sociocultural issues muted and economic matters and ideology dividing along partisan lines, the candidate of the majority party, not the incumbent, was in the driver's seat. Carter won primarily because he was a Democrat and secondarily because his personal assessment was more favorable than Ford's.

In 1980, being a Democrat was not enough. Poor performance ratings overcame the advantage partisanship and incumbency normally bring to a President of the majority party, particularly one who was perceived as the more centrist of the two major candidates at the beginning of the campaign. In 1976, Carter was judged on the basis of his potential *for* office. In 1980 he was judged on the basis of his performance *in* office. As the results of the election indicate, that judgment was very harsh.

Reagan's victory was overwhelming. He won forty-four states with 489 electoral votes, compared with only six states and 49 electoral votes for Carter. Reagan received 51 percent of the popular vote, Carter 41 percent, and Anderson less than 7 percent, with the balance divided among the minority party candidates. Reagan's popular margin was over 8 million votes.

Not since 1888 had an elected incumbent Democratic President been denied reelection. President Ford lost in 1976, but he had not been elected to office. Only two Presidents since the Civil War, William Howard Taft and Herbert Hoover, lost their bids for reelection by larger margins than Carter. Even Hoover, in the midst of the Great Depression, won more electoral votes. Carter failed to carry a single large industrial state. His vote fell behind his 1976 percentages in every single state, and in approximately half the states, it dropped at least 10 percent. Why did he lose so badly? What happened to his electoral support over the four years?

The partisan predisposition of the electorate did not change appreciably. Between 1976 and 1980 the Republican party did not gain adherents at the expense of the Democrats. Public opinion did move slightly toward conservative policy positions, but the proportion of conservatives to liberals within the electorate remained approximately the same as it had since 1972.

Whereas long-term factors still seemed to benefit the candidate of the majority party, Jimmy Carter, short-term considerations did not. Personal evaluations and policy assessments were not nearly as favorable as they had been in 1976. Of these, the judgments of Carter's performance in office were the most important.

Carter started the campaign with the lowest approval rating of any President since the ratings were first begun in 1952. In July 1980, only 21 percent of the adult population approved of the way in which he conducted his Presidency. After the Democratic convention, his ratings improved, but during the course of the campaign they declined once again. In contrast, the personal assessments of Reagan became more favorable, although his overall evaluation was still negative at the end of the campaign.

These evaluations of the candidates colored the electorate's perceptions of Carter's and Reagan's ideological and policy positions. At the outset Carter was viewed as a centrist candidate and Reagan as the more extreme. By the conclusion of the campaign, this perception was reversed. Carter was seen as liberal, somewhat to the left of the electorate, and Reagan as more centrist.[55] Similarly, the policy-related assessments of the candidates also changed. Over the course of the campaign the public identified with Reagan's stands on a variety of issues more than with Carter's.

Analysts at the University of Michigan have concluded that these perceptual shifts, which occurred among liberals, moderates, and conservatives, resulted from voters' allowing their impressions of the candidates to affect their judgments of the candidates' positions. As they became more disillusioned with Carter, they became more supportive of Reagan and more likely to vote for him. To rationalize that vote it was necessary to perceive his opinions and attitudes as closer than Carter's to their own.[56] Many people did so.

The issues themselves seemed to benefit Reagan. Concerns about the economy, persistently high inflation, large-scale unemployment, the decreasing competitiveness and productivity of American industry all worked to the out-party's advantage. For the first time in many years, the Republicans were seen as the party better able to invigorate the economy, return prosperity, and lower inflation. The Democratic party and Carter were blamed for the problems.

Criticism of Democratic programs and elected officials extended to the government in general. A majority of Democrats and an overwhelming 87 percent of the Republicans believed that the government in Washington had become too large and powerful. In previous years, beliefs about the functions and responsibilities of government had divided along partisan lines, with Democrats more supportive of a larger governmental role than Republicans. Reagan's appeal, "to get the government off the backs of the people," struck a responsive cord, at least in the abstract.[57]

Frustration over the Soviet invasion of Afghanistan and the United States' failure to obtain the release of American hostages in Iran contributed to Carter's negative evaluation and to changing public attitudes toward defense spending. In 1980 most Americans supported increased military expenditures, a position with which Reagan was closely identified. Only on social issues, such as the ERA and abortion, was Carter more in tune with public opinion.[58]

The issues, when combined with personal assessments, contributed heavily to Carter's negative assessment. They explain why he lost even though he was the majority party's candidate. Twenty-seven percent of the Democrats who supported Carter in 1976 deserted him in 1980. Approximately 80 percent of these deserters voted for Reagan. They represented all ideological groups, not just conservatives.[59] Carter's share of the independent vote also declined substantially—almost 13 percent.

Anderson benefited from the disaffected liberal vote but was unable to attract a solid core of supporters. His candidacy did not appeal to ethnic, racial, or religious groups who were unhappy with the nominees of the major parties. Nor was Anderson able to differentiate his policy positions sufficiently from Carter's and Reagan's to generate an issue-oriented vote. In the end, his winning of no electoral votes and only 6.5 percent of the popular vote demonstrates the resiliency of the major parties and the legitimacy which their labels provide candidates for office.

In summary, Carter was repudiated by the voters because of his performance in office. In 1976 he won because he was a Democrat and because he provided more potential for strong and effective leadership than his opponent, Gerald Ford. In 1980 he lost despite the fact that he was a Democrat because he no longer provided greater potential than his opponent. His record as President doomed his candidacy.

Reagan, in contrast, won primarily because he was the option who had become acceptable and not primarily because of his ideology, or even his specific policy positions. While there was a desire for change, there was little direct ideological or issue voting.[60] Nor did Reagan's personal appeal contribute significantly to his victory. According to Miller and Wattenberg, "Reagan was the least positively evaluated candidate elected to the presidency in the history of the national election studies, which date back to 1952. Of all the candidates prior to 1980, only McGovern and Goldwater—each the victim of a landslide vote—had received lower ratings than did Ronald Reagan. The difference of course is that Reagan's opponent—Jimmy Carter—was seen even less favorably."[61] Nonetheless, it was Reagan who offered the potential for change. When judged against Carter's performance, this potential seemed more appealing.

If this analysis is correct, then Reagan did not receive an ideological or issue mandate from the voters despite his sizable victory and his party's gains in Congress.[62] The electorate desired change, agreed on many of the problems, but lacked a knowledge of and consensus on the solutions. Reagan's charge was to provide new and strong leadership, and, by so doing, invigorate the country's economy, strengthen its defenses, enhance its prestige, and maintain peace. How he would do this was for him to determine.

Figure 8–1   THE PRESIDENT'S MANDATE

Source: Copyright 1982 by Herblock in *Washington Post.*

CONVERTING ELECTORAL CHOICE INTO PUBLIC POLICY

The President's Imprecise Mandate

It is not unusual for the meaning of the election to be imprecise. The reasons that people vote for a President vary. Some do so because of his party, some because of his issue stands, some because of their assessment of his potential or his performance. For most, a combination of factors contributes to their voting decision. This combination makes it difficult to discern exactly what the electorate means, desires, or envisions by its electoral choice. The President is rarely given a clear mandate for governing.

Assuming that party is the principal influence on voting behavior, what cues can a President cull from his political connection? Party platforms contain a laundry list of positions and proposals, but there are problems in using them as a guide for new administrations. First and foremost, the presidential candidate may not have exercised a major influence on the platform's formulation or, second, may have had to accept certain compromises in the interests of party unity. It is not unusual for a nominee to disagree with one or several of the platform's positions or priorities. Carter personally opposed the party's abortion stand in 1980 and had major reservations about reducing unemployment through a $12 billion jobs program.

In addition to containing items the President-elect may oppose, the platform may omit some that he favors, particularly if they are controversial. There was no mention of amnesty in the 1976 Democratic platform, although Carter had publicly stated his intention to pardon Vietnam draft dodgers and war resisters if he was elected.

The platform's omission of these controversial issues was not unusual. In order to unite the party and not divide it, platforms try to avoid controversy when possible. Moreover, they cannot anticipate all the issues of a campaign. In this sense, the platform must constitute an incomplete policy agenda for a President, especially a new one.

Another limitation to using a platform as a guide to the partisan attitudes and opinions of the public is that most people, including party rank and file, are unfamiliar with most of its contents.[63] The platform per se is not the reason people vote for their party's candidates on election day.

Despite these constraints, a surprising number of party positions and promises do find their way into public policy.[64] This suggests that platforms are consensus documents that do represent the interests of a significant portion of the population. Increasingly, platforms have also become instruments of, by, and for organized interests within the party. The clout of these groups after the election may also account for the number of campaign promises that get enacted into law. The conversion of platform positions into adminsitration policy also indicates that the presidential nominee must be sympathetic to much of what the platform proposes, whether he affected its formulation or not. Incumbents, especially those seeking re-election, normally exercise considerable influence on its content. In 1964 and 1972, party platforms were actually drafted by White House aides.

In addition to the platform, are there any other partisan indicators to which a President might look for guidance? The parties' electoral images—the Democrats' in domestic affairs and the Republicans' in foreign affairs—suggest broad emphases but not specific direction. The issue positions and candidate evaluations of the voters are also important, but neither offers detailed guides to agenda building. Why not?

The electorate's positions on the issues are not always clear or consistent. While pollsters can discern a mood or even a range of views, they have difficulty evaluating, much less measuring, their precise impact on the vote. Not only do people with similar attitudes and beliefs vote for a candidate for different reasons, but people with very different attitudes and beliefs vote for the same candidate. Politicians, of course, encourage this by fudging their positions on the issues in the general election. In short, the campaign may identify problems, but the vote rarely points to specific solutions.

Instead of looking to the electorate for direction, successful candidates tend to look to themselves. They should. As mentioned in chapter 3, the specificity with which issues are discussed and the perceived differences between the candidates' positions have a lot to do with the impact of the issues on voting behavior. In other words, candidates affect the degree to which issues are important.

Expectations and Performance

When campaigning, candidates also try to create impressions of leadership, conveying such attributes as assertiveness, decisiveness, compassion, and integrity. Kennedy promised to get the country moving, Johnson to continue the New Frontier–Great Society program, Nixon to bring us together. These promises created expectations of performance regardless of the policy stands. In the 1976 election, Jimmy Carter heightened expectations by his constant reference to the strong, decisive leadership he intended to exercise as President. During the campaign, he was projected as a person who understood the nation's problems and would do something about them. "You can depend on it," he repeated over and over again in his acceptance speech to the Democratic convention. In 1980 he was less emphatic, emphasizing continuity, not change. In contrast, Reagan indicated his determination to steer a new and steadier course than Carter.

All new administrations and to some extent reelected ones face diverse and often contradictory expectations. By their ambiguity, candidates encourage voters to see what they want to see and believe what they want to believe. Disillusionment naturally sets in once a new President begins to make decisions. Some supporters feel deceived and others satisfied. Reagan's appeal to conservative voters during the campaign and his inability to meet some of their expectations as President constitute one of numerous examples that could be identified in any administration.

One political scientist, John E. Mueller, has referred to the disappointment which groups may experience with an administration as "the coalitions of minority variable."[65] In explaining declines in popularity, Mueller notes that the President's decisions inevitably alienate parts of the coalition that elected him. This alienation, greatest among independents and supporters who identify with the other party, produces a drop in popularity over time.[66]

The campaign's emphasis on personal and institutional leadership also inflates expectations. By creating impressions of assertiveness, decisiveness, and potency, candidates help shape public expectations of their performance in office. Jimmy Carter contributed to the decline in his own popularity by promising more than he could deliver. Carter's problem was not unique to his Presidency. It is one that other successful candidates have faced and will continue to face. How can impressions of leadership be conveyed during the campaign without creating unrealistic and unattainable performance expectations of the President?

The Electoral Coalition and Governing

Not only does the selection process inflate performance expectations and create a set of diverse policy goals, it also *lessens* the President's power to achieve them. His political muscle has been weakened by the decline in the power of party leaders, and the growth of autonomous state and congressional electoral systems.

In the past, presidential candidates were dependent on the heads of the state parties for delegate support. Today, they are not. In the past, the state party organizations were the principal units for conducting the general election campaign. Today, they are not. In the past, partisan ties united legislative and executive officials more than they currently do.

Today, presidential candidates are more on their own. They essentially designate themselves to run. They create their own organizations, mount their own campaign, win their own delegates, and set their own convention plan. However, they pay a price for this independence. By winning their party's nomination, they gain a label but not an organization. In the general election, they have to expand their prenomination coalition, working largely on their own. Planning a strategy, developing tactics, writing speeches, formulating an appeal, organizing interest groups, and, perhaps with the help of the party, conducting a grass roots registration and get-out-the-vote effort are all part of seeking the Presidency.

The personalization of the presidential electoral process has serious implications for governing. To put it simply, it makes it more difficult. The electoral process provides the President with fewer political allies in the states and in Congress. It makes his partisan appeal less effective. It fractionalizes the bases of his support.

The establishment of candidate campaign organizations and the use of out-of-state coordinators have weakened the state parties. This has created competition, not cooperation. The competition cannot help but deplete the natural reservoir of partisan support a President needs to tap when he alienates parts of his electoral coalition.

Moreover, the democratization of the selection process has also resulted in the separation of state, congressional, and presidential elections. In the aftermath of Watergate, Jimmy Carter made much of the fact that he did not owe his nomination to the power brokers within his party or his election to them or members of Congress. The same can be said for members of Congress and, for that matter, governors and state legislators. Carter was not dependent on them nor were they dependent on him for their nomination and election. The increasing independence of Congress from the Presidency decreases legislators' political incentives for following the President's lead.

The magnitude of the President's problem is compounded by the public expectation of his legislative leadership. Yet that leadership is difficult to achieve because of the constitutional and political separation of institutions. Thus, the weakening of party ties during the electoral process carries over to the governing process, with adverse consequences for the President.

Finally, personality politics has produced factions within the parties. It has created a fertile environment for the growth of interest group pressures. Without strong party leaders to act as brokers and referees, groups vie for the nominee's attention and favor during the campaign and for the President's after the election is over. This group struggle provides a natural source of opposition and support for almost any presidential action or proposal. It enlarges the arena of policymaking and contributes to the multiplicity of forces that converge on most presidential decisions.

Personality Politics and Presidential Leadership

What is a President to do? How can he meet public expectations in light of the weakening of partisanship and the increased sharing of policymaking powers? How can a President lead, achieve, and satisfy pluralistic interests at the same time?

Obviously, there is no set formula for success. Forces beyond the President's control may affect the course of events. Nonetheless, there are three maxims that every President should follow in his struggle to convert promises into performance and perhaps also to get reelected.

1. He must define his own priorities rather than have them defined for him.
2. He must build his own coalitions rather than depend solely or even mostly on partisan support.
3. He must take an assertive public posture rather than let his words and actions speak for themselves.

Priority setting is a necessary presidential task. Without it, an administration appears to lack direction and leadership. People question what the President is doing and have difficulty remembering what he has done. This happened to Carter during his first three years in office and contributed to the decline of his performance ratings in the public opinion polls. Senior aides of the Reagan administration understood the lesson well. They limited the issues, controlled the agenda, and, for the most part, focused the media on Reagan's policy objectives.

Presidential campaigns are not likely to provide a limited agenda.

In fact, they usually do just the opposite. The promises made during the preconvention contest, the pledges contained in the party's platform, and the positions taken during the general campaign constitute a wide range of policy objectives that may or may not be consistent with one another. This provides the President with more discretion than direction. If he is skillful, he can actually manufacture a mandate. Reagan did so in 1980. Claiming that he was elected to implement his economic program, he appealed for public support and then used this support to win congressional backing for his budget and revenue proposals.

While the absence of a clear electoral mandate can actually help the President, allowing him flexibility in designing his program, it can also hurt him. Priority setting often takes time, valuable time at the beginning of an administration when presidential popularity tends to be highest. A failure to act initially may make later actions more difficult. When unity fades and partisan divisions reemerge, a President may prolong his honeymoon, but he cannot do so indefinitely.

Extending the campaign debate over goals and policies into the new administration is also likely to reduce presidential support. The losers within the President's electoral coalition are not likely to keep their arguments and protests private for long, particularly if they represent vocal constituencies. One way a President can counter this debate is to preempt it by taking a position at the beginning of his administration. Another is to appoint loyalists who are on the same ideological and partisan wavelengths as he.

In addition to establishing priorities and positions, the President has to get them adopted. His electoral coalition does not remain a cohesive entity within the governing system. This forces a President to build his own alliances around his policy objectives. Constructing these alliances requires different organizing skills from winning an election. Partisanship is no longer as effective an appeal and as cohesive an instrument. Recruiting public officials who have their own constituencies demands a variety of inducements and tactics. It also requires time. The President cannot do it alone.

As campaign organizations are necessary to win elections, so governing organizations are necessary to gain backing for presidential policies. Several offices within the White House have been established to provide liaison and mobilize support for the President on Capitol Hill, in the bureaucracy, and with outside interest groups. By building and mending bridges, a President can improve his chances for success. He can commit, convince, cajole, and otherwise gain cooperation despite the constitutional and political separation of institutions and powers.

Unlike winning the general election, making and implementing public policy is not an all-or-nothing proposition. Assessments of performance are based on expectations, somewhat as they are in the primaries. Part of the President's image problem results from the contrast between an idealized concept of what his powers are or ought to be and his actual ability to get things done. This is why a President needs a public relations staff and why some grandstanding is inevitable.

If a President cannot achieve what he wants, he can at least shift the blame for failure. He can at least look good trying and perhaps even claim partial success. And finally, he can always change his public priorities to improve his batting average. Public appeals may or may not generate support within the governing coalitions, but they can boost support outside them and within the electoral coalition the next time around.

SUMMARY

Americans are fascinated by presidential elections. They want to know who will win, why the successful candidate has won, and what the election augurs for the next four years. Their fascination stems from four interrelated factors: elections are dramatic; they are decisive; they are participatory; and they affect future policy and leadership.

Presidential elections provide entertaining news for millions of people. They select the nation's most visible leader to serve in its most charismatic office. They give citizens a voice in that selection, and they provide guidance for the new administration.

These factors suggest why so much attention has been devoted to predicting and analyzing presidential elections. Public opinion polls constantly monitor the attitudes and views of the electorate. Gallup, Harris, and other pollsters reflect and, to some extent, contribute to public interest by the hypothetical elections they conduct. Private surveys also record shifts in popular sentiment, helping clients to know what to say, to whom to say it, and, in some cases, even how to say it.

These polls have become fairly accurate measures of opinion at the time they are taken. Based on probability theory, they utilize standard sampling procedures. These procedures enable researchers to calculate how representative the sample is likely to be. Gallup, Harris, Roper, and others have had good track records since 1948, although they underestimated the size of Reagan's landslide in 1980.

In addition to predicting the results, polls may affect the results, although usually not directly. They have a greater impact on politicians, contributors, and campaign workers than they do on the general public. Practitioners use polls as a guide; the public reads them as news.

The format of the election forces voters to choose among several candidates. They cannot articulate their policy views when voting for President. However, the reasons for their vote can be partially discerned through pre- and postelection surveys.

The most thorough analyses have been conducted by the Center for Political Studies of the University of Michigan. Using party identification as a base, Michigan analysts have discussed the results of presidential elections in terms of their deviation from the expected partisan vote. Deviations have been caused primarily by evaluations of the candidates and their ideological-issue stances. The declining intensity of partisan attitudes and the increasing number of independent voters have contributed to the impact of these short-range factors on voting behavior.

In 1960, it was Kennedy's religion that seemed to account for the closeness of the popular vote. In 1964, it was Goldwater's uncompromising ideological and issue positions that helped provide Johnson with an overwhelming victory in all areas but the Deep South. In 1968, it was the accumulation of grievances against the Democrats that spurred the Wallace candidacy and resulted in Nixon's triumph. In 1972, ideology, issues, and the perception of McGovern as incompetent split the Democratic party, with over 40 percent of the Democrats, 66 percent of the independents, and most of the Republicans voting for Nixon. In 1976, however, partisanship was reinforced by issue, ideological, and personal evaluations to the benefit of the majority party nominee. In 1980, it was not. On the contrary, short-term factors overcame the advantage that partisanship and incumbency normally bring to a major party President seeking reelection. Carter lost primarily because of his poor performance evaluation, which made the candidacy of his opponent more attractive.

When combined, the long- and short-term influences on voting behavior create a diverse and inflated set of expectations for the successful candidate, expectations upon which his Presidency is likely to be judged. That these expectations may be conflicting, unrealistic, or in other ways unattainable matters little. A President is expected to lead, to achieve, and to satisfy the interests of a heterogeneous coalition. His failure to do so will produce public criticism and ultimately result in declining popularity.

The President has a problem. The election provides him with an open-ended mandate that means different things to different people, including the President, but does not give him the political clout to get things done.

Parties have become structurally weaker and electoral systems more autonomous. Candidates now have to create their own organization to win the election, and Presidents have to build their own alliances to govern. In the past, the electoral and governing coalitions were connected by partisan ties. Today, those ties are looser.

This situation has presented serious governing problems for the President. He must establish his own priorities. He must construct his own policy alliances. He must articulate his appeal clearly and convey it to the public.

With fewer natural allies, declines in popularity are inevitable and more serious. They detract from the President's ability to accomplish his goals. The growing influence of personality on people and events makes the President's job much tougher.

NOTES

1. Michael Wheeler, *Lies, Damn Lies, and Statistics* (New York: Dell, 1976), p. 84.

2. Moreover, the 2 million people who returned the questionnaire were not necessarily even typical of those who received it. By virtue of responding, they displayed more interest and concern than the others.

3. Archibald Crossley predicted that Roosevelt would receive 53.8 percent of the vote, George Gallup estimated that he would receive 55.7 percent, and Elmo Roper forecast 61.7 percent. Roosevelt actually received 62.5 percent.

4. "Gallup Opinion Index," December 1980, 120.

5. "What Went Wrong?" *Opinion Outlook,* 1 (November 17, 1980), 7.

6. Ibid.

7. Gallup and Roper used quota samples in the elections from 1936 to 1948. A quota sample, also referred to as a stratified sample, divides the population into the categories which the researcher intends to use in the analysis. These may include sex, race, religion, and/or socioeconomic variables. The percentage of each group in the sample should equal its percentage in the population as a whole. To gain sufficient numbers, the surveyor must meet the quota for each group.

8. Here's how the Gallup organization describes its sampling procedure:

The design of the sample used by the Gallup Poll for its standard surveys of public opinion is that of a replicated probability sample down to the block level in the case of urban areas and to segments of townships in the case of rural areas.

After stratifying the nation geographically and by size of community in order to insure conformity of the sample with the latest available estimates by the Census Bureau of the distribution of the adult population, over 350 different sampling locations or areas (Census Tracts of Census Enumeration Districts) are selected on a mathematically random basis from within cities, towns, and counties which have in turn been selected on a mathematically random basis. The interviewers have no choice whatsoever concerning the part of the city, town, or county in which they conduct their interviews.

Approximately five interviews are conducted in each such randomly selected sampling point. Interviewers are given maps of the area to which they are assigned, with a starting point indicated; they are required to follow a specified direction. At each occupied dwelling unit, interviewers are instructed to select respondents by following a prescribed systematic method and by a male-female assignment. This procedure is followed until the assigned number of interviews has been completed.

"Gallup Opinion Index," December 1980, 70.

9. Such a sample will also yield a level of significance of .05. The level of significance indicates the odds of being wrong in generalizing from the sample to the population *even with the sampling error.* A .05 level of significance means that in all probability, five times out of one hundred, the sample will not reflect the population. Unfortunately, survey researchers never know which five times they will be wrong.

10. Telephone interviews cost approximately half those of the person-to-person sessions but are considered to be less effective. They do not facilitate rapport between the interviewer and the respondent. Moreover, it is also extremely difficult to obtain income and race information over the phone.

11. Charles H. Backstrom and Gerald D. Hursh, *Survey Research* (Evanston, Ill.: Northwestern University Press, 1963), p. 33.

12. If it is desired to break down the sample and generalize about specific groups within it, then a larger sample will probably be needed. It is necessary to have a sufficient number in each group (age, sex, religion, income, race, etc.) in order to generalize from that group to the population as a whole. Ibid., p. 27.

13. A list of the candidates is then provided, and respondents are asked to indicate their preferences. Frequently this is done on a card and actually placed in a sealed ballot box to improve the accuracy of the response. There is a tendency for people to tell the interviewers what they think they want to hear. Thus, the vote for socially unpopular candidates such as Goldwater and McGovern would be underestimated by an oral response.

14. Harris polls are conducted until noon on Sunday. The final weekend polls, by necessity, are conducted via the phone.

15. Paul Wilson, "Election Night 1980 and the Controversy over Early Projections," in William C. Adams (ed.), *Television Coverage of the 1980 Presidential Campaign* (Norwood, N.J.: Ablex, 1983). Joan Bieder, "Television Reporting," in Gerald Benjamin (ed.), *The Communications Revolution in Politics* (New York: Academy of Political Science, 1982), pp. 37–41.

16. The need for quick reporting eliminates those precincts that use paper ballots, which must be counted by hand, or punched ballots, which normally are tabulated by machine at the county board of elections. Thus, the media depend on those precincts that use automatic voting machines, which tend to be concentrated in urban areas.

17. NBC, however, waited until the polls closed within a state before predicting that state's vote.

18. Harold Mendelsohn and Irving Crespi, *Polls, Television, and the New Politics* (Scranton, Pa.: Chandler, 1970), pp. 234–236.

19. Sam Tuchman and Thomas E. Coffin, "The Influence of Election Night Television Broadcasts in a Close Election," *Public Opinion Quarterly*, 35 (1971), 315–326.

20. Raymond Wolfinger and Peter Linquiti, "Tuning In and Turning Out," *Public Opinion*, 4 (1981), 57–59.

21. For a discussion of the concept of the normal vote and its application to electoral analysis, see Philip E. Converse, "The Concept of a Normal Vote," in Angus Campbell, Philip E. Converse, Warren E. Miller, and Donald E. Stokes (eds.), *Elections and the Political Order* (New York: Wiley, 1966), pp. 9–39; Warren E. Miller and Teresa E. Levitin, *Leadership and Change* (Cambridge, Mass.: Winthrop, 1976), pp. 37–40.

22. For an analysis of the components of the 1952 presidential election, see Angus Campbell, Philip E. Converse, Warren E. Miller, and Donald E. Stokes, *The American Voter* (New York: Wiley, 1960), pp. 524–527.

23. Ibid., pp. 527–528.

24. Ibid.; Donald E. Stokes, Angus Campbell, and Warren E. Miller, "Components of Electoral Decision," *American Political Science Review*, 52 (1958), 382.

25. Philip E. Converse, Angus Campbell, Warren E. Miller, and Donald E. Stokes, "Stability and Change in 1960: A Reinstating Election," in Campbell et al., *Elections and the Political Order*, p. 92.

26. Ibid., pp. 88–89.

27. Kennedy's Catholicism may have enlarged his Electoral College total by 22 votes. See Ithiel deSola Pool, Robert P. Abelson, and Samuel Popkin, *Candidates, Issues and Strategies* (Cambridge, Mass.: MIT Press, 1965), pp. 115–118.

28. Kennedy addressed a group of Protestant ministers in Houston, Texas. In his opening remarks, he advocated a complete separation of church and state. He then replied to questions about how his Catholicism would affect his behavior as President. His responses, which received considerable media coverage, appeared to satisfy the apprehensions of a significant portion of the Protestant community.

29. Converse et al., "Stability and Change in 1960," p. 87.

30. Miller and Levitin, *Leadership and Change*, p. 52.

31. For a discussion of the 1964 presidential election, see Philip E. Converse, Aage R. Clausen, and Warren E. Miller, "Electoral Myth and Reality: The 1964 Election," *American Political Science Review*, 59 (1965), 321–336.

32. Ibid., pp. 330–331.

33. Norman H. Nie, Sidney Verba, and John R. Petrocik, *The Changing American Voter* (Cambridge, Mass.: Harvard University Press, 1976); Miller and Levitin, *Leadership and Change*; Gerald Pomper, "From Confusion to Clarity: Issues and the American Voter, 1956–1968," *American Political Science Review*, 66 (1972), 415–428.

34. Nie, Verba, and Petrocik, *The Changing American Voter*, p. 307.

35. Philip E. Converse, Warren E. Miller, Jerrold G. Rusk, and Arthur C. Wolfe, "Continuity and Change in American Politics: Parties and Issues in the 1968 Election," *American Political Science Review*, 63 (1969), 1,097.

36. Wallace claimed that there was not a dime's worth of difference between the Republican and Democratic candidates. He took great care in making his own positions distinctive. The clarity with which he presented his views undoubtedly contributed to the issue orientation of his vote. People knew where Wallace stood.

37. In the South, the breakdown of the Wallace vote was 68 percent Democratic and 20 percent Republican. Outside the South, it was 46 percent Democratic and 34 percent Republican. Converse et al., "Continuity and Change," p. 1,091.

38. Daniel A. Mazmanian, *Third Parties in Presidential Elections* (Washington, D.C.: Brookings Institution, 1974), p. 71.

39. Converse et al., "Continuity and Change," p. 1,085.

40. Arthur H. Miller, Warren E. Miller, Alden S. Raine, and Thad A. Brown, "A Majority Party in Disarray: Policy Polarization in the 1972 Election" (paper presented at the annual meeting of the American Political Science Association, New Orleans, Louisiana, September 4–8, 1973), p. 73.

41. Ibid.

42. Miller and Levitin, *Leadership and Change*, p. 164.

43. Miller et al., "A Majority Party in Disarray," p. 18.

44. Ibid., p. 74.

45. Samuel Popkin, John W. Gorman, Charles Phillips, and Jeffrey A. Smith, "Comment: What Have You Done for Me Lately? Toward an Investment Theory of Voting," *American Political Science Review*, 70 (1976), 799–802.

46. David RePass, "Comment: Political Methodologies in Disarray: Some Alternative Interpretations of the 1972 Election," *American Political Science Review*, 70 (1976), 816.

47. Ibid. See also Gerald Pomper, "From Confusion to Clarity: Issues and American Voters, 1956–1968"; David E. RePass, "Issue Salience and Party Choice," *American Political Science Review*, 65 (1971), 389–400.

48. Nie, Verba, and Petrocik, *The Changing American Voter*, p. 295.

49. See Michael Margolis, "From Confusion to Confusion: Issues and Voters, 1952–1972," *American Political Science Review*, 71 (1977), 31–43; Hugh L. LeBlanc and Mary Beth Merrin, "Independents, Issue Partisanship and the Decline of Party," *American Politics Quarterly*, 7 (1979), 240–255; David RePass, "Comment: Political Methodologies in Disarray," pp. 814–831.

50. Arthur H. Miller, "The Majority Party Reunited? A Comparison of the 1972 and 1976 Elections," in Jeff Fishel (ed.), *Parties and Elections in an Anti-Party Age* (Bloomington: Indiana University Press, 1978), pp. 133–134.

51. Ibid.

52. Arthur H. Miller and Warren E. Miller, "Partisanship and Performance: 'Rational' Choice in the 1976 Presidential Elections" (paper presented at the annual meeting of the American Political Science Association, Washington, D.C., September 1–4, 1977).

53. Ibid., p. 99.

54. Ibid., p. 109.

55. Mainstream candidates tend to do better than those with more extreme political and ideological views. In 1964 and 1972, voters perceived conservative Republican Barry Goldwater and liberal Democrat George McGovern as less competent than their more centrist opponents. In 1980 this trend was reversed. It was Carter who was seen as the less competent candidate. John R. Petrocik and Sidney Verba with Christine Schultz, "Choosing the Choice and Not the Echo: A Funny Thing Happened to *The Changing American Voter* on the Way to the 1980 Election" (paper delivered at the annual meeting of the American Political Science Association, New York, September 3–6, 1981), p. 25.

56. In the words of Arthur H. Miller and Martin P. Wattenberg, "the voters were less supportive of Carter's perceived positions because they had rationalized them on the basis of evaluations of his [Reagan's] past performance; not because they had shifted to a more conservative set of policy preferences." Arthur H. Miller and Martin P. Wattenberg, "Policy and Performance Voting in the 1980 Election" (paper delivered at the annual meeting of the American Political Science Association, New York, September 3–6, 1981), p. 15.

57. A majority of voters would still increase government spending for health, education, cities, crime, and the environment. Ibid., p. 8 and Table 4.

58. Ibid., p. 11.

59. Ibid., pp. 7 18.

60. Ibid., p. 7; Warren E. Miller, "Policy Directions and Presidential Leadership: Alternative Interpretations of the 1980 Presidential Election" (paper delivered at the annual meeting of the American Political Science Association, New York, September 3–6, 1981).

61. Miller and Wattenberg, "Policy and Performance Voting in the 1980 Election," p. 6.

62. When asked in a nationwide poll following the election whether Reagan's victory was a mandate for more conservative policies or a rejection of Carter and his presidency, 63 percent of those responding saw it as a rejection of Carter and only 24 percent viewed the election as a conservative victory. A CBS/*New York Times* exit poll on election day also found little support for the conservative mandate thesis. John F. Stacks, "New Beginnings; Old Anxieties," *Time,* February 2, 1981, p. 22; Adam Clymer, "Displeasure with Carter Turned Many to Reagan," *New York Times,* November 9, 1980, p. 28.

63. In fact, it may even be difficult to obtain a complete copy of it. The number of platform summaries that are printed and circulated greatly exceeds the number of copies of the platforms that are available across the country during the campaign.

64. Paul David, "Party Platforms as National Plans," *Public Administration Review,* 31 (1971), 303–315; Jeff Fishel, "Agenda-Building in Presidential Campaigns: The Case of Jimmy Carter" (paper presented at the annual meeting of the American Political Science Association, Washington, D.C., September 1–4, 1977).

65. John E. Mueller, *War, Presidents and Public Opinion* (New York: Wiley, 1973), pp. 205–208 and 247–249.

66. Ibid.

Selected Readings

Abramson, Paul R., John H. Aldrich, and David W. Rohde. *Change and Continuity in the 1980 Elections.* Washington, D.C.: Congressional Quarterly Press, 1982.

Converse, Philip E., Angus Campbell, William E. Miller, and Donald E. Stokes. "Stability and Change in 1960: A Reinstating Election," *American Political Science Review,* 55 (1961), 269–280.

Converse, Philip E., Aage R. Clausen, and Warren E. Miller. "Electoral Myth and Reality: The 1964 Election," *American Political Science Review,* 59 (1965), 321–336.

Converse, Philip E., Warren E. Miller, Jerrold G. Rusk, and Arthur C. Wolfe. "Continuity and Change in American Politics: Parties and Issues in the 1968 Election," *American Political Science Review*, 53 (1969), 1,083–1,105.

Mendelsohn, Harold, and Irving Crespi. *Polls, Television, and the New Politics.* Scranton, Pa.: Chandler, 1970.

Miller, Arthur H. "The Majority Party Reunited? A Comparison of the 1972 and 1976 Elections," in Jeff Fishel (ed.), *Parties and Elections in an Anti-Party Age.* Bloomington: Indiana University Press, 1978.

Miller, Arthur H., Warren E. Miller, Alden S. Raine, and Thad A. Brown. "A Majority Party in Disarray: Policy Polarization in the 1972 Election," *American Political Science Review*, 70 (1976).

Miller, Warren E., and Teresa E. Levitin. *Leadership and Change.* Cambridge, Mass.: Winthrop, 1976.

Pomper, Gerald M., with colleagues. *The Election of 1980.* Chatham, N.J.: Chatham House, 1981.

Roll, Charles W., Jr., and Albert H. Cantril. *Polls: Their Use and Misuse in Politics.* New York: Basic Books, 1972.

Schneider, William, "The November 4 Vote for President: What Did It Mean?" in Austin Ranney (ed.), *The American Elections of 1980.* Washington, D.C.: American Enterprise Institute, 1981.

Wheeler, Michael. *Lies, Damn Lies, and Statistics.* New York: Dell, 1976.

Afterword

REFORMING
THE SYSTEM

Introduction

The American political system has changed substantially in recent years. Party rules, finance laws, and media coverage are very different than they were two decades or even one decade ago. The Electoral College also no longer functions as it was originally designed to do.

Have these changes been beneficial? Has the system been improved? Are further structural or operational changes desirable? These questions have elicited a continuing and sometimes spirited debate.

Critics have alleged that the electoral process is too long, too costly, and too burdensome, that it wears down candidates and numbs voters. They have said that many qualified people are discouraged from running for office and much of the electorate is discouraged from participating in the election. Other criticisms are that the system benefits the rich, encourages factionalism, weakens parties, and focuses undue emphasis on the candidates and not on the issues. It has also been contended that voters do not receive the information they need to make an intelligent, rational decision.

In contrast, proponents argue that the political system is more democratic than ever. More, not fewer, people are involved, particularly at the nomination stage. Candidates, even lesser-known ones, have ample opportunity to demonstrate their competence, endurance, motivation, and leadership capabilities. Parties remain important as vehicles through which the system operates and by which governing is accomplished. Those who defend the process believe voters do receive as much information as they desire and that most people can make intelligent, informed, rational judgments.

The old adage "where you stand influences what you see" is applicable to the debate about electoral reform. No political process is neutral. There are always winners and losers. To a large extent the advantages which some enjoy are made possible only by the disadvantages which others face. Rationalizations aside, much of the debate about the system, about equity, representation, and responsiveness, revolves around a very practical, political question: Who exercises the greatest influence?

Proposals to change the system need to be assessed in the light of who gains and who loses. They also should be judged on the basis of how such changes would affect the operation of the political system. This section will discuss some of these proposals and the impact they could have on the road to the White House. The chapter is organized into two parts, one dealing with the more recent changes in party rules, campaign finance, and media coverage, and the other dealing with the long-term issue of the Electoral College.

MODIFYING THE RECENT CHANGES

Party Rules

Of all the recent changes that have occurred in the nomination process, none has caused more persistent controversy than the reforms governing the selection of delegates. Designed to encourage grass roots participation and broaden the base of representation, these reforms have also lengthened the nominating period, made it more expensive, generated candidate-based organizations, weakened state party leaders, converted conventions into coronations, and loosened the ties between the parties and their nominees. As a consequence, governing has been made more difficult.

Since 1968, when the Democrats began to rewrite their rules for delegate selection, the party has struggled with these unintended repercussions. Each succeeding presidential election has seen a new Democratic commission recommend new changes to the party rules, changes which have attempted to reconcile expanded participation and representation with the traditional need to unify the party for a national campaign. While less reform conscious than the Democrats, the Republicans have also tried to steer a middle course between greater rank-and-file involvement and more equitable representation on the one hand and the maintenance of a successful electoral and governing coalition on the other.

How to balance these oft-competing goals has been the critical issue. Those who desire greater public participation have lauded the trend toward more primaries and a larger percentage of delegates selected in them. Believing that the reforms have opened up the process and made it more democratic, they favor the continued selection of pledged delegates based on the proportion of the popular vote a candidate receives. In contrast, those who believe that greater control by state and national party leaders is desirable argue that the reforms have gone too far. They would prefer fewer primaries, a smaller percentage of delegates selected in them, and more unpledged delegates, elected officials, and party leaders attending the nominating conventions. They would also favor a larger involvement by the national party in the presidential campaign. Giving federal funds to the party, and not to the candidate, has been proposed as one way to achieve this latter objective.

While the strong party advocates appear to be on the ascendancy, having dominated the latest series of Democratic party reforms, widespread public support continues for simplifying the process and extending it to what some consider to be its logical conclusion—a national primary. While party leaders including members of the reform commissions have opposed such a proposal and Congress has been cool to the idea, the general public seems to be more favorably disposed. Gallup polls taken over the last twenty years indicate that a majority of the electorate would prefer such an election to the present system.[1]

Most proposals for a national primary call for a one-day election to be held in early August. Candidates who wish to enter their party's primary would be required to obtain a certain number of signatures, equal to approximately 1 percent of the vote in the last presidential election. Any aspirant who wins a majority would automatically receive the nomination. In some plans a plurality would be sufficient provided it was at least 40 percent. In the event that no one received 40 percent, a runoff election would be held three weeks later between the top two finishers. Nominating conventions would continue to select the vice presidential candidates and decide on the platforms.

A national primary would be consistent with the one person-one vote principle. All participants would have an equal voice in the selection. No longer would those in the early, small primary and caucus states exercise disproportionate influence.

It is likely that a national primary would stimulate turnout. It would certainly provide greater incentive for voting than currently exists, particularly in those states that hold their nomination contests after the apparent winner has emerged. A national primary would probably result in nomination by a more representative electorate than is currently the case. Moreover, by holding the vote on one day in the summer, a shorter campaign could be expected. This would reduce the physical strain on the candidates and condense the barrage of election news and information that besieges voters for many months.

A single primary for each party would accelerate a nationalizing trend and might improve government at the national level. Issues that affect the entire country would be the primary focus of attention. Thus, candidates for the nation's highest office would be forced to discuss the problems they would most likely confront as President.

Moreover, the results of the election would be clear-cut. The media could no longer interpret primaries and caucus returns as they saw fit. An incumbent's ability to garner support through the timely release of grants, contracts, and other spoils of government might be more limited in a national contest. On the other hand, such an election would undoubtedly discourage challengers without national reputations. No longer would an early victory catapult a relatively unknown aspirant into the position of a serious contender and jeopardize a President's chances for renomination. In fact, lesser-known candidates such as George McGovern and Jimmy Carter would find it extremely difficult to raise the money, build an organization, and mount a national campaign within the relatively short period in which such a contest would be waged. This would seem to ensure that competent, experienced political leaders would be selected as their party's standard-bearers—or, depending on one's perspective, that older, tired, Washington-based politicians would be chosen.

From the standpoint of the party, a national primary would further weaken the ability of its leaders to influence the selection of the nominee. A successful candidate would probably not owe his victory to party officials. Moreover, a postprimary convention could not be expected to tie the nominee to the party although it might tie the party to the nominee at least through the election. The trend toward personalizing politics would continue.

Whether the primary winner would be the party's strongest candidate is also open to question. With a large field of contenders, those with the most devoted supporters might do best. On the other hand, candidates who do not arouse the passions of the diehards, but who are more acceptable to the party's mainstream, might not do as well. Everybody's second choice might not even finish second unless a system of approval voting were used. Approval voting, which allows the electorate to list their top two or three choices in order, would complicate the election, confusing the result and adding to the costs of conducting it.[2]

In addition to weakening the party, a national primary would further strain the decentralized character of the political system. It would lessen the ability of states to determine when and how their citizens would participate in the presidential nomination process. The clout of state party leaders and elected officials to affect the process and influence the outcome would suffer. These consequences would undoubtedly make it difficult to mobilize wide support for such a plan.

To allow the states some discretion yet to continue to encourage greater participation by rank-and-file voters, a series of regional primaries has been proposed. One plan, introduced by Senator Robert Packwood of Oregon, would divide the country into five regions: the Northeast, South, Midwest, Great Plains, and Far West. Each state within a region would be required to hold its primary (if it chose to have a primary) on the same day. The dates for each region would be chosen at random and scheduled one month apart beginning in March of the election year. To discourage early campaigning, the order in which each of the five regions would hold their elections would not be announced until seventy days before the first contest. Delegates would be awarded in proportion to the popular vote a candidate received provided that it was at least 5 percent of the total.

Regional primaries would facilitate a more concentrated campaign than the present system. Lesser-known candidates would still have a chance to demonstrate their potential. Turnout would be encouraged by the regional media blitz. The allocation of delegates would reflect the popularity of the candidates within the area. Conventions would still be necessary to ratify the selection of the winner or to choose among the leading candidates. Other convention functions, such as determining the vice presidential nominee, writing a platform, and rallying the party faithful, would also continue.

The regional plan is not without its shortcomings, however. Like the national primary, it would probably weaken the party's organizational structure and encourage the formation of separate candidate groups in much the same manner as the present system does. Unlike the national primary, it might exacerbate sectional rivalries and result in a hopelessly deadlocked convention with few unpledged delegates to break the impasse. Moreover, a series of regional primaries would not substantially reduce the length of the preconvention period, the personal hardships and financial costs of competing in it, nor the effect of early regional victories on the nomination. It would, however, deny a state the option of setting its own primary date. For this reason alone, some state officials could be expected to oppose it, with those from New Hampshire and Iowa in the lead.

Finance Laws

Affecting the changes in party rules have been new finance laws. Enacted in the 1970s in reaction to secret and sometimes illegal bequests, to the disparity in contributions and spending among the candidates, and to the spiraling costs of modern campaigns, particularly the costs of television advertising, the new laws are designed to improve accountability, subsidize nominations, and fund the general election, thereby controlling expenditures in the presidential campaign. Many of these objectives have been achieved, but in the process other problems have been created.

The laws have taken campaign finance out of the back rooms and put it into the public spotlight. However, they have also created a nightmare of compliance procedures and reporting requirements. Detailed records of practically all contributions and expenditures must now be kept by campaign organizations and periodically submitted to the Federal Elections Commission. A good accountant and attorney are now as necessary as a pollster, image maker, and grass roots organizer.

The law limits the amounts wealthy individuals can donate to presidential nominating campaigns but not the amount they can spend independently. It has created incentives for broad-based public support but has not lessened the need for frequent appeals for funds. It has eliminated the burden of raising money during the general election but has created severe budget constraints on the candidates.

Nor has government support equalized the financial plight of the major party candidates. Republicans still enjoy an advantage by virtue of their party's superior organizational and financial base at the national, state, and local levels. Incumbents are also benefited by their capacity to make news, affect events, and use the perquisites of office.

While the law has hurt third parties, it has not buttressed the two major parties. On the contrary, federal subsidies and support have contributed to party factionalism and have encouraged the formation of separate candidate organizations.

Several changes have been proposed to alleviate these problems. Compliance procedures could be eased. For example, the size of the contribution that must be reported could be increased and the number of reports might be reduced. This would relieve campaign organizations of some of the burdens of record keeping but it would also mean that less detailed information would be available less promptly to the public.

Independent spending cannot be prevented, but the contribution limits could be increased, particularly for individual donors. This would provide candidates with more money and reduce their dependence on outside groups. Party organizations should benefit from a decline in PAC activity. They would have more incentive to create and maintain a structure that could mobilize the vote for their nominees. The problem with increasing the amount individuals could give is that the wealthy would gain greater influence, and grass roots solicitation might suffer.

Similarly, the national party's contribution might be increased. This could strengthen its role in the presidential campaign, but it could also divert funds from other candidates and accentuate the financial advantage which the Republicans presently enjoy.

Finally, more money could be given by the federal government if more money were available. With only 25 percent of the population contributing to the campaign fund, however, a large increase would require funding from the general treasury, placing election funds in competition with other programs. Another possibility would be to permit private donations in the general election, but this raises the perennial problem of benefitting those in the upper-income groups.

The difficulty in designing finance laws is that competing needs have created contradictory goals. Freedom of speech implies the right to give and to spend. Equality of opportunity requires that the wealthy not be advantaged. Yet campaign appeals to the entire electorate are very expensive. If the legislation of the 1970s is any indication, there are no easy solutions.

Media Coverage

A third significant change in the electoral process concerns the way in which information about the campaign is communicated to the voters. Beginning in the 1950s, television became the principal medium through which candidates made their appeals and by which these appeals were assessed. Since then, television's emphasis on the contest, the drama, and the style of the campaigning has affected public perceptions of the candidates and influenced images created by them.

Changes in party rules and finance laws have also contributed to the media's impact. The increasing number and complexity of preconvention contests have provided the media with greater inducements to cover these events and interpret their results. The desire of the party to obtain maximum exposure for its nominating convention has further extended such coverage and interpretation. The limited funds for presidential campaigns have also increased the importance of news about the election and may have contributed to its impact on the voters. Today, candidates do not leave their coverage to chance. They attempt to influence it by carefully releasing favorable information, staging events, and paying for many commercial messages.

Is the coverage adequate? Do voters receive sufficient information from the media to make an intelligent decision? Many believe they do not. Academics especially have urged that greater attention be paid to policy issues and less to the horse-race. One proposal would have the networks and wire services assign special correspondents to cover the issues of the campaign much as they assign people to report on its color, drama, and personal aspects.

In addition to criticizing the media's treatment of the issues, academics and others have frequently called into question the amount and accuracy of election reporting. The law states that if the networks provide free time to some candidates, they must provide equal time to all running for the same position. This "equal time" provision has in fact resulted in no free time, although coverage of presidential debates as news events has circumvented the rule to a large extent. Networks are also required to be impartial in their coverage. Station licenses can be challenged and even revoked if biases are consistently evident in the presentation of the news.

Other than requiring fairness, preventing obscenity, and insuring that public service commitments are met, there is little the government can do without impinging on the freedom of the press. The media are free to choose which elections and candidates to emphasize, what kind of coverage to provide, how to interpret the results of primaries and caucuses, and even to predict who will win before the election is concluded.

Forecasting the returns on election night has caused particular controversy. Since 1964, when a Johnson landslide was predicted before the polls on the West Coast had closed, proposals have been advanced to limit or prohibit these glimpses into the immediate future.[3] One, sponsored by the League of Women Voters, would request the networks and wire services voluntarily to desist from making any forecast until voting across the continental United States has been completed. A second, introduced in the form of legislation in both houses of Congress, would establish a uniform hour at which all polls in the country would close: 12 P.M. in the East (EST), 9 P.M. on the West Coast, and 5 P.M. in Hawaii and Alaska. To equalize the number of hours in which people could vote, one recommendation would permit voting in the evening before the election on the West Coast. A third proposal, the most far-reaching, would eliminate the polls altogether and have all votes cast by mail.

Each of these proposals has encountered criticism. Could the networks be expected to comply voluntarily, given the competitive character of news reporting? Could uniform hours for the entire country be agreed upon? What about the logistical problems this would cause on the West Coast and the increased costs it would produce in the East if the polls were kept open three to four more hours? Besides, there still would be no guarantee that early forecasts could be eliminated. They could still be made on the basis of exit polling even if exit polling were made more difficult by restricting network interviewers to a certain distance from the polls. Voting by mail would be expensive, time-consuming, and subject to the most potential fraud.

In addition to the obvious First Amendment problems which such proposals would engender, the restrictions on the media might meet other objections. Americans seem to want their election returns reported rapidly. After a lengthy campaign, workers and sympathizers are eager to know the results and celebrate or commiserate. Second, the presidential transition is short enough without having to wait another few days for every state to conclude its official count. Even exit polls have value. Knowledge about the beliefs, attitudes, and motivations of the voters is useful information, particularly for those who are elected. In a democracy, it is essential to get as clear a reading of the pulse of the electorate as possible. At the very least this prevents mythological mandates from being claimed and implemented.

THE ELECTORAL COLLEGE

Even more fundamental to the operation of a democratic political process is the manner in which the winner is determined. The Electoral College has been criticized on the grounds that it is undemocratic and potentially unreflective of popular choice. Over the years, there have been numerous proposals to alter it. The first was introduced in Congress in 1797. Since then, there have been over 500 others. The first actual modification occurred in 1804 with the ratification of the Twelfth Amendment. While other constitutional amendments have tangentially affected presidential elections, none has changed the basic structure of the college.

In urging changes, critics have pointed to the college's archaic design, its electoral biases, and its potentially undemocratic results. In recent years, five major plans (the automatic, proportional, district, direct election, and national bonus plans) have been proposed to allieviate some or all of these problems. This section will examine these proposals and the impact they could have on the way in which the President is selected.

The Automatic Plan

The actual electors in the Electoral College have been an anachronism since the development of the party system. Their role as partisan agents is not and has not been consistent with their exercising an independent judgment for President. In fact, sixteen states plus the District of Columbia prohibit such a judgment by requiring electors to cast their ballots for the state's popular winner. While these laws are probably not enforceable because they seem to clash with the Constitution, they strongly indicate an expectation of how electors should vote.

The so-called automatic plan would do away with the potential danger of electors' exercising their personal preferences. First proposed in 1826, it has received substantial support since that time, including the backing of Presidents John Kennedy and Lyndon Johnson. The plan keeps the Electoral College intact but eliminates the electors. Electoral votes are automatically credited to the candidate who has received the most popular votes within the state.

Other than removing the potential problem of faithless or unpledged electors, the plan would do little to change the system. It has not been enacted because Congress has not felt the problem of faithless electors to be of sufficient magnitude to justify a constitutional amendment.

The Proportional Plan

The election of the entire slate of electors has also been the focus of considerable attention. If the winner takes all the electoral votes, the impact of the majority party is increased within the state and the larger, more competitive states are benefited.

From the perspective of the minority party or parties within the state, the selection of an entire ticket is not desirable. In effect, it disenfranchises them. Knowing that the popular vote winner will take all the votes often works to discourage a strong campaign effort by a party which has little chance of winning. This has the effect of reducing voter turnout and can theoretically lead to the perpetuation of one-party dominance at the presidential level within the state.

One way to rectify this problem would be to have proportional voting. Such a plan has been introduced on a number of occasions. Under a proportional system, the electors would be abolished, the principle of winner-take-all would be eliminated, and a state's electoral vote would be divided in proportion to its popular vote. A majority of electoral votes would still be required for election. If no candidate received a majority, most proportional plans call for a joint session of Congress to choose the President from among the top two or three candidates.

The proportional proposal would have a number of major consequences. It would decrease the influence of the most competitive states, where voters are more evenly divided, and increase the importance of the least competitive ones, where they are likely to be more homogeneous. Under such a system, it would be the size of the victory that counts. To take a dramatic example, if the electoral votes of Vermont and New York in 1960 had been calculated on the basis of the proportional vote for the major candidates within the states, Nixon would have received a larger margin from Vermont's 3 votes (1.759 to 1.240) than Kennedy would have gotten from New York's 45 (22.7 to 22.3).[4] Similarly, George Wallace's margin over Nixon and Humphrey in Mississippi in 1968 (3.8) would have been larger than Humphrey's over Nixon in New York (2.3).

While the proportional system rewards large victories in relatively homogeneous states, it also seems to encourage competition within those states. Having the electoral vote proportional to the popular vote provides an incentive to the minority party to mount a more vigorous campaign and establish a more effective organization. However, it might also cause third parties to do the same, thereby weakening the two-party system.

Finally, operating under a proportional plan would in all likelihood make the Electoral College vote much closer, thereby decreasing the President's mandate for governing. Carter would have defeated Ford by only 11.7 electoral vote in 1976 and Nixon would have won by only 6.1 in 1968. (See Table 1.) In at least one recent instance, it might also have changed the election results. Had this plan been in effect in 1960, Richard Nixon would probably have defeated John Kennedy by 266.1 to 265.6. However, it is difficult to calculate the 1960 vote precisely because the names of the Democratic presidential and vice presidential candidates were not on the ballot in Alabama. Only the names of the electors appeared.

Table 1　VOTING FOR PRESIDENT, 1952–1980: FIVE METHODS FOR AGGRE-GATING THE VOTES

Year	Electoral College	Proportional Plan	District Plan	Bonus Plan	Direct Election (percentage of total vote)
1952					
Eisenhower	442	288.5	375	544	55.1%
Stevenson	89	239.8	156	89	44.4
Others	0	2.7	0	0	.5
1956					
Eisenhower	457	296.7	411	559	57.4
Stevenson	73	227.2	120	73	42.0
Others	0	7.1	0	0	.6
1960					
Nixon	219	266.1	278	219	49.5
Kennedy	303	265.6	245	405	49.8
Others	0	5.3	0	0	.7
1964					
Goldwater	52	213.6	72	52	38.5
Johnson	486	320.0	466	588	61.0
Others	0	3.9	0	0	.5
1968					
Nixon	301	231.5	289	403	43.2
Humphrey	191	225.4	192	191	42.7
Wallace	46	78.8	57	46	13.5
Others	0	2.3	0	0	.6
1972					
Nixon	520	330.3	474	622	60.7
McGovern	17	197.5	64	17	37.5
Others	1	10.0	0	0	1.8
1976					
Ford	240	258.0	269	240	48.0
Carter	297	269.7	269	399	50.1
Others	1	10.2	0	0	1.9
1980					
Reagan	489	272.9	396	591	50.7
Carter	49	220.9	142	42	41.0
Anderson	0	35.3	0	0	6.6
Others	0	8.9	0	0	1.7

Source: Figures on Proportional and District Vote supplied to the author by Joseph B. Gorman of the Congressional Research Service, Library of Congress.

The District Plan

The district electoral system is another proposal aimed at reducing the effect of winner-take-all voting. While this plan has had several variations, its basic thrust would be to keep the Electoral College but change the manner in which the electoral votes within the state are determined. Instead of selecting the entire slate on the basis of the statewide vote for President, only 2 electoral votes would be decided in this manner. The remaining votes would be allocated on the basis of the popular vote within individual districts (probably congressional districts). A majority of the electoral votes would still be necessary for election. If the Electoral College were not decisive, then most district plans call for a joint session of Congress to make the final selection.

For the very smallest states, those with 3 electoral votes, all three electors would have to be chosen by the state as a whole. For others, however, the combination of district and at-large selection would probably result in a split electoral vote. On a national level, this would make the Electoral College more reflective of the partisan division of the newly elected Congress rather than of the popular division of the national electorate.

The losers under such an arrangement would be the large, competitive states and, most particularly, the organized, geographically concentrated groups within those states. Third and minority parties might be aided to the extent that they were capable of winning legislative districts. It is difficult to project whether Republicans or Democrats would benefit more from such an arrangement, since much would depend on how the legislative districts within the states were apportioned. If the 1960 presidential vote were aggregated on the basis of 1 electoral vote to the popular vote winner of each congressional district and 2 to the popular vote winner of each state, Nixon would have defeated Kennedy 278 to 245 with 14 unpledged electors. In 1976 the district system would have produced a tie, with Carter and Ford each receiving 269 votes. (See Table 1.) The state of Maine is the only state which presently chooses its electors in this manner.

The Direct Election Plan

Of all the plans to alter or replace the Electoral College, the direct popular vote has received the most attention and support. Designed to eliminate the college entirely and count the votes on a nationwide basis, it would elect the popular vote winner provided the winning candidate received a certain percentage of the total vote. In most plans, 40 percent of the total vote would be necessary. In some, 50 percent would be required. In the event that no one got the required percentage, a runoff between the top two candidates would be held to determine the winner.[5] Lincoln was the only plurality President who failed to attain the 40 percent figure. He received 39.82 percent, although he probably would have received more had his name been on the ballot in nine southern states.

A direct popular vote would, of course, remedy a major problem of the present system—the possibility of electing a nonplurality President. It would better equalize voting power both among and within the states. The large, competitive states would lose some of their electoral advantage by the elimination of winner-take-all voting. Party competition within the states and perhaps even nationwide would be increased. Turnout should also improve. Every vote would count in a direct election.

However, a direct election might also encourage minor parties, which would weaken the two-party system. The possibility of denying a major party candidate 40 percent of the popular vote might be sufficient to entice a proliferation of candidates and produce a series of bargains and deals in which support was traded for favors with a new administration. Moreover, if the federal character of the system were changed, it is possible that the plurality winner might not be geographically representative of the entire country. A very large sectional vote might elect a candidate who trailed in other areas of the country. This would upset the representational balance that has been achieved between the President's electoral constituency and Congress's.

The organized groups that are geographically concentrated in the large industrial states would have their votes diluted by a direct election. Take Jewish voters, for example. Highly supportive of the Democratic party since World War II, Jews constitute approximately 3 percent of the total population but 14 percent in New York, 4 percent in Pennsylvania, and 4 percent in California. These three states, the largest in population, have 20 percent of the electoral votes needed for victory. Naturally, the impact of the Jewish vote is magnified under the present Electoral College arrangement.[6]

The Republican party has also been reluctant to lend its support to direct election. As the minority party, its chances for winning would not seem to be improved by the substitution of a popular vote for the present Electoral College system. While Benjamin Harrison was the last Republican President to win even though he lost the national vote, Gerald Ford came remarkably close in 1976. On the other hand, Richard Nixon's Electoral College victory in 1968 could conceivably have been upset by a stronger Wallace campaign in the southern border states.

Another potential problem could surround a very close election. The winner might not be evident for days, even months. Voter fraud could have national consequences.[7] Under such circumstances, challenges by the losing candidate would be more likely.

The contingency provision in the event that no one receives the required percentage has its drawbacks as well. A runoff election would extend the length of the campaign and add to its cost. Considering that some aspirants begin their quest for the Presidency more than two years before the election, a further protraction of the process might unduly tax the patience of the voters and produce a numbing effect. Moreover, it would also cut an already short transition period for a newly elected President and further drain the time and energies of an incumbent seeking reelection.

There is still another difficulty with a contingency election. It could reverse the order in which the candidates originally finished. This might undermine the mandate of the eventual winner. It might also encourage spoiler candidacies. Third parties and independents seeking the Presidency could exercise considerable power in the event of a close contest between the major parties. Imagine Wallace's influence in 1968 in a runoff between Humphrey and Nixon.

Nonetheless, the direct election plan is supported by public opinion and has been ritualistically praised by recent Presidents. A 1980 Gallup Poll found 67 percent of the public favoring a direct election over the present electoral system.[8] Carter and Ford have both urged the abolition of the Electoral College and its replacement by a popular vote. Yet, for many of the reasons noted, some Democrats and Republicans have worked behind the scenes to prevent such a constitutional amendment from being adopted. In July 1979, the Senate voted 51 to 48 in support of a constitutional amendment for the direct election of the President and Vice President. The vote fell 15 short of the required two-thirds needed for passage. Senator Birch Bayh of Indiana, the architect and principal advocate of the bill, attributed its defeat to pressure on liberal senators from such groups as the Urban League and the American Jewish Congress.[9] Additionally, conservative senators of both parties opposed the bill. The continuing opposition suggests that only the election of a nonplurality President or some other electoral crisis could generate sufficient support to establish the direct popular election of the President.

The National Bonus Plan

A new proposal, known as the national bonus plan, has recently been advanced by a task force of social scientists, journalists, and political practitioners.[10] The plan would retain the electoral vote but weight it more heavily toward the popular vote winner. A pool of 102 electoral votes (2 for each state plus the District of Columbia) would automatically be awarded on a winner-take-all basis to the candidate who received the most popular votes. This bonus would be added to the candidate's regular electoral vote total. A majority of the electoral vote would still be required for election. If no one received the requisite votes (321 under the bonus plan), a runoff would be held between the two candidates who had the most popular votes. Other features of the task force proposal include the elimination of the position of elector, the automatic recording of electoral votes for the popular vote winner within the state, and the adoption of automated vote-counting procedures for all states.

The major objective of the national bonus plan is to make the outcome of the presidential election more democratic. The bonus practically assures that the popular vote winner will also be the electoral vote winner. Moreover, it reduces the chances for deadlock in the Electoral College.

Proponents of the bonus plan argue that it would contribute to the vitality of the two-party system by promoting competition in one-party states. The importance placed on winning the most popular votes in the country should also encourage greater citizen participation and voter turnout. Minor parties and independent candidates would be discouraged by the bonus provision.[11]

Had this system been in effect in 1976, Carter would have won a much larger Electoral College victory. In 1960, Kennedy also would have been a more decisive winner, assuming he had the most popular votes. However, the 1960 vote count problem in Alabama and possibly in Illinois suggests one of the difficulties with the bonus plan. In close elections, the Electoral College winner cannot be determined until the popular vote count is completed and a winner certified. Fraud and election irregularities would present the same kinds of problems for the national bonus plan as they do for direct election. In general, many of the disadvantages of direct election would also apply to the bonus plan.

By turning a close popular vote into a sizable Electoral College victory, the national bonus plan presents the elected President with an enlarged, and to some extent unrepresentative, mandate. In this sense, it may create unrealistic public expectations of him and his administration.

SUMMARY

There have been continuities and changes in the way we select a President in recent years. The procedures for conducting the general election and the method for determining who wins resemble those of past elections. However, the rules for choosing delegates, the laws regulating contributions and spending, and the medium through which appeals are generated depart significantly from the practices of previous years.

The question is, have these changes been beneficial or harmful? Have they functioned to make the system more efficient, more responsive, and more likely to result in the choice of a well-qualified candidate? Political scientists disagree in their answers.

Much of the current controversy over campaign reform has focused on party rules. Designed to encourage greater rank-and-file participation in the selection of delegates, the new rules have helped democratize presidential nominations. In the process, however, they have also factionalized and personalized the parties and weakened the position of their leadership. These unintended consequences have stimulated a debate over the merits of the changes. Recently, a consensus has emerged within the hierarchy of the Democratic party that its reforms have gone too far and that modifications are necessity. Some of these modifications have already been adopted by the party for delegate selection in 1984. The Republicans have not changed their rules for 1984 but neither had they imposed national guidelines on their state parties as the Democrats had.

Despite the inclination of Democratic party leaders to retrench or, at the very least, control the undesirable effects of their reform, a majority of the electorate would go even further in the opposite direction. They would have more participatory democracy, not less. According to a recent Gallup Poll, the public supports abolishing the present patchwork of state caucuses and primaries and replacing it with a single, national primary election.[12]

New finance legislation has also been designed to reform the process by improving accountability, equalizing contributions, and controlling spending. The law has enhanced public information but it has done so only by increasing the burden on candidate organizations of keeping detailed records and submitting frequent reports. The law has succeeded in decreasing the influence of large donors but not the influence of professional fund raisers. It has also contributed to the factionalizing of parties, encouraging multiple candidacies for the nomination. Moreover, it has weakened parties by giving aid directly to the candidates and encouraging the formation of their own separate organizations and of political action committees. Whether the end result has been to lessen the advantage of wealth and effectively open the process to a much larger group of aspirants is difficult to say. A consensus on how to improve the law is not apparent, although many proposals have been advanced.

Media coverage has also been consistent with the democratizing trends. It has brought more people into contact with presidential candidates than in the past, but that contact has also tended to be indirect and passive. The reporting of information about personalities and events far exceeds that of substantive policy issues. Television, in particular, is often blamed for the average voter's low level of knowledge and for exercising undue influence on the electorate. Its campaign coverage has been chided for being too extensive and too little, too critical and too laudatory. Its emphasis on who is ahead during the campaign and who has won on election night has also been seen as affecting who votes and who wins.

Whether or not these accusations are accurate, they are widespread. They have generated complaints by candidates and others and have produced many suggestions for change, such as providing greater coverage of non–front-runners, giving more attention to policy matters, placing less stress on the horse-race aspects of the campaign, and exercising more restraint in election-night forecasts.

Few changes are likely, however. The public seems less concerned about media coverage than do the candidates and the critics. Moreover, any nonvoluntary attempt to affect that coverage is apt to run into the First Amendment guarantees which the media enjoy.

Finally, the Electoral College continues to be a source of dialogue and concern. It is the most undemocratic feature of a political system that has become more democratic.

However, while the equity of the college has been questioned, none of the proposals to alter or abolish it, except the direct election of the President, has received much political support. Most of these plans would eliminate the electors but not the collegial system of counting votes. One would allocate a state's electoral vote in proportion to its popular vote; another would determine the state's electoral vote on the basis of separate district and statewide elections; a third would use the winner-take-all method within the states but add a bonus to the popular vote winner in the nation as a whole. Only one proposal—direct election—would abolish the Electoral College entirely.

Each of these proposals has merits, but none is problem-free. Each provides advantage to some and disadvantage to others. With no public outcry for change, Congress has been reluctant to alter the present system. Moreover, it seems unlikely to do so until an electoral crisis or unpopular result forces its hand.

Does the system need to be reformed? The answer depends on who asks the question and whether they benefit or are hurt by the process. Only if enough people believe that the system does not work very well is change likely to occur, and even then there is no guarantee that it will produce the desired effect. Politics is the art of the possible. Success is achieved only by those who can adjust quickly to the change and profit from it.

NOTES

1. *Gallup Opinion Index,* January 1980, 19.

2. Steven J. Brams and Peter C. Fishburn, "Approval Voting," *American Political Science Review,* 72 (1978), 831–847.

3. For an excellent discussion of the details of these proposals and their likely consequences see Paul Wilson, "Election Night 1980 and the Controversy Over Early Projections," in William C. Adams (ed.), *Television Coverage of the 1980 Presidential Campaign* (Norwood, N.J.: Ablex, 1983).

4. Wallace S. Sayre and Judith H. Parris, *Voting for President* (Washington, D.C.: Brookings Institution, 1970), p. 122.

5. Other direct election proposals have recommended that a joint session of Congress decide the winner. The runoff provision was contained in the resolution that passed the House of Representatives in 1969. A direct election plan with a runoff provision failed to win a two-thirds Senate vote in 1979.

6. Kennedy carried New York by approximately 384,000 votes. He received a plurality of more than 800,000 from precincts that were primarily Jewish. Similarly in Illinois, a state he carried by less than 9,000, Kennedy had a plurality of 55,000 from the so-called Jewish precincts. Mark R. Levy and Michael S. Kramer, *The Ethnic Factor* (New York: Simon & Schuster, 1972), p. 104.

7. If the leading candidate's margin hovered around 40 percent, the total number of ballots would have to be determined before the final percentages could be calculated. Controversy might be heightened by the possibility of a runoff.

8. *Gallup Opinion Index,* December 1980, 59.

9. Ward Sinclair, "Senators Soundly Defeat Direct Presidential Ballot," *Washington Post,* July 11, 1979, p. A-2.

10. *Winner Take All: Report of the Twentieth Century Fund Task Force on Reform of the Presidential Election Process* (New York: Holmes and Meier, 1978), pp. 3–16.

11. Ibid., p. 6.

12. *Gallup Opinion Index,* December 1980, 59.

PART V

APPENDIXES

Appendix A
Results of Presidential Elections, 1860–1980

Year	Candidates Democrat	Candidates Republican	Electoral Vote Democrat	Electoral Vote Republican	Popular Vote Democrat	Popular Vote Republican
1860(a)	Stephen A. Douglas / Herschel V. Johnson	Abraham Lincoln / Hannibal Hamlin	12 / 4%	180 / 59%	1,380,202 / 29.5%	1,865,908 / 39.8%
1864(b)	George B. McClellan / George H. Pendleton	Abraham Lincoln / Andrew Johnson	21 / 9%	212 / 91%	1,812,807 / 45.0%	2,218,388 / 55.0%
1868(c)	Horatio Seymour / Francis P. Blair Jr.	Ulysses S. Grant / Schuyler Colfax	80 / 27%	214 / 73%	2,708,744 / 47.3%	3,013,650 / 52.7%
1872(d)	Horace Greeley / Benjamin Gratz Brown	Ulysses S. Grant / Henry Wilson		286 / 78%	2,834,761 / 43.8%	3,598,235 / 55.6%
1876	Samuel J. Tilden / Thomas A. Hendricks	Rutherford B. Hayes / William A. Wheeler	184 / 50%	185 / 50%	4,288,546 / 51.0%	4,034,311 / 47.9%
1880	Winfield S. Hancock / William H. English	James A. Garfield / Chester A. Arthur	155 / 42%	214 / 58%	4,444,260 / 48.2%	4,446,158 / 48.3%
1884	Grover Cleveland / Thomas A. Hendricks	James G. Blaine / John A. Logan	219 / 55%	182 / 45%	4,874,621 / 48.5%	4,848,936 / 48.2%
1888	Grover Cleveland / Allen G. Thurman	Benjamin Harrison / Levi P. Morton	168 / 42%	233 / 58%	5,534,488 / 48.6%	5,443,892 / 47.8%
1892(e)	Grover Cleveland / Adlai E. Stevenson	Benjamin Harrison / Whitelaw Reid	277 / 62%	145 / 33%	5,551,883 / 46.1%	5,179,244 / 43.0%
1896	William J. Bryan / Arthur Sewall	William McKinley / Garret A. Hobart	176 / 39%	271 / 61%	6,511,495 / 46.7%	7,108,480 / 51.0%
1900	William J. Bryan / Adlai E. Stevenson	William McKinley / Theodore Roosevelt	155 / 35%	292 / 65%	6,358,345 / 45.5%	7,218,039 / 51.7%

Year	Candidates	Electoral Vote	%	Popular Vote	%
1904	Alton B. Parker / Henry G. Davis	140	29%	5,028,898	37.6%
	Theodore Roosevelt / Charles W. Fairbanks	336	71%	7,626,593	56.4%
1903	William J. Bryan / John W. Kern	162	34%	6,406,801	43.0%
	William H. Taft / James S. Sherman	321	66%	7,676,258	51.6%
1912(f)	Woodrow Wilson / Thomas R. Marshall	435	82%	6,293,152	41.8%
	William H. Taft / James S. Sherman	8	2%	3,486,333	23.2%
1916	Woodrow Wilson / Thomas R. Marshall	277	52%	9,126,300	49.2%
	Charles E. Hughes / Charles W. Fairbanks	254	48%	8,546,789	46.1%
1920	James M. Cox / Franklin D. Roosevelt	127	24%	9,140,884	34.2%
	Warren G. Harding / Calvin Coolidge	404	76%	16,133,314	60.3%
1924(g)	John W. Davis / Charles W. Bryant	136	26%	8,386,169	28.8%
	Calvin Coolidge / Charles G. Dawes	382	72%	15,717,553	54.1%
1928	Alfred E. Smith / Joseph T. Robinson	87	16%	15,000,185	40.8%
	Herbert C. Hoover / Charles Curtis	444	84%	21,411,991	58.2%
1932	Franklin D. Roosevelt / John N. Garner	472	89%	22,825,016	57.4%
	Herbert C. Hoover / Charles Curtis	59	11%	15,758,397	39.6%
1936	Franklin D. Roosevelt / John N. Garner	523	98%	27,747,636	60.8%
	Alfred M. Landon / Frank Knox	8	2%	16,679,543	36.5%
1940	Franklin D. Roosevelt / Henry A. Wallace	449	85%	27,263,448	54.7%
	Wendell L. Willkie / Charles L. McNary	82	15%	22,336,260	44.8%
1944	Franklin D. Roosevelt / Harry S. Truman	432	81%	25,611,936	53.4%
	Thomas E. Dewey / John W. Bricker	99	19%	22,013,372	45.9%
1948(h)	Harry S Truman / Alben W. Barkley	303	57%	24,105,587	49.5%
	Thomas E. Dewey / Earl Warren	189	36%	21,970,017	45.1%

Appendix A

Results of Presidential Elections, 1860–1980 (Continued)

Year	Candidates Democrat	Candidates Republican	Electoral Vote Democrat	Electoral Vote Republican	Popular Vote Democrat	Popular Vote Republican
1952	Adlai E. Stevenson John J. Sparkman	Dwight D. Eisenhower Richard M. Nixon	89 17%	442 83%	27,314,649 44.4%	33,936,137 55.1%
1956(i)	Adlai E. Stevenson Estes Kefauver	Dwight D. Eisenhower Richard M. Nixon	73 14%	457 86%	26,030,172 42.0%	35,585,245 57.4%
1960(j)	John F. Kennedy Lyndon B. Johnson	Richard M. Nixon Henry Cabot Lodge	303 56%	219 41%	34,221,344 49.8%	34,106,671 49.5%
1964	Lyndon B. Johnson Hubert H. Humphrey	Barry Goldwater William E. Miller	486 90%	52 10%	43,126,584 61.0%	27,177,838 38.5%
1968(k)	Hubert H. Humphrey Edmund S. Muskie	Richard M. Nixon Spiro T. Agnew	191 36%	301 56%	31,274,503 42.7%	31,785,148 43.2%
1972(l)	George McGovern Sargent Shriver	Richard M. Nixon Spiro T. Agnew	17 3%	520 97%	29,171,791 37.5%	47,170,179 60.7%
1976(m)	Jimmy Carter Walter F. Mondale	Gerald R. Ford Robert Dole	297 55%	240 45%	40,828,657 50.1%	39,145,520 48.0%
1980	Jimmy Carter Walter F. Mondale	Ronald Reagan George Bush	49 10%	489 90%	35,483,820 41.0%	43,901,812 50.7%

Source: *Congress and the Nation* (Washington, D.C.: The Congressional Quarterly, 1977, 1981), Vol. IV, p. 27; Vol. V, p. 1,147. Copyrighted material reprinted with permission of Congressional Quarterly Inc.

(a) 1860: John C. Breckenridge, Southern Democrat, polled 72 electoral votes; John Bell, Constitutional Union, polled 39 electoral votes.
(b) 1864: 81 electoral votes were not cast.
(c) 1868: 23 electoral votes were not cast.
(d) 1872: Horace Greeley died after election, 63 Democratic electoral votes were scattered. 17 were not voted.
(e) 1892: James B. Weaver, People's party, polled 22 electoral votes.
(f) 1912: Theodore Roosevelt, Progressive party, polled 88 electoral votes.

(g) 1924: Robert M. LaFollette, Progressive party, polled 13 electoral votes.
(h) 1948: J. Strom Thurmund, States' Rights party, polled 39 electoral votes.
(i) 1956: Walter B. Jones, Democrat, polled 1 electoral vote.
(j) 1960: Harry Flood Byrd, Democrat, polled 15 electoral votes.
(k) 1968: George C. Wallace, American Independent, polled 46 electoral votes.
(l) 1972: John Hospers, Libertarian party, polled 1 electoral vote.
(m) 1976: Ronald Reagan, Republican, polled 1 electoral vote.

Appendix B
1980 Presidential Election Results*

State	Ronald Reagan (Republican) Votes	%	Jimmy Carter (Democrat) Votes	%	John B. Anderson (Independent) Votes	%	Ed Clark (Libertarian) Votes	%	Barry Commoner (Citizens) Votes	%	Other Votes	%
Alabama	654,192	48.8	636,730	47.5	16,481	1.2	13,318	1.0	517	0.0	20,721	1.5
Alaska	86,112	54.4	41,842	26.4	11,156	7.0	18,479	11.7			805	0.5
Arizona	529,688	60.6	246,843	28.2	76,952	8.8	18,784	2.2	551	0.1	1,127	0.1
Arkansas	403,164	48.1	398,041	47.5	22,468	2.7	8,970	1.1	2,345	0.3	2,594	0.3
California	4,524,835	52.7	3,083,652	35.9	739,832	8.6	148,434	1.7	61,063	0.7	29,214	0.4
Colorado	652,264	55.0	368,009	31.1	130,633	11.0	25,744	2.2	5,614	0.5	2,186	0.2
Connecticut	677,210	48.2	541,732	38.5	171,807	12.2	8,570	0.6	6,130	0.4	836	0.1
Delaware	111,252	47.2	105,754	44.8	16,288	6.9	1,974	0.9	103	0.0	529	0.2
District of Columbia	23,313	13.4	130,231	74.9	16,131	9.3	1,104	0.6	1,826	1.1	1,284	0.7
Florida	2,046,951	55.5	1,419,475	38.5	189,692	5.2	30,524	0.8			285	0.0
Georgia	654,168	41.0	890,955	55.8	36,055	2.2	15,627	1.0	104	0.0	8	0.0
Hawaii	130,112	42.9	135,879	44.8	32,021	10.6	3,269	1.1	1,548	0.5	458	0.1
Idaho	290,699	66.4	110,192	25.2	27,058	6.2	8,425	1.9			1,470	0.3
Illinois	2,358,094	49.7	1,981,413	41.7	346,754	7.3	38,939	0.8	10,692	0.2	13,874	0.3
Indiana	1,255,656	56.0	844,197	37.6	111,639	5.0	19,627	0.9	4,852	0.2	6,062	0.3
Iowa	676,026	51.3	508,672	38.6	115,633	8.8	13,123	1.0	2,273	0.2	1,934	0.1
Kansas	566,812	57.8	326,150	33.3	68,231	7.0	14,470	1.5			4,132	0.4
Kentucky	635,274	49.0	617,417	47.7	31,127	2.4	5,531	0.4	1,304	0.1	4,974	0.4
Louisiana	792,853	51.2	708,453	45.8	26,345	1.7	8,240	0.5	1,584	0.1	11,116	0.7
Maine	238,522	45.6	220,974	42.3	53,327	10.2	5,119	1.0	4,394	0.8	675	0.1
Maryland	680,606	44.2	726,161	47.1	119,537	7.8	14,192	0.9			7,972	0.3
Massachusetts	1,056,223	41.8	1,053,800	41.7	382,539	15.2	22,038	0.9	2,056	0.1	4,218	0.1
Michigan	1,915,225	49.0	1,661,532	42.5	275,223	7.0	41,597	1.1	11,930	0.3	9,479	0.5
Minnesota	873,268	42.6	954,173	46.5	174,997	8.5	31,593	1.5	8,406	0.4	4,749	0.5
Mississippi	441,089	49.4	429,281	48.1	12,036	1.4	5,465	0.6			1,546	0.1
Missouri	1,074,181	51.2	931,182	44.3	77,920	3.7	14,422	0.7	573	0.0		
Montana	206,814	56.8	118,032	32.4	29,281	8.1	9,825	2.7				

Appendix B
1980 Presidential Election Results* (Continued)

State	Ronald Reagan (Republican) Votes	%	Jimmy Carter (Democrat) Votes	%	John B. Anderson (Independent) Votes	%	Ed Clark (Libertarian) Votes	%	Barry Commoner (Citizens) Votes	%	Other Votes	%
Nebraska	419,214	65.6	166,424	26.0	44,854	7.0	9,041	1.4			4,193	1.7
Nevada	155,017	62.5	66,666	26.9	17,651	7.1	4,358	1.8			344	0.1
New Hampshire	221,705	57.7	108,864	28.4	49,693	12.9	2,064	0.5	1,320	0.4		
New Jersey	1,546,557	52.0	1,147,364	38.6	234,632	7.9	20,652	0.6	8,203	0.3	18,276	0.6
New Mexico	250,779	55.0	167,826	36.8	29,459	6.5	4,365	0.9	2,202	0.5	1,606	0.3
New York	2,893,831	46.7	2,728,372	44.0	467,801	7.5	52,648	0.8	23,186	0.4	36,121	0.6
North Carolina	915,018	49.3	875,635	47.2	52,800	2.9	9,677	0.5	2,287	0.1	416	0.0
North Dakota	193,695	64.2	79,189	26.3	23,640	7.8	3,743	1.2	429	0.2	849	0.3
Ohio	2,206,545	51.5	1,752,414	40.9	254,472	5.9	49,033	1.2	8,564	0.2	12,575	0.3
Oklahoma	695,570	60.5	402,026	35.0	38,284	3.3	13,828	1.2				
Oregon	571,044	48.3	456,890	38.7	112,389	9.5	25,838	2.2	13,642	1.2	1,713	0.1
Pennsylvania	2,261,872	49.6	1,937,540	42.5	292,921	6.4	33,263	0.7	10,430	0.2	25,475	0.6
Rhode Island	154,793	37.2	198,342	47.7	59,819	14.4	2,458	0.6	67	0.0	593	0.1
South Carolina	441,841	49.4	430,385	48.2	14,153	1.6	5,139	0.6				
South Dakota	198,343	60.5	103,855	31.7	21,431	6.5	3,824	1.2			2,177	0.2
Tennessee	787,761	48.7	783,051	48.4	35,991	2.2	7,116	0.4	1,112	0.1	250	0.1
Texas	2,510,705	55.3	1,881,147	41.4	111,613	2.5	37,643	0.8	453	0.0	2,585	0.2
Utah	439,687	72.8	124,266	20.6	30,284	5.0	7,156	1.2	1,009	0.1	75	0.0
Vermont	94,628	44.4	81,952	38.4	31,761	14.9	1,900	0.9	2,316	1.1	1,750	0.3
Virginia	989,609	53.0	752,174	40.3	95,418	5.1	12,821	0.7	14,024	0.8	742	0.3
Washington	865,244	49.7	650,193	37.3	185,073	10.6	29,213	1.7	9,403	0.5	1,986	0.1
West Virginia	334,206	45.3	367,462	49.8	31,691	4.3	4,356	0.6			3,268	0.2
Wisconsin	1,088,845	47.9	981,584	43.2	160,657	7.1	29,135	1.3	7,767	0.3		
Wyoming	110,700	62.6	49,427	28.0	12,072	6.8	4,514	2.6			5,233	0.2
Total	43,901,812	50.7	35,483,820	41.0	5,719,722	6.6	921,188	1.1	234,279	0.3	252,475	0.3

Source: *Congressional Quarterly*, XXXIX (January 17, 1981), 138. Copyrighted material reprinted with permission of Congressional Quarterly Inc.
*Total popular vote: 86,513,296; Reagan's plurality: 8,417,992.

Date	State and Method
Sept. 7, 1982	Arizona (R-election of committee)
Sept. 11, 1982	Arkansas (R-election of committee)
Jan. 24, 1984	Hawaii (R-C)
Feb.	South Carolina (R-C)
Feb. 1–Mar. 15, 1984	Maine (R-C)
Feb. 6–Mar. 7, 1984	Wyoming (R-C)
Feb. 11	Democrats Abroad (mail ballots may be posted)
Feb. 16, 1984	Alaska (R-C)
Feb. 19, 1984	Puerto Rico (R-P)
Feb. 27	Iowa (C)
March and April	Virginia (R-C)
Mar. 4, 1984	Maine (C)
Mar. 6, 1984	New Hampshire (P), Vermont (Advisory P)
Mar. 10, 1984	Kentucky (R-C), South Carolina (R-P)
Mar. 13, 1984	Alabama (P), Democrats Abroad (deadline for mail ballots), Florida (P), Georgia (P), Hawaii (D-C), Massachusetts (P), Nevada (C), Oklahoma (D-C), Rhode Island (P), Washington (C)
Mar. 13–15, 1984	Wyoming (D-C)
Mar. 14, 1984	Alaska (D-C), Delaware (D-C)
Mar. 14–28, 1984	North Dakota (D-C)
Mar. 17, 1984	Arkansas (D-C), Latin American Democrats (D-C), Michigan (D-C) Mississippi (D-C) Kentucky (D-C), South Carolina (D-C)
Mar. 18, 1984	Puerto Rico (D-P)
Mar. 20, 1984	Illinois (P), Minnesota (C)
Mar. 24–31, 1984	Missouri (R-C)
Mar. 24, 1984	Kansas (D-C)
Mar. 24 or 26, 1984	Virginia (D-C)
Mar. 25	Montana (D-C)
Mar. 27, 1984	Connecticut (P)
Mar. 31, 1984	Wisconsin (D-C)

(*table continues*)

Date	State and Method
Late March and early April	Guam (R-C)
Apr. 2, 1984	Oklahoma (R-C)
Apr. 3, 1984	Wisconsin (D-Advisory P; R-P)
Apr. 7, 1984	Louisiana (P)
Apr. 14, 1984	Arizona (D-C)
Apr. 16, 1984	Utah (C)
Apr. 17, 1984	Missouri (D-C)
Apr. 24, 1984	Pennsylvania (P), Vermont (C)
By Apr. 30, 1984	Delaware (R-C)
May 1, 1984	Wash D.C. (P), Tennessee (P)
May 3, 1984	Virgin Islands (R-C)
May 5, 1984	Guam (D-C), Texas (D-C/Advisory P; R-P)
May 7, 1984	Colorado (C)
May 8, 1984	Indiana (P), Maryland (P), North Carolina (P)
May 15, 1984	Nebraska (P), Oregon (P)
May 22, 1984	Idaho (D-Advisory P; R-P), New York (P)
May 24, 1984	Idaho (D-C)
June 5, 1984	California (P), Mississippi (R-P), Montana (Advisory P), New Jersey (P), New Mexico (P), Ohio (P), South Dakota (P), West Virginia (P)
By June 12, 1984	Virgin Islands (D-C)
June 12, 1984	North Dakota (D-Advisory P; R-P)

Source: Joseph B. Gorman, "Delegate Selection for 1984: Dates of Presidential Primaries or First Step in Caucus/ Convention Process," *Congressional Research Service,* Library of Congress (July 6, 1983).
   *Note that no entry in this chronological listing has been made for: Kansas (R-C) and Michigan (R-C). Abbreviations: D/Democrats; R/Republicans; C/caucus; P/primary

INDEX